THE UNIVERSITY OF
WINCHESTER

Martial Rose Library
Tel: 01962 827306

13 MAY 2013

24 MAY 2013

30 SEP 2013

27 FEB 2014

19 JAN 2015

To be returned on or before the day marked above, subject to recall.

Also available

Science 5–11
A Guide for Teachers
Alan Howe, Dan Davies, Kendra McMahon, Lee Towler and Tonie Scott
1–84312–319–3

Geography 3–11
A Guide for Teachers
Hilary Cooper, Simon Asquith and Chris Rowley
1–84312–421–1

modern foreign languages 5–11

issues for teachers

Jane Jones and Simon Coffey

 **David Fulton** Publishers

This edition reprinted 2009 by Routledge
2 Park Square, Milton Park, Abingdon, Oxon, OX14 4RN
Simultaneously published in the USA and Canada
By Routledge
270 Madison Avenue, New York, NY 10016

First published in Great Britain in 2006 by David Fulton Publishers

10 9 8 7 6 5 4 3 2

David Fulton Publishers is a division of Granada Learning Limited

British Library Cataloguing in Publication Data
A catalogue record for this book is available from the British Library.

ISBN: 1 84312 390 8 (9781843123903)

Typeset by RefineCatch Limited, Bungay, Suffolk
Printed and bound in Great Britain

Contents

Acknowledgements

This book would not have been possible without the suggestions and ideas of a great many teachers, headteachers, advisers, inspectors, researchers, colleagues in higher education and children, all of whom, too numerous to mention by name, have made contributions in many ways in the light of their interest in primary Modern Foreign Languages (primary MFL).

The authors would, however, like to thank the following colleagues: Chris Andon, Nick Andon, Lis Bundock, Professor Margaret Cox, Jane Garrett, Sue Gibbs, Stephanie Gorecki, Muriel Grosbois, Margaret Haste, Alison Hurrell, Jane Nimmo, Liz Scott, Michaela Thomas and Marc Van den Brande, for their very precious support. They have all generously contributed in different ways such as drawings, graphics, teaching ideas and plans, research support and critical insights.

Introduction – new beginnings for primary MFL learning

Primary MFL started out as an experiment initiated by teachers who, quite some time ago, saw benefits in early foreign language learning. We call it an adventure due to its pioneering and exploratory character, thereby giving credit to those enthusiasts who laid the foundations for children to have an enjoyable learning experience in today's tightly packed curriculum. The last few years have seen an ever accelerating series of 'bangs' in the form of, among other things, burgeoning primary school early foreign language learning experiences across the nation, albeit unevenly spread. The National Advisory Centre on Early Language Learning (NACELL), a plethora of official frameworks for learning and teaching, and the government's Pathfinder initiative, that has provided targeted funding for primary MFL, have all resulted in a seriously high profile for the whole enterprise. This is nothing short of a paradigmatic change in attitude on the part of leaders and, indeed, other stakeholders – a change reflected in the place afforded foreign language learning in the curriculum provision of many primary schools.

The DfES recognised these developments and this enthusiasm and invited practitioners at all levels to contribute to a roadmap for the subject, the national Key Stage 2 Framework for Languages 2005. This document provides the early language learning adventure with a structure and thus turns it into a project by offering clear guidelines, measurability and accountability in terms of progress and assessment. The parameters of this project allow schools and language teachers to build on previous experiences with primary MFL as well as to develop and experiment with ideas.

The national Key Stage 2 Framework can thus be regarded as a much needed frame of reference. Researching for this book we have identified central current issues facing schools and questions they will be faced with when implementing the Framework with the objective of providing quality language teaching and learning. Our book goes beyond the scope of the recently published Key Stage 2 document in that we use research and snapshots from the world of primary

MFL teaching to translate theoretical discussions into practice which we present to teachers and parties interested in primary MFL as suggested planning and teaching approaches.

We do, however, refer to the Key Stage 2 Framework objectives where these are concordant with the examples of effective practice the authors have seen on school visits. Although we have had to be selective in our coverage of key areas and in the numbers of examples we incorporate, we have integrated feedback and the views of teachers and pupils from dozens of primary schools we visited around the UK and in Europe where primary MFL has often been successfully embedded in the primary curriculum.

Our main focus in the following chapters will be on issues affecting developments on the national level but we will, where appropriate, discuss European research, since for some time now a number of countries have quite independently commissioned their own research into learning and teaching modern foreign languages at primary level. Scotland has been a pioneer in this respect with a bold and committed national primary MFL provision that has provided important insights and research findings for other countries.

Each chapter of our book begins with a brief summary of the content and key questions to be explored. We present examples of practice from Key Stage 1 and Key Stage 2 teachers who do not make any great claims for their teaching other than that they enjoy their primary MFL experiences and try their professional best for their pupils and colleagues. We have analysed the practice of these teachers in order to establish indicators of 'practice that works' and that can be transferred into other teaching and learning contexts. Each chapter concludes with a summary of key points and questions to the reader on what the authors believe are key issues for deliberation.

Our discussion of primary MFL begins in Chapter 1 by considering reasons for an early start, drawing on a range of research findings and on areas of considerable consensus in the community. It is within a school community that primary MFL will be implemented and to do this successfully requires a strongly supportive leadership of the shared or distributed kind, as discussed in Chapter 2. This is followed by practical discussion of how MFL can be implemented and Chapter 3 deals with planning issues that concern teachers' choice and deployment of time and resources. We suggest ways to plan, what to take into account and what could be included in long- and short-term planning (schemes of work and lesson plans). This teacher focus on planning continues in Chapter 4 where choices about the effective use of MFL-specific and improvised materials are discussed and exemplified with reference to teaching the four skills of listening, speaking, reading and writing. We explore the issues surrounding the teaching and learning of specific skills, such as how and when to incorporate reading and writing into MFL to support language awareness, both in terms of 'oracy' in MFL and first language literacy. The theme of cross-curricular learning and embedding MFL into the curriculum is emphasised in Chapter 5 and we provide case study examples of how MFL can be integrated into other areas of the curriculum. We link this to successful whole-child learning and advocate the hugely important motivational aspect of language learning through 'meaning-making' rather than rote-learning foreign language phrases out of context.

We then highlight children's learning needs in Chapter 6 and consider learner and learning strategies that can promote and support learning to enable pupils to become competent strategic language learners. In Chapter 7 we emphasise that primary MFL, like any other subject, needs to assess the children's learning, particularly through formative assessment in a supportive, 'laddered' and progressive way.

ICT, now embedded across the primary curriculum, offers new and exciting opportunities to support MFL learning for individual work, group work and teacher-led classwork. In Chapter 8 we discuss some simple and some more challenging ways in which new technologies can support the teacher and enhance pupils' language learning. One of the major benefits of ICT use is in opening the classroom door and bridging children's experience to target language communities; indeed developing cultural awareness and genuine intercultural understanding is a key objective of primary MFL (an objective now officially enshrined in the Key Stage 2 Framework). Chapter 9 considers what exactly we mean by 'teaching cultural awareness' and how we can encourage pupils to embrace difference and otherness. We give some snapshot examples of how we have seen cultural input integrated into MFL teaching across Key Stages 1 and 2 and how whole-school initiatives can raise cultural awareness.

It is crucial that primary MFL is not perceived as an isolated entity but seen in a context of the whole school, as well as that of transition, as we assert in Chapter 10. MFL provision needs to be considered and planned on a cross-phase basis to ensure progression in learning and across the different school phases.

Progression is equally important with respect to the professional development of teaching staff. In our discussion of this topic in Chapter 11 we focus on general principles and look at questions arising from it but we do not 'advertise' any specific course provision, or material, or the work of any LA or other authority.

This book then is not an apologia for the Key Stage 2 Framework for Languages, but drawing on previous debate, research and discussion with primary modern foreign language teachers, its purpose is to contribute to the hugely stimulating debate about the issues of early foreign language learning and to involve all those who have an interest in the subject.

CHAPTER

1

Starting early – what do younger language learners do better?

THIS CHAPTER CONSIDERS the rationale for an early start to language learning since it is important that this is made explicit; it cannot simply be assumed. There are many reasons for beginning learning a language early, not least of all the greater openness of early learners to new sounds and their natural curiosity to engage with new activities. MFL teaching and learning in the UK has redefined itself for the twenty-first century. Children are now being taught to be able to speak a given foreign language, as well as to be equipped with a range of foundational language learning skills which reinforce whole-curriculum learning and encourage increased social and cultural awareness of difference. These aims are expressed in the national Key Stage 2 Framework, key aspects of which we outline in this chapter. In keeping with the ethos of the Framework we encourage a cross-curricular perspective of MFL, particularly with respect to linking it to literacy development. The emphasis in this chapter is very much on promoting an unmissable, enjoyable learning experience for pupils and teachers.

Key issues

- MFL learning needs to go beyond the mimicry stage of parrot-fashion learning to encourage creative use of language and experimentation.

- Popular opinion suggests the younger the learner of a language the more effective is learning. Is there real evidence for this assertion and are there real long-term benefits?

- Failure to engage with MFL learning represents a myopic view of language education and a missed opportunity at many levels.

- Progressive cross-phase learning between primary and secondary school is essential to a child's successful school-based language learning trajectory.

- Is one language easier to learn than another? Which language(s) should we be teaching?

Introduction – can parrots talk?

Parrots are birds of immense fascination, given their natural curiosity, varied personalities and propensity for mimicry. It appears that a certain African Grey parrot, Alex, has been trained to use words to identify objects, describe them, count them, and even answer questions about them such as 'how many red squares?, seemingly with some 80 per cent success. The parrot on the cover of the book can be seen as a symbol of these skills and reminds us of much that we observe in children who show inquisitiveness as well as learning capacity. The primary MFL classroom provides an opportunity for all children to demonstrate more than their powers of mimicry. While teachers sometimes talk of children parroting words and phrases – a natural part of the early stage of language learning – children have the cognitive flexibility and physiological apparatus to become competent and creative language users. Babies visibly enjoy babble and infants thrive on constant chatter and verbal interrogation of their world. As toddlers grow into children and their language use becomes more sophisticated they retain the flexibility to unconsciously absorb and 'parrot' new words in their mother tongue or in any language that they come into contact with, as any parent can testify who has spent some length of time abroad with young children engaged in social contact in a foreign language.

Children at this age are focused on the nature of the communication afforded by language use and are not concerned with the cultural load of which words

FIGURE 1.1 Parrot

and which language they are using. This natural, uninhibited use of language makes early learners particularly receptive in MFL and it is a foundation to build upon.

Younger learners bring motivational capital to language learning and this has to be maintained throughout the entire primary phase and into the secondary school phase of learning to ensure the success of the primary MFL project.

One of the concerns expressed in the MFL community of practice, that is the group of professionals interested in the promotion of skilled MFL teaching, has been about the decline in interest that is often characteristic of the secondary stage of learning. After many discussions with secondary teachers and interviews with Year 7 children, it appears that there is some justification for this. Let us, by way of illustration, consider comments from two groups of Year 7 pupils. Children in a Year 7 class in a specialist language college (SLC) in the London area, gave the following answers when asked to describe the differences in the way MFL is taught at secondary level:

'Here the teacher just says it without explaining and expects you to understand.'

'At primary school we did colours and answered questions. Here the words are harder.'

'It's annoying here because there are so many noisy boys who don't do what the teacher says. At primary school it was quiet.'

'At primary we did all computer games but here it's just tests and work off the board. More homework here. [when asked what sort of homework] Just revision.'

Given its language college status, associated funding and requirements, MFL clearly enjoys an important place in the curriculum at this school. However, the children's views are not necessarily more favourable than those of pupils in a non-specialist comprehensive. Significantly, several Year 7 students who were interviewed as a group were unaware that their school was a specialist language college! Many specialist language colleges do excellent work in collaboration with their primary colleagues but it would be wrong to assume an SLC designation *per se* is a guarantee of effective teaching.

We also interviewed pupils in another group of Year 7 attending a non-specialist comprehensive at the same time during their first Autumn term, where one pupil supported by others in the group expressed enthusiasm for the French and German teacher and the languages thus:

'I just love it. I can't stop speaking French! Ça va? Tu vas bien? [to the author in the interview]. Miss gets us to sing and move around all the time [seat-dancing movements]. It's not embarrassing as we all do it. The PowerPoints are excellent. Miss gets us to work in teams and we get points when we say something good. If you are not sure, she helps us then comes back to us and asks us again. The German lessons are fun too [group bursts out into a volley of German phrases]. I can't wait to do Spanish.'

This comment is a testimony to particular primary and secondary teachers who, working together without any SLC framework, have succeeded in maintaining cross-phase interest, motivation and progression in language learning, arguably the cornerstones of this book. Without continuity and coherence of learning on a progressive basis, primary MFL is likely to be perceived yet again as a failed project (see the report by Burstall *et al.* (1974) on the perceived ineffectiveness of primary MFL). If this is the case, an evident lack of success could lead to considerable disquiet on the part of secondary colleagues, and probably sceptical primary teachers who might feel inclined to challenge the rather over-generalised, albeit contested notion, that provides the basis for primary MFL: 'the younger the better'.

A head start for the younger learner?

Age-related issues have been discussed extensively and written about with considerable authority by, for example, Martin (2000) and Johnstone (1994). It seems that decisions about when to introduce foreign language learning depend in different countries on local and/or national schooling contextual or politically influenced factors. In various European countries the 'optimum starting age' for language learning has been researched yet there is contradictory evidence on almost every count. Across Europe we can find starting ages ranging from 5 to 11, even younger in some countries and in many private schools, for example. Research on the optimum age includes the field of neurobiology and has led to an ongoing debate. The Swiss linguist Georges Lüdi, from the University of Basel, recently working with colleagues in neurobiology on brain activation and the capacity for the development of early bilingualism has asserted, for example, that the optimum age for the development of early bilingualism is before the age of 3! Lüdi does however stress the need to be conscious of children's individuality and their flexibilities in different areas of acquisition and at different ages. While the neurobiological research of languages has yet to come to a conclusive result and the Swiss context is somewhat different to the primary school classrooms under discussion in this book, as well as our language learning aims being rather more modest, nonetheless such new research continues to fuel the 'optimum age' debate.

In view of the discussion of 'earlier the better', Martin rightly questions the meaning of 'better' in respect of children's learning: is it 'proficiency and the ultimate level of attainment' or 'the rate of acquisition . . . and . . . which aspects of language learning are they best at?' (Martin 2000: 10). However we choose to interpret 'better', the key lies, according to Martin, in the planning of an appropriate age-related programme that capitalises on what younger learners can do better and with the greatest enthusiasm in order to maximise their advantages. Similarly, MFL provision at the secondary level needs to be planned to exploit the advantages of the secondary-aged learner by consolidating and building on, but not repeating, terrain already covered. It can be seen from this that the case for an early start is not so much age-dependent but rests on a range of other more influential factors. These are reflected in the following statement of Jurgen Meisel of the University of Hamburg (cited by George Lüdi in an address to the Education Department in Basel, 16 June 2004), according to which 'monolingualism can be regarded as resulting from an impoverished environment where an opportunity to exhaust the potential of the language faculty is not fully developed'.

Primary MFL provides, assuming training, funding and support for teachers and schools, added-value in the primary classroom and indeed the whole school environment. It provides language learning opportunities and can make the most effective use of children's full language learning potential and thus give that all important head start.

The Key Stage 2 Framework for Languages 2005

The value of language learning to a child's cognitive, social and cultural development is, at least some might say, enjoying official recognition with the launch of the National Language Strategy's Framework for Primary Languages at KS2. Andrew Adonis, Parliamentary Under-Secretary of State for Schools, introduces the Framework with the following words:

> *The centrepiece of the National Language Strategy 'Languages for All Languages for Life' is our commitment to give every child between the ages of 7 and 11 the entitlement to learn a new language. This marks a fundamental shift in our approach to language learning in this country and, by 2010, will transform the shape of language learning in our schools*
>
> **(Key Stage 2 Framework for Languages 2005: 1)**

A considerable amount of research has led to the formulation of the KS2 Framework. An investigation of the 19 Pathfinder LAs showed some outstanding cases of strongly networked and sustainable MFL provision through outreached clusters of primary schools and local specialist language colleges. Findings recently presented by Lid King, National Director of Languages, confirmed that 'best practice' was found where:

- MFL was started early, from Year 3 rather than introduced in Years 5 and 6

- primary schools worked with secondary schools and Higher Education institutions

(Lid King speaking at 'Spanish: the Primary Challenge', 25 November 2005)

However, in some cases, we have seen MFL provision delivered in a patchy, incoherent way, dependent on the goodwill and enthusiasm of a few teachers rather than on joined-up whole-school initiatives. There is a clear need for guidance which is captured aptly in the following four 'challenges' (the '4 Cs') facing primary MFL that King went on to outline in the exposition of the KS2 Framework:

– curriculum: the need for guidelines, progression, (a framework)

– continuity: links to secondary stage, successful transfer, language diversification

– competence: CPD, language training, teacher training

– collaboration: how to get various partners working together. While this may be relatively easy at the level of national agencies, how do initiatives successfully filter down to the local level of school and regional networks? ICT offers a solution here.

Given the importance of the document, it is appropriate to include a brief outline of its structure. The Framework consists of three parts:

i.   Learning objectives

ii.   Guidance documents

iii. Planning and exemplar materials (still unreleased at the time of writing)

The 'Learning objectives' are listed within the following five strands, the first three are progressive, linear strands and the last two are designed to be transversal, 'conceived of as both arising from and supporting the core teaching and learning strands rather than as existing independently from them' (Key Stage 2 Framework for Languages 2005: 6):

–   oracy
–   literacy
–   intercultural understanding
–   knowledge about language
–   language learning strategies

The key emphasis of the Framework is on developing language skills, which are not necessarily specific to a particular language but are intended to be embedded across the whole-school learning experience of pupils and to develop skills which can lead to ongoing learning. The KS2 Framework has broken new ground in its endorsement of an early start for MFL learning, beginning in Year 3. The debate about the optimal learning age will certainly continue as different research projects have yielded mixed findings relating to the long-term effectiveness of an early start.

The earlier the better? What are the advantages of an early start?

Throughout this book, we address KS2 teaching and include KS1 as we believe, in line with Sharpe and Driscoll, that 'foreign language learning should begin at the start of compulsory primary schooling' (Sharpe and Driscoll 2000: 83). However, we recognise that the gains of such an early start may not always be clearly quantifiable linguistically. Much of the research looking into the nature and benefits of early language learning has tried to measure the success of children's 'acquisition rate'

compared to peers who did not have an early start. The most famous example of this was Burstall *et al.*'s NFER report (1974) which ultimately led to the disintegration of the pilot Primary French Project started in the 1960s.When children who had studied French at primary were compared to those who had not and to older secondary children who had studied French for the same period of time, it was found that children who had started learning earlier did not demonstrate greater proficiency. It could be argued though that the research data were flawed as they were based on testing linguistic gains when children had already moved on to the secondary school and so had started learning French 'again' as beginners in Year 7 along with peers who had not previously learnt any foreign language in their primary school.

In linguistic terms, there is some evidence to show that an early start helps to improve foreign language listening skills, and pronunciation (Vilke 1988; Singleton 1989). These studies seem to concur with Lenneberg's (1967) 'critical period hypothesis' which claimed that the brain of a child before puberty was more receptive to imitating native-like pronunciation (though subsequent evidence of successful acquisition in older children has contested this theory).

Contentious gains in linguistic proficiency cannot be the only reason for advocating an early start for language learners; the main benefits early MFL learning engenders lie rather as reflected in the rationale KS2 Framework in:

- enjoyment of languages
- mutual reinforcement of first language development (the long-term affects of which will be monitored in the light of the KS2 Framework once implemented)
- international awareness and enhanced understanding.

In the long term a more formal investigation confirming connections between early language learning and these advantages is required. This needs to take into consideration that the learning must already be embedded in a progressive trajectory which crosses the school phases both vertically through the years and horizontally across the curriculum.

Continuity, progression and cohesion in language learning: the wider context

Primary MFL is not an isolated entity and any debate on the subject needs to take account of the secondary school stage of learning as we discuss at length in Chapter 10. Our main concern in this book remains to discuss questions about the 5–11 age range, which need to be considered within the context of a primary to secondary continuum of learning. Transfer at 11 merely reflects the organisation of schooling in England and functions as a stepping-stone from one stage of learning to another, where one stage consolidates and builds upon the learning of the earlier stage. This requires planning that is progressive in content and in terms of the development of skills, for example, building on the extensive 'learning through the ears' approach at KS1 advocated by Eric Hawkins (2005: 10) through song and rhyme (also appropriate for Foundation Stage children), towards 'a wider, richer concept of literacy' at KS2 (ibid. 2005: 10).

We have seen simple but very effective planning of this kind, for example a three colour-coded mind map, indicating previous learning objectives, learning intentions for the present and learning expectations for the immediate future (see Chapter 3 for more about planning). Erika Werlen's extensive research on primary MFL, carried out in Baden Württemberg in Germany and discussed in Chapter 10, stresses the importance of cross-phase planned continuity and progression to avoid truncating the child's language learning experience. Werlen emphasises the need for elements of continuity, for example of teaching approach, in both phases as well as challenge in new but connected learning, to avoid demotivation, recognising the strengths of both the younger and the older learner and to progress learning. Without attention to cross-phase cohesive provision and sustained progressive learning opportunities, the rationale for early learning in school might well be considerably weaker.

Cohesive primary MFL learning enables children to learn in such a way that they understand content and contexts relating to their own experiences. When this is embedded across the whole curriculum it provides a powerful way to develop basic communicative and intercultural competence as well as a range of language and social skills. In this way, primary MFL is an integrative, authentic and emancipatory learning experience which can also be fun, and enjoyable learning, whatever the language.

Which language?

There is much popular wisdom propagated about which language should be taught in schools. Most of the ideas exchanged are based on an idea of maximum 'usefulness' of a given language. This usefulness is sometimes understood in relation to the language that we have the greatest contact with (in tourism or business), or even in terms of the language with the largest number of speakers (Mandarin Chinese) though, historically, sheer numbers of speakers have never motivated learners to learn a language unless there is attached a commensurate prestige or utilitarian value.

Many adults in the UK associate language learning at school with French only and this can reflect negatively or positively on the attitudes they convey to their children. Many parents continue to enjoy learning and rekindle their own French through their child's experience of language learning whereas others may have an entrenched dislike for French and encourage their child to learn another language.

Parental attitudes and other 'learnt' ideas are clearly visible when asking children which language they prefer, for example the child cited in Chapter 4 ('French is hard to pronounce').

French has always been, by far, the most taught modern foreign language in the UK and this picture looks set to continue for the time being though diversification is taking place. For several reasons French remains the obvious choice:

- it is the language of our nearest neighbours and most countries have a tradition of familiarity with their neighbouring language and culture;
- the important historical and cultural links between Britain and France;
- French is ingrained into our education system and into our psyches as 'the' foreign language with most MFL material aimed at French and French attracting the highest number of students, thereby language-qualified staff;
- although now no longer comparable with English, French retains international prestige as an international language of culture;
- as a mother tongue or second language French connects a wide range of different societies around the world (la Francophonie);
- the linguistic effects of history have resulted in enormous lexical congruity between English and French.

There is an increasing interest in other languages, those being mainly German and Spanish. In certain areas, community languages are gaining ground, taught as MFL as well as 'second language', and this move is to be equally welcomed. There should be, following King's presentation of the KS2 Framework, no 'constraint on which language is to be taught, including community languages' (King 2005) but the authors recognise that there are practical limitations:

> The injunction to 'diversify' is a longstanding *cri de coeur* of policy makers in the field of MFL teaching in schools. To a considerable extent it has been a cry in the wilderness so far as it seems to have come to little in the face of the massive inertia of the self-perpetuating system through which French teachers reproduce themselves from generation unto generation.
>
> (Sharpe 2001: 73)

In contrast to this it was found in the recent DfES survey (Report 572, 2004) that:

> Although the provision of primary MFL is at an early stage in England, there is already some evidence of diversification. In some schools a range of foreign languages are offered whereas in others one foreign language is offered. French is the language most commonly taught. It is offered by 40% of all schools teaching KS2 pupils. It is the only language offered by 32%. Spanish is offered in 6%, German in 4% and Italian in 2%. In 8% of schools teaching KS2 pupils, more than one language is offered.
>
> (DfES Report 572, 2004: 94)

The report cites the various reasons, staffing issues being the most prominent:

> Reasons for offering a particular language varied, but clear trends are evident. 60% of schools with primary MFL offered a particular language because there was a teacher available with expertise to teach it. Among schools that had ceased offering primary MFL, 27% had done so because the teacher had left the school. 36% of schools with primary MFL offered a particular language because it was part of the local secondary school curriculum and 24% because resources were available.
>
> (DfES Report 572, 2004: 94)

Perceived easiness was the other main reason that the authors were given for the choice of a particular language. This was particularly true in the case of Spanish and Italian. Several MFL coordinators and headteachers mentioned that they would like to adopt Spanish because children find it easier than French, especially in writing. One MFL primary specialist, though herself a German and French specialist, gave the following response when asked about the dominance of French at her school:

> *'We're largely led by staffing and material factors though we would like to introduce Spanish instead of (that is, not as well as) French. Although I don't really speak Spanish yet I know that pupils find Spanish easier because of the regular phonetic spelling and also they're more motivated to do Spanish and parents sometimes ask me why we don't do it. Let's face it, who goes to Germany on holiday, and fewer people go to France these days.'*

Parental attitudes or preferences to teaching styles or the teachers themselves clearly influence the choice of one language in favour of another. In our view *all* languages have the capacity to enrich the lives of children through the enjoyment, curiosity and greater sense of understanding engendered by the learning of a different cultural space.

Conclusion

There is, as the research referred to in this chapter has shown, clear evidence that children are capable of far more even at an early stage than mere copying of sounds and symbols when learning modern foreign languages. Their language learning skills are independent of a specific language. The efforts of enthusiastic MFL primary school teachers have now been officially recognised as has primary MFL as a subject in its own right. Based on the guidelines laid down in the national Framework, providing there is sufficient funding and well trained teaching staff so as to ensure the best language learning provision based on a whole-school approach, there is now a genuine opportunity to build on and maintain children's natural interest in foreign languages.

Comenius, some three and a half centuries ago, also had parrots in mind when he emphasised the inclusive nature of language learning and saw it as inseparable from the development of the whole person:

The study of languages . . . should be joined to that of objects, that our acquaintance with the objective world and with language . . . may progress side by side. For it is people we are forming and not parrots.

(Comenius 1657: 203-4)

Professor Richard Johnstone of the University of Stirling, eminent in the field of primary MFL, gave a warning in a speech to MFL teacher educators in the early 1990s concerning the need to avoid ready assumptions about early learning, in his words putting 'too many eggs in the early learning basket'. With this in mind we can see few reasons to delay further a start to language learning in the primary school as outlined in the KS2 Framework. It matters – for 'every child matters' – that all children have an opportunity to engage in language learning. Well trained and confident teachers can, with their enthusiasm and with appropriate support, capitalise on the evidence of pupil enjoyment in language learning and the development of self in many primary classrooms and open doors onto the world more widely for their pupils.

Issues for reflection

- What is your own general view in the debate on 'the earlier the better?' and for what reasons?

- What do younger learners do better and what do older learners do better according to your own observations?

- What do your own experiences and engagement with MFL in the first few years at secondary school alert you to in respect of primary MFL?

- What are the factors shaping the language of choice at your school?

- Do you have a preference for a particular MFL? If so, can you analyse the origin of this preference?

2

Leading the way – the importance of a shared leadership approach

THE VAST LITERATURE on change management indicates clearly that any curriculum change or innovation needs the active support from the headteacher to be successful. Although the role of the head is central, it is insufficient in itself. If such change, specifically in the case of primary MFL, is to become embedded in the curricular fabric of the school and to be a sustainable option that will endure and continue to develop, the support of a leadership in the broadest sense is required. Alongside the headteacher, the role of the subject leader and other parties interested in primary MFL is central. Success needs to be sustained and we need to explore issues of sustainability and the nature of a school culture that can nurture a whole-school perspective on primary MFL to this end. This chapter identifies what seem to be the key supportive factors for primary MFL in the school culture.

Key issues

- Leadership is crucial in the implementation of curriculum innovation and development.
- Radiating from various pulse points and not just from the top leadership is more effective than otherwise as a shared endeavour.
- Subject leadership is vital for quality subject provision.
- Shared leadership is a powerful tool for collaborative staff learning and professional development.
- Such collaboration is nurtured by a 'warm' and open school culture.
- Leaders will have to decide how to interpret the KS2 Framework in a way that best suits the needs of their school community.
- Sustainable provision for modern foreign language teaching and learning needs to be planned for as part of the ongoing school development or improvement plan.
- An international mindset is central as part of the leadership vision and an identifiable part of the leadership factor where primary MFL is concerned.

Introduction

An experienced primary school teacher told us: 'I am a language specialist and taught French in primary schools in the 70s when it was in vogue. Part of the reasons for the decline was the lack of specialist teachers, lack of coherence across and even within schools and teachers who tried to deliver a secondary model to young children.'

The DfES entitlement for KS2 learners seeks to address the issues raised in this quote by requiring adequately qualified and trained teachers and suitable transition arrangements from KS2 to KS3. Government funding has been provided for the purposes of training and cross-sector collaboration with strong expectations of leadership from those in the various driving seats. Leadership is an essential factor driving and supporting successful change management, and is, therefore, fundamental to an effective and sustainable primary modern foreign language provision. The DfES Research Report 572 (2004: 103) made three recommendations specifically in terms of leadership, asserting that:

1 Key personnel were needed in each LA to promote primary MFL and to develop networks.

2 Leadership from central government was needed to support schools in the target to meet the entitlement.

3 Schools themselves should take a lead on planning for a minimum time allocation for the learning of the foreign language to include 30 minutes protected time a week.

While the first two recommendations are perhaps somewhat self-evident, the third could be contested on the grounds of the amount of protected time, for each stakeholder will have a view on the minimum recommendation. Establishing the principle of protected time is important as it marks a move for primary language learning towards equality of status as a core subject within the whole primary curriculum provision. Leadership, as understood in a broader sense, is essential for this to happen. Leaders comprise heads, subject coordinators or subject leaders and others with a leadership role; in short, those with the power and resources to sanction and make such provision operational and to provide a mechanism to scaffold sustainability. We define leaders, along with Peter Senge, as people who 'lead through developing new skills, capabilities and understandings. And they come from many places in the organisation' (Senge 1990: 15).

The 'leadership factor' has been shaped considerably by, for example, the NACELL observatory of practice developed and supported by the National Languages Centre, research over the years and very recent snapshots that have been taken for this book of 'practice that works'. It is these types of visions and practices of leadership that fuel the existing revolutionary picture of primary language learning that might otherwise have remained part of a very incomplete patchwork of activity, or marginalised in relation to the status of and priority afforded 'core' subjects.

The power of leadership

'Our children's development is poor in English. Learning a foreign language does not help this factor and adds to the learning failure of some children.'

'We are striving to raise academic achievement in the core subject areas and our timetable reflects this. We would find it difficult to accommodate yet another subject area without compromising existing provision.'

'The pressures on staff to deliver an ever changing curriculum mean that there is little energy to develop foreign language learning unless there is consistent long term support.'

Teachers with experiences of previous but not always satisfactory early language learning experiments have expressed concerns regarding future teaching of primary language learning and its sustainability with the government's commitment to a foreign language entitlement for all Key Stage 2 pupils. There are certainly many schools where heads have chosen not to develop primary MFL for their pupils for a variety of reasons – following the prerogative of leadership that leaders can choose to make things happen or not. Leadership has to attend to views that are similar to those of the three heads quoted above on language development, in particular the time and energy to innovate, but fortunately there are many teachers and heads who have offered different more positive arguments. In recent years many leaders, with their different yet interlinking primary MFL stakeholders, be they schools, LAs or training institutions, have made primary foreign language learning happen and have put it indelibly on/in the curriculum of many a primary school, as we mentioned in our Introduction. Keith Sharpe ended his book on the 'what, why and how of early MFL teaching' (Sharpe 2001: 198) with the somewhat prophetic suggestion that: 'Much could be gained by extending the initiative within an overall policy of gradualism rather than a "big bang" approach to making MFL a statutory part of the National Curriculum.' In a relatively short period of time this wish has been met since the early language learning experience is being shepherded into the KS2 curriculum over what will have been, in effect, an eight-year period (2001–2009 if the beginning of the school year 2009–2010 is the starting point), a fairly gentle gradient.

The central role of the head as a driving force

Leadership and headship should not be seen as synonymous, nor is it true to say that leadership is a prerogative of headteachers alone, although the role of the head is essential. When asked about the 'push' factor behind one school's successful venture into early language learning – Spanish in this case – across the school, the LA advisor replied 'Headteacher, headteacher, headteacher!'. The headteacher's own perspective is that she empowered others: 'I acted as a catalyst and supported those teachers who were enthusiastic about foreign language teaching. Personally I hardly know any Spanish!'

Barthes (1990) refers to a 'community of leaders' as the potential for shared leadership. A more shared or distributed pattern of leadership can help to secure a measure of sustainability where primary language learning is fragile without which the 'bang' of recent enthusiasm might be in danger of dissipating. In essence though, nothing happens without the active support of headteachers who command the position as well as resource power to enable early foreign language learning to become a part of their school's curriculum.

The subject leader – manager of the internal and external environments

Effective subject leadership becomes all the more important if headteachers do not have any foreign language capability. In one particular school, subject leadership was an enterprise mainly shared between several class teachers and a parent modern linguist although one of the teachers held the formal responsibility for ensuring coherence of provision and its coordination. The current preoccupation with middle management, and 'leading from the middle', recognises the importance of the subject leader as a key agent of change as well as for school improvement, and research has demonstrated unequivocally that leadership is central in achieving these missions (Harris 2003). Subject leaders might be considered as lead professionals, with a significant role in helping to develop subject expertise in colleagues as well as demonstrating best practice in their subject. This is a much needed function in the still emerging revolutionary area that is primary modern foreign language learning. A subject leader in one of the schools we visited has developed her confidence in primary MFL over the years, and was clear about how she was now able to offer differentiated support to colleagues: 'Some teachers are still scared of foreign languages and even if they have a certain level of competence themselves they don't want to display their lack of competence in front of children. I suppose it's a bit like singing, some people like to do it, some people don't apart from in a car. Different teachers need different support and they also need different levels of support.'

This subject leader had a clear understanding of the monitoring aspect of her role: 'My role is basically to monitor the provision of MFL in the school to standardise the provision for the children and to ensure progression.' This definition of role reflects very well the mentoring, managing and monitoring dimensions of a subject leader's

role as identified in the research undertaken by Busher and Harris (2000) and the five interlocking processes that, they maintain, are the hallmark of effective planning and that help to create an effective subject area:

Working with staff

Establishing baselines: measuring current performance

Having a clear vision of where to go

Creating sensible maps, timetables and ladders to achieve the preferred goals

Devising a means of monitoring progress on the road to achieving the goals (target setting).

These processes could indeed serve as an emergent job description for the primary language subject leader. While subject leadership is seemingly located more often than not within a discourse of secondary school subjects, it plays, encompassing subject *coordination*, a vital role in the primary school. This particularly holds true as subject leadership aims to focus on the attendant concerns of teaching, learning, assessment, staff management and resources in the internal arena of the school as well as connecting to external links such as partner secondary schools, the LA, parents and the community at large.

Having identified two key leadership roles and emphasised the importance of sharing leadership, let us at this point situate the full range of leadership in the context of a school. The following case study snapshot, in which the headteacher and others with leadership responsibilities for primary modern foreign language learning and teaching describe what leadership looks like in a real-life primary school context. It provides valuable data for highlighting issues concerning leadership. The school that is spotlighted has a vibrant, continuously evolving and evidently sustainable provision, and is illuminative of key issues that are important in developing and sustaining an effective provision, and which are supported as being so by a considerable canon of research (Fullan 1991; Fullan and Hargreaves 1992; MacBeath 1998; Sergiovanni 2001; Stoll and Fink 1996).

Case study: the 'ancient mariner's' tale

The school is a mixed primary school located in a medium-sized town where unemployment is high. Of the 200-plus pupils on roll, its Additional Educational Needs register shows some 40 per cent of children in need of support for learning or behavioural difficulties. The school represents an oasis of learning and calm behaviour for many children with unsettled backgrounds and has invested heavily in literacy support. The current headteacher who has been in post for some six years is a confirmed Francophile herself; indeed she sets the tone for language learning. As a Church-aided school, she begins the day with greetings and prayers in French in whole-school assembly. Pupils respond with their return greeting in French.

A previous head, with great vision and before the primary MFL initiative of the last decades, introduced French to pupils in the late 1960s. This was not due to the Nuffield experiment of the time but based solely on the head's belief that pupils could benefit from learning and enjoying French in the way that he had done as part of his time in the Merchant Navy. Despite the retirement of the charismatic 'ancient mariner', the French experiment remained operational yet unsystematic, although successive heads reacted favourably to the LA's enthusiastic efforts in wanting to be part of the LA's primary French project, subsequently extended to other languages.

The current head consolidated the previous patchy provision of language learning for Years 5 and 6 and extended provision to the whole school, including Year 1 pupils. The deputy head, the leader for early years, has overseen this move into the early years. The provision has grown organically, very much in graduated form, as teachers have developed the confidence and have planned an ever-developing scheme of work together. The primary MFL coordinator has been both a KS1 and KS2 teacher. All teachers, for the most part, teach their own classes, using course materials provided by the county but supplemented by an array of additional resources bought by the school or made by the teachers themselves. The coordinator attends the county twilight training sessions and all teachers have had some training using in-house expertise and are well supported by the coordinator as well as the LA primary MFL adviser.

Recent appointments to posts at the school have been made in open competition taking into consideration candidates' qualifications for MFL gained during their school careers and their teacher training. The chair of governors is a modern linguist who helped to launch the language learning enterprise and initially coached the Key Stage 2 school teachers in the early 1990s. She retains a leadership role as adviser and as monitoring governor. It has been the tradition for some years that the governor organises an Easter holiday project connected to some aspect of cultural learning and including some language work. This has been very popular; for example it attracted some 80 children's efforts on a project about Belgium and the 'Swiss Miss' project. While French is the main language taught, some pupils at some point get bursts of Spanish and German when they are in the classes of teachers with knowledge of these languages. The school's input to training future teachers of primary languages is considerable. In any one year, the tally of trainee teachers would typically include several postgraduate trainees, two students training on the undergraduate route, and trainees from France as part of the reciprocal training arrangements of a local teacher training institution.

All teachers are enabled through the support of the subject leader to make an input of a progressive and cyclical nature, for example the younger children learn greetings in French just as they practise greetings in English as a social activity in class. Sometimes they do this activity in a circle time activity as part of their

PHSE programme. Greetings are recycled continuously as children move up the school and are extended to other languages and to more complex varieties of expression. The headteacher is an opportunist. A graduate MFL trainee, who is a native speaker, was asked to provide a 'life saver' of target language commands for all staff. Native-speaking French trainees have been asked to make signs in French for around the school. A French-speaking Belgian parent has coached the teachers in pronunciation and simple phrases in after-school sessions. One teacher has some Spanish and another some German so these languages, rather precariously, are added to the linguistic menu, extra spice as it were that could arguably be left out of the recipe. French predominates for historical reasons and because of the active support of the head for French.

Crucially in terms of primary–secondary liaison, an MFL teacher, actually the head of department from one of the local secondary schools, comes in to support the Key Stage 2 teachers and to teach Year 6 children occasionally. This provides a high level of coaching for the teachers and some high quality teaching for the pupils, as well as very transparent continuity of provision from KS2 to KS3. Leadership is enacted by many in their different but complementary roles. Nonetheless, the head-teacher is pivotal in her central role as 'project leader', as shown in the web of leadership diagram (Figure 2.1).

Let us now elaborate the 'who does what, why and how' in terms of leadership. Table 2.1 shows a breakdown of roles in tabular form.

Leadership roles

Table 2.1 is not designed as a hierarchical list; it locates the head at the top on account of her position of power. She also provides instructional leadership and leads by example using French incidentally throughout the school day and awarding foreign language stickers for good work, good effort, improvement, etc. The head works in tandem with the subject leader whose seminal role we have already commented upon at length and with the deputy headteacher who is responsible for the early years and intends to involve children from Year 1 in the project. While excluding the Reception class children – 'They have too much to learn at this stage and it [primary MFL] might bewilder them' – Years 1 to 3 have a brief timetabled slot and teachers are asked to make incidental use of French. Since none of the other teachers are language specialists the support of the subject leader is again essential to the successful teaching of French. The subject leader's role extends to coaching all colleagues at both Key Stages, teachers and teaching assistants who are, in turn, expected to demonstrate dimensions of subject leadership through their own roles in the classroom. The leadership of the subject area at primary level is complemented by that of secondary colleagues who, where they have time and funding to be able to do so, visit the primary school to model and share subject expertise.

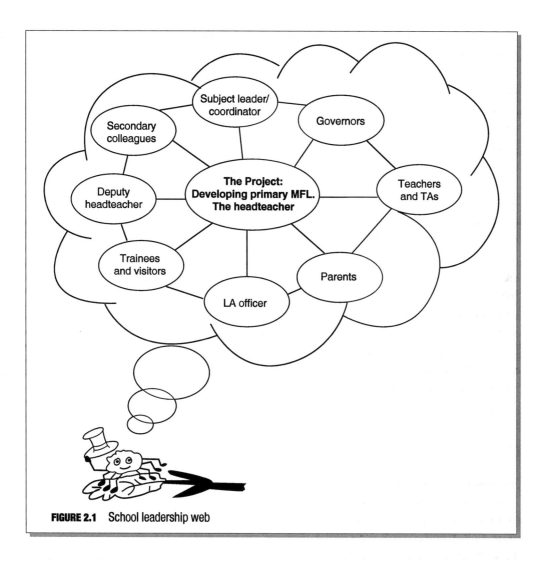

FIGURE 2.1 School leadership web

Some school governing bodies talk of a 'dream ticket' comprising accountant, lawyer and architect (modern version of 'butcher, baker and candlestick maker') as useful persons to have available to dispense free advice. We could also add a governor modern linguist where primary MFL is concerned as potentially very useful. The MFL governor in the case study school helped kick-start the provision at a time when the LA made materials available to schools but most of the teachers needed support in developing confidence in their use of language and in the use of appropriate teaching methods; the governor modelled teaching strategies, created materials and coached colleagues. The DfES Research Report (2004) identified the important role of governors, whether directly as in this case study, or indirectly, with goodwill and support for the school's primary MFL development in evidence. However, a governor's role is often transitory and time-bound to a term of office

TABLE 2.1 The who, why, how of leadership in the case study school

Lead role – who?	Motivation – why?	How leadership demonstrated
Headteacher	Personal 'crusade' on behalf of the pupils deriving from own experiences of travel	Whole-school drip-feed approach and international mindset; use of position and resource power
Subject leader/coordinator	Own enjoyment and belief in value of language learning for pupils	Lead subject teacher and coach to peers; professional development opportunities taken and shared with colleagues, e.g. new ideas and materials obtained shared with colleagues in staff meetings
Deputy headteacher	Belief in opportunities for early years	PMFL developed as part of basic skills and developing bi-literacy
Teachers and teaching assistants	Wish to have ownership of MFL teaching in their own classroom	Developing subject expertise over time with possibility to coach others
Secondary school teachers	To ensure coherence across key stages and cross-sector collaboration	Modelling subject expertise, both linguistic and pedagogical
Governor	Belief in language learning as life opportunity	Provision of materials; annual project for pupils; coaches headteacher; monitoring school development plan with regard to foreign language learning
Parents	Wish to be involved in life of school; one uses her foreign language competence to help staff lacking in confidence	Foreign language lessons by one parent for teachers with particular focus on pronunciation; others provide cultural artefacts and share knowledge
Trainee teachers and foreign visitors	Specialist subject provision in class	Class inputs and whole-school tasks such as notices around the school in French and German
LA adviser	Strong belief in early language learning	Wide range of training provision, resources and one-to-one support

so does not score over-highly on sustainable grounds. It would be ideal if the school could create a sustainable structure of governing support with, for example, one governor role attached to primary MFL, another to monitor and support primary–secondary liaison and perhaps a third to support the international dimension of the school. All these roles have an expectation of leadership. In a similar way, the potential for parental leadership will be dependent on the skills and knowledge parents can offer. A school could undertake a kind of 'audit' of the languages parents know actively and, in their quest to involve them in their children's learning of a foreign language, help parents to be able to practise with their children and identify any possible leadership role such as in the case study school context. A practical, working example of parents in partnership is that of a French-speaking Belgian mother who was at hand for support in this school over a sustained period of time. The teachers felt very comfortable practising pronunciation with her and she assumed a role in coaching the teachers. Ever an opportunist, the head welcomed visitors to the school including a considerable number from European educational institutions wanting to come on study visits. Where they were French or German speaking, they were asked to take a lead in certain events, in assembly, in MFL lessons, by designing materials, a good example of reciprocal support. Trainee teachers with an MFL specialism can also be asked to utilise their specialist knowledge for the benefit of the school and take a lead in a similar way. Where primary MFL is buoyant in a school, the school acts as a magnet to potential visitors.

The DfES (2004) research found conclusively that those LAs with primary language coordinators or advisers had the most extensive and potentially sustainable practice. This is due to the wide range of resources they make available, the expert coaching and professional development on offer, the networking opportunities and the sheer excellence and exuberance of colleagues in LA primary MFL leadership roles – not least in the instance of the case study school where bespoke support over the years had helped nurture the MFL culture in the school.

The leadership vision and visions into practice

What then can be inferred from this case study about ways in which leadership permeates and sustains the language learning enterprise? How does leadership manifest itself with respect to primary MFL? How exactly does it support primary language learning? A key issue is the personal engagement of the headteacher and her leadership vision based on a strong personal commitment. When asked where her personal commitment came from, the subject coordinator of this school replied: 'Well, it's partly because I like France so much.' She continued: 'I think it is very restricting when people think they can get on in life just by speaking English. It's arrogant and it doesn't do much for a person's ability to communicate with other people.'

In Chapter 1, we looked at reasons in favour of an early language learning opportunity. These positions have been more than adequately debated over the years and a measure of consensus has been achieved as to the value of the enterprise – positive attitudes towards foreign language learning and towards other cultures, linguistic sensitivity, cultural awareness, enjoyment in learning. What is striking in the testimonies of the case study head is the 'bigger picture' vision for the learners: 'Learning French opens horizons. The world is theirs. Learning a language enables them to have greater opportunities.' The desire to introduce children to the joys of foreign language learning derives in part from a personal successful and enjoyable voyage into 'otherness' by those involved in leading the project. As the headteacher said, echoing the feelings of her subject leader: 'I didn't enjoy learning French at school and couldn't see the point but then we started to spend our holidays in France and we have friends who live there and I think it is rude not to know something of the language and the culture.' Here we have a Francophile headteacher who now enjoys learning the language herself and visiting France (as, coincidentally, does the school's subject leader). It is clear from this example and from what we know about the importance of directive, visionary leadership that the personal drive of the head is a key motivating factor in successfully embedding MFL into the fabric of a school. MFL provision might be also influenced by an opera-loving Italophile or indeed a person with no specific predilection for a particular country and language but simply, and this is the essential ingredient, a desire to broaden the cultural and linguistic horizons of the school, its pupils and staff.

While joyous and inspiring, visions need to be made concrete and operational as Trethowan (1991: 3) writes: 'There must be absolute clarity in the leader's mind about what constitutes the key features of the vision. The vision has to be hard, well thought out, practical . . . related to time and place.' The leaders have to take decisions about who will teach, how they will teach, which language and what time allocation will be given: 'The central decisions that must be made by school managers – Who? What? When? How?' (Key Stage 2 Framework 2005: 19). Furthermore, leaders decide what they will use to support their teaching and on ways to monitor and assess teaching and learning. They also need to take into consideration means to ensure progression and how they will interpret the Key Stage 2 Framework in a way that matches the needs and resources of the school and be quite clear about the value of the enterprise. CILT, The National Centre for Languages, deriving from its Development of Early Language Learning (DELL) project, has identified seven curricular models that schools could adopt, according to their special circumstances and needs. Each model has a different emphasis and a different way of incorporating the MFL provision into the curriculum but common to all is a clear delineation of learning purpose, systematic arrangements for supporting the learning, evident leadership across sectors and a shared learning culture. However, in a telephone poll of 15 heads carried out by the authors across three LAs, it was found that every school had its own unique arrangements, some loosely related to the DELL models, others on a 'pick and mix' basis, but all of them very idiosyncratic and in harmony with their own particular culture.

The school culture – a culture of learning together

Each school is unique and creates, based on its own way of organising itself, its individual culture. A school culture at its simplest is, as Nias *et al.* (1989) wrote:

'influenced by particular sets of circumstances (for example buildings, personnel, organisational arrangements) and expressed in special ways (for example, through language, rituals and symbols) or quite simply "the way things get done" '.

The case study school has an identifiable culture of learning together and specifically one that celebrates language learning. The research of Jennifer Nias (ibid. 181) and colleagues in primary schools emphasised the importance of a 'warm' culture in which to innovate and create, for it is not so much the single bearing of the head herself but rather the culture that is created for the possibility of innovation and experimentation. There are some elements of a school culture that are stable and are resistant to change which can be a positive factor, as with the upholding of traditions such as that of teaching French initiated some thirty years ago in the case school. Sometimes this stability can be problematic in that many individuals prefer to stay within their 'comfort zone' and will resist innovation and change especially if they are not convinced that it will be of benefit or if they do not have ownership of the change. Other aspects of the school culture such as planned curriculum development, policy construction and professional development are manageable and more susceptible to change, especially where the critical mass of staff is involved in the development from the early stages of planning. A top-down management approach never really works but then a bottom-up approach is not without its difficulties, as is known from cases where teachers were enthusiastic about foreign language teaching but the headteacher remained sceptical.

It has long been recognised that leaders create cultures and that creating a culture for learning is crucial. A primary language learning scenario is likely to be a learning experience for many of the teachers and others involved in terms of linguistic and pedagogical competence, for enthusiasm alone takes one only so far and cannot be a sound basis for sustainable learning. However, teachers who are motivated by the experience of their own learning are likely to excite their pupils in turn. Such enthusiasm is tangible in the subject leader and the headteacher in the case study school. A learning-centred head will give strong messages about learning and about professional development. The research of Earley and Weindling (2004) included ten case studies of highly effective heads that showed without exception that headteachers paid great attention to the development of leadership capacity throughout the school. Middle managers or coordinators, for example, gained confidence and shaped the rest of the staff's perceptions of them as experts in their fields. Leadership can thus be defined as: 'that part of a manager's work concerned with helping people to tackle prescribed tasks to the optimum of their ability' (Day *et al.* 1998: 41).

The case study school subject leader has risen to the challenge and having been encouraged and empowered by the headteacher now feels able to coach her colleagues in their classrooms and assume the role of leader of learning, and, with the help of the LA adviser, provide support for teachers with limited experience of primary MFL, as well as continuing support for subject leaders.

To summarise, features of a school culture conducive to developing sustainable primary MFL provision include:

- receptivity to experimentation on the part of the teachers;

- active encouragement by, and the involvement of, the head;

- a 'slowly but surely' approach where all can engage with innovation at their own pace;

- collaborative learning at an organisational level coupled with differentiated provision;

- empowering staff through the development of leadership skills and opportunities to share leadership;

- creating a network of support both within the school and beyond by engaging with other schools, associated institutions, the LEA and the school community; and crucially for primary MFL,

- a deep-seated wish to provide opportunities to 'expand horizons' and to move beyond the parochial.

An international mindset

The notion of 'expanding horizons' though well intentioned and sincere can be a very nebulous concept and yet the intercultural dimension or what we call the 'international mindset' has arguably never been so important in primary schools. As the headteacher of the case study school commented, never have children been forced to be so politically aware or needed to begin to understand their developing role as active citizens in a European and indeed global context.

This head and the subject leader choose to engage with cross-bordering in their own personal lives and, with their colleagues, to welcome the opening of borders in the school, given the increasing diversity of language and cultures incoming children bring and the many visitors from abroad who enrich the school's cultural fabric and language learning environment. Such a 'border free leadership' perspective implies that, in the cosmopolitan school, school leaders will have to deal with international issues and not just local ones and develop an 'international mindset', articulating a vision that meets the needs of learners from all over the world. In this one small primary school, there are such learners: 'We have children from across the world . . . Italy, France, and bilingual families from North Africa . . . Dutch, Japanese, children from all sorts of cultural backgrounds.'

While the children's cultures and heritages are already welcomed and celebrated and the parents invited as much as possible into the school, part of this school's international project is to consider how to exploit further the languages that the children have as part of a language learning project that goes beyond the teaching of French. When school leaders actively develop an international mindset, then they 'walk their talk'. They enjoy and encourage travel, real or virtual, and provide opportunities for the learners to experience such enjoyment, with trips and exchanges, e-links and participation in Comenius projects, or other EU-funded actions, or town-twinning links, for example. In so doing, school leaders become part of the international community of leadership.

Conclusion

This chapter has sought to underline the importance of leadership in the development of primary MFL, to define and illustrate the concept of shared leadership and to emphasise the importance of planning for sustainability in order to avoid the disappointment of the project fizzling out through a lack of key leadership skills. A successful primary MFL project is a whole-school enterprise. The image of creeping ivy can be used to illustrate how primary MFL has crept into the primary curriculum unremittingly, like the tenacious ivy, and has, in many respects and in many areas and in a great many individual schools, developed secure roots that are important for sustainability. Sustainability, we are asserting, derives from developing leadership skills and sharing leadership to create a kind of leadership web that provides at least second level support and expertise. This forms a solid resource basis for the important decision-making about primary MFL policy and the implementation of the provision.

Some schools' arrangements are fragile because of a lack of secure leadership, especially subject leadership scaffolding which may mean that the ivy could so easily lose its grip. This has happened in many a secondary school where especially the second and/or third language (usually languages other than French) have disappeared. This is particularly true in cases where all the subject expertise was invested in one person. Sustainability needs to be considered from the very start of the project and become part of the school and staff development/improvement/ learning plan. Some heads and other leaders prioritise the development of primary MFL as a performance objective and/or as part of their leadership training. In so doing, they illustrate the concept of leadership as learning and establish themselves as lead learners in their primary MFL learning community.

Issues for reflection

- Look at a particular school with which you are associated and identify the leadership web. Who leads and on what? Where is leadership lacking or where could it be improved?
- How can leadership skills and capability be developed to undertake the roles needed to support a strong web?
- What resources are needed to develop leadership capability?
- What are the key factors in planning for primary MFL sustainability?

Planning and use of resources – doing the groundwork

IN THIS CHAPTER we will consider how to approach planning MFL teaching and learning. Planning issues that we discuss are those of setting achievable targets – learning intentions – and using resources effectively. We will suggest ways in which teachers can improvise and adapt material from different sources, not forgetting that the greatest resources available are the teacher and the pupils themselves! We use the metaphor of the Russian doll to emphasise the interconnected nature of micro- and macro-planning and we include examples of lessons plans and schemes of work to illustrate the mesh between learning objectives and the integrated use of resources within short-term, medium- and longer-term planning.

Key issues

- MFL is most effectively delivered when teaching is embedded within a longer-term view to ensure cohesion and progression.

- As with other subjects, it is important that teachers are sympathetic with the aims and objectives which constitute the scheme of work and that these are meaningfully conveyed to pupils.

- Resources are overwhelmingly identified by primary teachers as the most important factor in enabling them to teach MFL in primary schools (DfES Report 572, 2004).

- The single most important resource in MFL teaching is the teacher and the quality of the teacher–pupil relationship.

- As teachers' confidence in MFL teaching grows they become less dependent on following prepared material and can instigate activities and adapt materials more freely.

- Primary teachers' expertise in using age-appropriate techniques and adapting re-sources for cross-curricular purposes means they are especially well placed to adapt MFL material to suit the particular needs of pupils.

Introduction

In recent years a plethora of MFL materials has become available on the market, many encouraging teachers to exploit new technologies (see Chapter 8) and many others updating old favourites by repackaging and using new images for the twenty-first century. For example, instead of the classic French 'prototype' family *Les Dupont* that many of us were familiar with from our textbooks of the 1960s and 1970s, children today are more likely to be presented with the daily routines, likes and dislikes of crazy animals or fantastic characters such as *Floridor* and *Yxtra*, the extraterrestrials from *La Planète X* who feature in the *Salut* series. Older children are often taught through easily identifiable celebrities such as *La famille Simpson* or footballers and pop singers presented in colourful moving images. Despite these changes and despite many developments in our understanding of child learning, however, the pedagogic rationale underlying many of the MFL materials available has hardly changed and many activities that can be seen today in a primary MFL lesson might have been seen thirty or forty years ago. Does the abundance of good quality materials blind us to what the learning objectives really are in primary MFL? In this chapter, we will look at ways of approaching planning which include setting achievable targets, considerations affecting which new language to present, how to present new language, how to encourage pupil participation in a way that maximises ownership of the new language, and the use of different resources which contribute to whole-child skills development for early learners.

Defining resources

The terms resources and materials are often used interchangeably to refer to any of the 'props' that might be used in the MFL class such as picture cards, posters, clothes, toys, OHTs, cue cards, worksheets, books, display items, tapes, songs, video-clips, etc. (ICT resources and activities will be dealt with separately in Chapter 8). Resources can be used in the classroom by the teacher, by the whole class, by pairs, groups and individual pupils. When used by the teacher they often function as a demonstration prop and we will see later in this chapter how new language might be presented. A broader definition of resources includes all support material which is used to help teachers plan and coordinate pupil learning within and away from the classroom. We are including here the syllabus or scheme of work which the teacher has been asked to, or has chosen to, follow, or which they have themselves created.

The scheme of work is a resource in that it functions as a framework that shapes and guides teachers' planning of *what* is to be taught, *when* (in sequence) and (in a good scheme of work at least) suggestions of *how* it will be included. In our view, the scheme of work is a bank of ideas best used when dipped into and tailored to personal preference and particular pupil needs rather than followed slavishly. The conventional structure of an MFL syllabus is discussed below and an approach to planning is suggested starting from lessons and building up to medium (termly), long (yearly) and whole-school schemes of work. Although we present the lesson first as a minimum unit of planning, in reality it is the longer-term overarching objectives which will form the starting point when planning MFL learning. The different levels of planning mesh together like a Russian doll. The end product is the classroom teaching and learning but this is encased in broader frames of planning which ensure coherence, variety and balance.

As with any other resource material, the scheme of work is there to provide guidelines and suggestions as a support mechanism. It is one of the advantages of the otherwise decidedly mixed blessing that MFL is not formally assessed in primary schools that teachers usually have greater autonomy in deciding what, when and how MFL should be taught, compared, for example, to the numeracy and literacy frameworks, although as these have become firmly established in practice these too

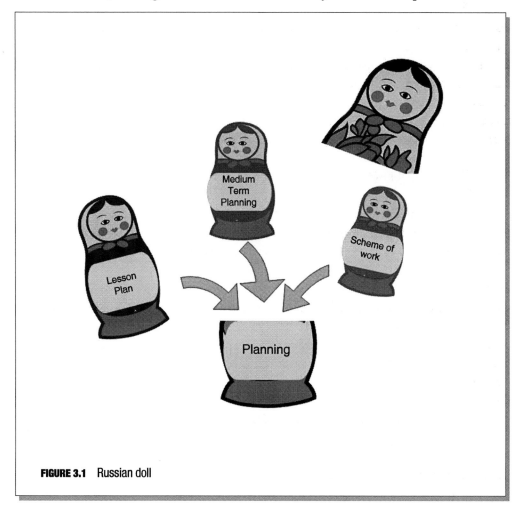

FIGURE 3.1   Russian doll

are becoming ever more flexible in recognition of teachers' desire to appropriate learning frames to suit their own styles and the specific localised needs of their pupils' learning context. This broader definition of resources was highlighted by the DfES Research Report (2004) into MFL provision at KS2, showing that 'local or in-house schemes of work' are the most popular syllabus plans, used by 34 per cent of respondents. These have often been adapted themselves from existing LA/QCA or coursebook-based schemes in the light of practitioners' experiences and beliefs as well as other localised circumstances such as material and time constraints. Since this research was conducted, the Key Stage 2 Framework has been introduced and the learning objectives listed in the Framework are also now being used to structure planning.

Among the resources used in teaching MFL in the classroom, audio tapes and CDs are the most popular, used by over half of respondents. These are often used for songs but also to provide non-specialist classroom teachers with an authentic source of native-speaker quality target language which they can then manipulate together with the children as a listening comprehension exercise, ensuring that pronunciation is accurate.

This use of audio material also highlights another valuable use for foreign language resources which is the teacher's own linguistic development away from pupils. Many teachers use textbooks and tapes to familiarise themselves with the language that they are going to teach rather than use the resource with the children. In this way, the resource is an excellent teacher support (and means of professional development) and the children have the benefit of the language being presented 'live' by their teacher, which may help them feel more secure with new input in the early stages. Later, of course, exposure to a variety of new voices, including native-speaker voices (on a tape or through the computer), will greatly enhance phonic awareness and add a cultural dimension to the learning.

Resource dependency

Teachers will depend on resources in MFL teaching to differing degrees and will naturally adapt them to their own personal styles. Heavy resource dependency can reflect less confidence in teachers' self-beliefs about themselves in their role as competent MFL teachers as well as being a time issue. The teachers we spoke to when researching this book who used MFL-specific (commercially produced) resources the least were those who were either most confident in the use of the foreign language (often having studied it to degree level or to A-level) or, more importantly, those who had gained in confidence through experience of teaching MFL and were now able to instigate activities more spontaneously using either materials not specific to MFL or by exploiting links to other subjects. These teachers had, over time, developed a repertoire of skills enabling them to use the patterns of language they were familiar with confidently and, with minimal or no resources, were able to organise activities to encourage pupil engagement with the foreign language. This might be something as simple as spontaneously giving an instruction or counting heads in the foreign language, or may be a last minute game of hangman (*le pendu*) on the whiteboard at the end of the day or longer activities in the MFL slot such as role-playing or singing without tapes or scripts.

The 'value-added' of using resources in MFL

Since the 'fuzzy felt' of the 1960s and the language 'labs' of the 1970s, MFL has often led the way in terms of innovative resources. Tape recorders and OHPs have long been the daily bread and butter of MFL lessons and are now being gradually replaced by interactive whiteboards (discussed in Chapter 8) which combine both sound and image. Nonetheless, the most essential resource by far is the teacher, their relationship with the children and their imagination in delivering MFL.

The teacher: the greatest resource of all

Primary MFL is now a fast-expanding commercial market and so many new resources and materials are being created and promoted, often via slick marketing brochures which promise all manner of successful learning outcomes for our pupils. While many of the new materials are indeed excellent, it is essential that they not be mistakenly seen as an end in themselves. Indeed, slick resources are, in our view, the *least* crucial element in the learning procedure. Before level of resources, we would rank as important the various constituents which determine pupil motivation, chiefly the interpersonal quality of the pupil–teacher relationship but also other variables such as teaching time (frequency of input), the value attributed to the subject (status within the school), links to whole school experience (as discussed in Chapter 5). We cannot emphasise enough that the teacher is the greatest resource of all! Nonetheless, attractive resources are of course intrinsically motivating and serve the needs of teachers. More importantly, curriculum planning must incorporate a range of activity types which will encourage both inclusion and real progression.

Planning

MFL provision, where provision is indeed *planned* to fit within a sequence of learning objectives rather than random snippets added at the whim of an enthusiastic teacher (though this is great too!), is nearly always presented according to the topic. This fits in with the dominant theory in language teaching theory which emphasises communicative language teaching (discussed in Chapter 5), suggesting that a 'logical' syllabus design reflects the following intersection: topic → language needed. The 'language needed' is often broken down into *key vocabulary* and *structure* (or grammar) and these can then be layered to form differentiated objectives. One example of how to plan a programme is provided in the QCA Schemes of Work for KS2. Also, the current Key Stage 2 Framework for languages has been designed to be used for 'curriculum design' around learning objectives that are skill based rather than topic based:

> *Schools can use the Framework creatively as a basis for long, medium and short-term planning, adapting it to meet the needs of their children and to match their own curriculum. The Framework does not prescribe specific topics or contexts for learning. It gives teachers the freedom to be creative and innovative and to devise programmes of work and activities, which will engage, excite and challenge children.*
>
> **(Key Stage 2 Framework for Languages 2005: 5)**

In the initial learning stages the topics are usually centred around formulaic phrases (greetings/introducing oneself/saying where one lives) and so the question of whether or not to 'teach' grammar (in the traditional sense of rules which are learnt and applied) does not arise. Most language phrases are therefore treated as 'vocabulary' in the sense of discrete lexical items. However, the questions of whether or not to explicitly teach grammar, how much, what type of grammar, etc., are relevant to primary MFL and once provision has been rolled out nationally to meet the 2010 entitlement target will become even more pressing as national levels increase and the need for greater coherence with secondary stage learning emerges.

Planning: the issue of grammar

The question surrounding the teaching of grammar – i.e. How explicit should it be? – is, like many such questions, something of a red herring. We do not advocate teaching mechanistic drills in MFL which have no contextually-bound meaning (that is, beyond the context of children doing what they are told to do as a classroom activity). However, we do believe that it is appropriate to explain to children how the language works if such an explanation is called for. In the same way as literacy teaching seeks to provide a basic tool kit for raising language awareness in English so teaching 'language awareness' in MFL further reinforces this aim.

The word 'grammar' tends to have negative associations for many of us who remember feeling bewildered by abstract explanations of case and gender declensions – among other seemingly impenetrable concepts – yet the problem may have been that these concepts were often presented divorced from context and without immediate opportunity for real practice. Within any communicative approach to language teaching the distinction between teaching 'grammar' and teaching 'language' or 'communication' becomes nonsensical. Sharpe (2001: 88–9) claims we have made a 'fetish' of grammar, by which he means that, while we should not make our exposition of language overly technical, grammar is simply part and parcel of what a language is. Even if we wish to focus on the socio-functional aspects of the language we are teaching, it would be unrealistic to do this without ever referring to the rules which have been formulated to help explain which words go where and why. The catchword is emphasis.

For example, if pupils have learnt to say 'I play football', 'I play basketball', etc., in Spanish, a logical next step might be, when discussing what the children did at the weekend, 'I played . . .'. If we want to teach *jugué* (I played) children do not need to overtly learn rules about forming the preterite, radical-changing verbs, adding a *u* to keep the *g* 'hard' before an *e*, including the accent to conserve the syllabic stress in regular preterite verbs, etc. Clearly, such grammatical description is inappropriate. To encourage the use of *jugué* we must convey a sense of 'pastness' to encourage pupils to use the word appropriately. One way to do this is to teach the words for today *(hoy)* and yesterday *(ayer)* and then miming and repeating

Hoy juego al fútbol

Ayer jugué al baloncesto

As pupils practise *juego* versus *jugué* they can be prompted by the words *hoy/ayer*, teacher hand movements suggesting now/in the past, pictures, dates on a calendar, etc. In this way pupils will arrive at their own translation of *jugué* without being confused and demotivated by cumbersome metalanguage and, with increased use, will naturally spot emerging patterns in the language they use. When this happens, some pupils may ask for explicit explanations and at such a time it is appropriate to help explicitly clarify rules for those pupils who wish to know them.

Planning: What to include?

As a starting point for planning let us now turn to a simplified system of approach which incorporates the *topic–language–resources* trichotomy. This could be a first lesson and/or constitute a first section of a scheme of work. Taking the classic beginners' first topic 'greetings' in Spanish, Table 3.1 is an initial draft of what might be included.

These rubrics may need further breaking down. We have stated the overall topic but what exactly do we want pupils to be able *to do* at the end of the learning sequence, i.e. what are the learning intentions? How long should the learning sequence be? How are we going to get them there? How do we know they have reached the set target? In other words, objectives need to be more precise. Now, there is a train of thought that would insist that primary MFL does not need to be so objectives-driven and that the overarching objective is to engender in pupils a positive attitude to language learning and an openness to language learning which will pave the way for later learning. We agree with this belief but would also argue that in order for progression to be assured and for MFL to be systematically embedded in the primary curriculum, coherent pedagogic planning is required as much as for any subject.

TABLE 3.1 The topic–language–resources trichotomy

Topic	Language needed	Resources
greetings	*¡Hola!*	■ video clips showing Spanish people greeting each other
	Buenos días	
	¿Qué tal?	■ smiley/grumpy/neutral faces to generate different answers
	¿Cómo estás?	
	bien, gracias	
	muy bien	
	fenomenal	
	bastante bien	
	fatal	
	¿Y tú?	

The objectives implicit in the topic used as an example here might be:

■ Pupils are able to do the following in Spanish:
  – say hello
  – ask 'How are you?' in two different ways
  – respond appropriately using a range of adjectives to express fine/great/terrific/not too bad/not great!

Inherent in these objectives lie other sets of expectations about the degree of accuracy in pronunciation, how quickly we expect pupils to be able to memorise the language and how soon we expect pupils to be able to produce the new language spontaneously. It is unlikely that all of the expressions given in the example could be covered in one lesson, even for older beginners. A first lesson for younger KS1 children might just focus on *¡Hola!* and *Buenos días* and practise these thoroughly before moving on.

Another objective which might be added for older KS2 children – or for more able pupils for an element of differentiation – is the exploitation of the written form (receptively in reading or productively in writing), a contentious issue discussed in the next chapter. Similarly, it might be a good idea to introduce at the outset the more formal *¿Cómo está usted?* to sensitise pupils to different forms of address in other languages. Indeed the Key Stage 2 Framework suggests as a learning objective for intercultural understanding that 'children should . . . learn about polite forms of address [and] know how to greet native speakers' (Framework objective IU3.3).

The decisions surrounding these objectives may be taken by the regular class teacher but she, unless she is also an MFL specialist, will usually seek the guidance of the MFL coordinator and a scheme of work. As teachers' confidence and experience grow they will naturally adapt their objectives to the pupils that they know and what they understand to be manageable and useful. In other words, teachers develop an intuition for MFL pedagogy.

As well as 'topic', we would expect to find the core 'language' to be taught explicitly listed in a scheme of work or syllabus, e.g.

Topic: Greetings

Learning outcomes: Pupils can understand and say Hello in Spanish

Language needed: *¡Hola!*

Let us move on to *how* these objectives can be achieved, bearing in mind that planning is circular and that methods and resources can be negotiated and modified as objectives become fine-tuned or reoriented once personal preferences, as well as logistics, come into play. In the example above we have listed a couple of resources that might be used for this simple interactional language but, of course, none are necessary! The language can be presented by a teacher and practised by pupils without any other resources. The QCA Scheme of Work, for example, suggests simply moving around the class and shaking hands with pupils to introduce 'Hello' in the foreign language. Pupils then greet each other using the new words. This is a useful suggestion and reminds us that, in terms of resources, simplicity is often the cornerstone. In the lesson plan exemplar given below children use finger puppets to practise saying *Guten Morgen* to each other. Similarly, exaggerated facial expressions or thumbs up/down gestures can be used to convey *bien, muy bien, fatal*, etc., as effectively as pictures to convey meaning and to gauge the level of understanding (see Chapter 7 on assessment issues).

Examples of lesson plans and a scheme of work

At the level of lesson plans, we need to consider how much is appropriate for the pupils' level. Let us look at some examples of how the broad-brush objectives mentioned above can be broken down and built into lesson plans, which then fit into a medium-term (one school term) scheme of work and then into a whole-school plan. These thoughtful examples were borrowed from a primary teacher (MFL specialist) in the north of England. Firstly, we see how she has planned two, initial 20-minute lessons for Year 1 beginners in German (Table 3.2).

We are then able to see how these two lesson plans fit into a medium-term plan or scheme of work (corresponding to seven 20-minute lessons or one school half-term) (Table 3.3).

TABLE 3.2 German lesson plan

GREETINGS AND INTRODUCTIONS (1)

Medium-term Plans for Y1 German Beginners. Thirteen 20 minute lessons. Part One, lessons 1 to 7, Greetings.

Week	Key Objectives	Key Structures and Vocabulary	Teaching Activities (20 minutes)	Resources	Expected Outcomes	Links
1	■ Know Germans often shake hands when greeting people. ■ Be able to say 'Guten Morgen' with good pronunciation. ■ Look forward with confidence to next German lesson.	Guten Morgen! Ganz still bitte!	1. Greet individually with handshake, Guten Morgen and a smile. 2. Shake hands. 3. Echo my GM in lots of different voices, and sing to tune of Alleluja, which emphasises syllables. 4. Teach children how to respond to 'Ganz still bitte'. 5. Hand out puppets to each child for them to say 'GM' with a partner. 6. Choose volunteers to show their 'role-play' to the class.	A finger puppet for each child.	Children will be able to use a finger puppet to say GM to a partner. Some children will show this to their class.	Cultural awareness of hand-shaking.
2	■ Be able to pick out the words GM from among the other words of a song.	Guten Morgen!	1. Class echo my GM, using different voices. 2. Children say 'GM' and shake hands of people nearby. 3. Listen to Detlev Jöcker's GM song from CD. Encourage children to count number of times they hear GM. Repeat as necessary.	CD player and 'Start German with a Song' CD by Detlev Jöcker, track 1, Guten Morgen.	Children will be able to join in singing the GM parts of the song. Some children will be confident enough to greet me individually in front of the class.	Turn-taking. Pair work.

4. Listen to song again and join in the GMs.

5. Invite individuals to say GM to me.

6. Pass round teddies. Children say GM to each one before they pass it on.

7. Play Jöcker song again.

8. CD can be left with class teacher to be played at other opportunities before next lesson.

Selection of friendly teddies.

Leave CD with class teacher for 'passive' listening opportunities before next lesson.

TABLE 3.3 Medium-term plan

Week	Key Objectives	Key Structures and Vocabulary	Teaching Activities (20 minutes)	Resources	Expected Outcomes	Links
1	■ Know Germans often shake hands when greeting people. ■ Be able to say 'Guten Morgen' with good pronunciation. ■ Look forward with confidence to next German lesson.	Guten Morgen! Ganz still bitte!	1. Greet individually with handshake, GM and a smile. 2. Shake hands. 3. Echo my GM in lots of different voices, and sing to tune of Alleluja, which emphasises syllables. 4. Teach children how to respond to 'Ganz still bitte'. 5. Hand out puppets to each child for them to say 'GM' with a partner. 6. Choose volunteers to show their 'role-play' to the class.	A finger puppet for each child.	Children will be able to use a finger puppet to say GM to a partner. Some children will show this to their class.	Cultural awareness of hand-shaking.
2	■ Be able to pick out the words GM from among the other words of a song.	Guten Morgen!	1. Class echo my GM, using different voices. 2. Children say 'GM' and shake hands of people nearby. 3. Listen to Detlev Jöcker's GM song from CD. Encourage children to count number of times they hear GM. Repeat as necessary. 4. Listen to song again and join in the GMs.	CD player and 'Start German with a Song' CD by Detlev Jöcker, track 1, Guten Morgen. Selection of friendly teddies.	Children will be able to join in singing the GM parts of the song. Some children will be confident enough to greet me individually in front of the class. Leave CD with class teacher for 'passive' listening opportunities before next lesson.	Turn-taking. Pair work.

	Learning objectives	Key language	Activities	Resources	Learning outcomes	Notes
			5. Invite individuals to say GM to me.			
			6. Pass round teddies. Children say GM to each one before they pass it on.			
			7. Play Jöcker song again.			
			8. CD can be left with class teacher to be played at other opportunities before next lesson.			
3	■ Know GM is suitable only for the morning. ■ Know there are other greetings, which can be used according to the time of day. ■ Begin to join in with parts of the Jöcker song other than GM.	Guten Morgen! Guten Tag! Guten Abend! Gute Nacht! Hier ist 'Grüne Spinne'!	1. Greet the children with GM and soft spider toy, Grüne Spinne, whose leg they can shake as they pass him around and greet him! 2. Discuss what if it were a different time of day. Consider English greetings we could use. (Be aware children may not be fully familiar with all English formal greetings.) 3. Use pictures to represent morning, afternoon, evening and night. Check children are very clear about which picture is for which. 4. Children echo my GM, GT, GA, GN in variety of voices, showing appropriate picture.	Soft toy with arms or legs to shake. Pictures representing morning, afternoon, evening and night.	Children will confidently shake hands and say GM to the new soft toy. Children will know English and be aware of German expressions for greetings at different times of day. Children will begin to imitate all words in the GM song, without necessarily understanding them yet.	Literacy links, with knowledge about formal use of their own language. Links in CD song to Wie geht's? part of topic in lesson 8 onwards.

(continued)

TABLE 3.3 Continued

Week	Key Objectives	Key Structures and Vocabulary	Teaching Activities (20 minutes)	Resources	Expected Outcomes	Links
			5. Finish with GM song from CD, children join in what they can, by listening to CD and watching my mouth shapes as I sing along.	Jöcker CD and player.		
4	■ Pronounce GM, GT, GA, GN with clarity and good pronunciation. ■ Learn new song. ■ Know how to order greetings according to time of day.	GM! GT! GA! GN! Ganz still bitte!	1. Greet with GM or GT, as appropriate. 2. Teach new song GM, GT, GA, GN to tune of Freres Jacques, with children filling in the echoed parts. 3. Look at pictures from last session and order according to time of day, asking children to name clues in picture which help us know which is which. 4. Sing new song, pointing to picture which corresponds to words as they are sung. 5. Remind children how to respond to 'Ganz still bitte'. 6. Hand out finger puppets. Children work with a partner to get their finger puppets to greet each other at 4 different times of day.	Pictures. One finger puppet per child.	Children will be able to join in with the echoed parts of the new song. Children will be keen to do a finger puppet role-play, and some children will be confident enough to show it to the class. (Pictures and some puppets can be left in a 'Deutsche Ecke' in the classroom for further informal opportunities for practice before next lesson.)	Order pics according to times of day.

No.	Objectives	Key language	Activities	Resources	Notes
			7. Confident pairs show their role-plays.		
5	■ Begin to sing GM, GT, GA, GN song independently. ■ Learn a new game 'Sprich oder schweig'. ■ As individuals, say the 4 greetings with confidence and accuracy.	GM! GT! GA! GN! Noch mal! Jetzt wollen wir 'Sprich oder schweig' spielen.	1. Sing GM, GT, GA, GN song to Frere Jacques tune and move towards children now singing both parts, not just echoes. Repeat, varying volume. 2. Explain the rules of 'Only repeat if it's true', where fingers are put on lips if it's not true. Say this game is called 'Sprich oder schweig' in German. Play it 'gently', using the pictures, acting as though the untrue statements are your genuine mistakes! 3. Pass round microphone. Children speak their favourite greeting into it. 4. Establish a pattern (e.g. GM, GT, GM, GT) and pass round microphone, children saying the greeting which fits. 5. Enjoy the Jöcker CD song again.	Pictures. Microphone (e.g. faulty toy echo mike). Jöcker CD and player.	Children will soon realise how to respond to 'Noch mal!'. Children will enjoy and be able to spot the teacher's 'mistakes' in 'Sprich oder schweig'. Some children will need support in following through the pattern.	Patterning skills
6	■ Get the gist of unfamiliar spoken German where gestures are used to support meaning.	GM! GT! GA! GN!	1. Sing GM, GT, GA, GN song together, pointing to appropriate picture cards as it is sung. 2. Divide class into 2, using target language and lots of body language. One half leads the	Picture cards.	Children now comfortable enough with German to cope with some target language instructions, where these involve an activity the children are already familiar with	Thinking skills involved in working out what's missing.

(continued)

TABLE 3.3 Continued

Week	Key Objectives	Key Structures and Vocabulary	Teaching Activities (20 minutes)	Resources	Expected Outcomes	Links
	■ Be confident as individuals to say the greeting which matches the missing picture card. ■ Respond appropriately to target language phrases to play 'Was fehlt?' game.	Ich teile euch in 2 Gruppen. Ihr beginnt. Was fehlt? Stimmt das? Ja/Nein. Mach(t) die Augen zu/auf!	song, the other follows, then swap. Point to appropriate picture cards as the children sing. 3. Quickly play 'Sprich oder schweig' with the pictures. 4. Explain they're going to play a game entirely in German, and they need to know 'Was fehlt?, Stimmt das?' and 'Ja/Nein' (lots of facial gestures, etc., to help, and echo in different voices). 5. Say 'Mach(t) die Augen zu!'/'Mach(t) die Augen auf!', accompanied by exaggerated gestures. Ask children to do this a few times till all respond confidently. Ask remainder, 'Stimmt das?' to encourage Ja/Nein response. 6. Lay out pictures in order. Use correct greeting for each one, then say 'Augen zu!' When all children have complied, remove one of the pictures. 'Mach die Augen auf! Was fehlt?'		(here, splitting into 2 groups), and where gestures and cognates ('beginnt' rather than 'fangt an') are used. Children will quickly respond to new phrases like 'Was fehlt?' and 'Stimmt das?' because of context within which they are used, intonation and gestures. *The plural or the singular forms of the imperative can be used. Plural is logical because of the number of children, but in reality many German primary teachers use the singular form so each child feels personally addressed.	

| 7 | ■ Children will use gesture clues to work out meanings of unfamiliar words.
 ■ Children will use all 4 greetings learned so far, plus 2 alternative goodbyes in a finger puppet role-play. | GM!
 GT!
 GA!
 GN!
 Was fehlt?
 Stimmt das?
 Ja/Nein.
 Auf Wiedersehen!
 Tschüss! | 7. Choose a child to repeat, maybe removing more than one or all of the pictures.
 8. End lesson by waving and saying 'Auf Wiedersehen' as you depart.

 1. Greet everyone in a variety of voices, and quickly play 'Was fehlt?' using pictures.
 2. Invite confident individuals to come to the front to take charge of game, using target language instructions to their classmates.
 3. Pretend to leave, saying 'Auf W!' (formal) and 'Tschüss!' (less formal). Return to discuss what they could mean. Practise echoing me with different voices.
 4. End task: Use finger puppets to greet someone. Children choose the situation (e.g. time of day, and formal or informal goodbye) in their role-play.
 5. Children perform. | Pictures.

 A finger puppet for each child. | Children will have the confidence and understanding to design a role-play with a partner, making appropriate use of words learned so far. |

43

As we can see, less is certainly more in primary MFL in terms of the content objectives. These remain modest, certainly in the early stages, but are such that they ensure maximum interactional value in the foreign language, for example, greetings dialogues, class instructions, numbers and colours, all of which can be used authentically almost from the start. We can also see how differentiation has been built into the pupil learning outcomes. A long-term (whole-school) plan might appear as in Table 3.4.

TABLE 3.4 Long-term plan

YEAR	AUTUMN TERM	SPRING TERM	SUMMER TERM
Y1	**Greetings** (hello, goodbye)	**Numbers** to 10	**Breakfast** foods
	About me (who, and how, I am) Taste Lebkuchen and say 'Merry Christmas'	**Colours**/Rainbows Easter rhyme and egg hunt	**Action songs**
Y2	**Starting school** (includes greetings-revision and classroom language as well as cultural info) **Toys** Christmas as Y1	**Farm animals** **Transport**	**Numbers** to 12 (with plus/minus, and odds and evens) *Dornröschen*
Y3	**Weather and Seasons** (loads of traditional rhymes) **Brothers & sisters** (to introduce some plurals)	**Colours** *Brauner Bär* story (colours, genders) Fasching	**Numbers** to 31 (and number magic) **Birthdays** (includes numbers to 31, months, and cultural awareness)
Y4	**Days of the week** (Minimonster) **Skills** (ich kann, ich . . . gern) Advent calendar, Sankt Nikolaus	**Clothes** **School equipment** (Schulranzen and cf. VP and GSE) **and activities**	*Die Raupe Nimmersatt* **Body parts and illness**
Y5	**Wild animals** (Lieber Zoo, and left right directions with e.g. Halle Zoo map) Sankt Martins Tag **Meine Familie + Where I live**	*Rotkäppchen* **School day** (days of week and subjects)	**Cafe** (e.g. Eiscafe and some money work) **Around town** (Rinteln)
Y6	**Time and timetables** (and more numbers) **Transport** *Ein Apfel für den Weihnachtsmann*	**Clothes show** (+ Adjectives) links with Faschingsverkleidung **Sport**	**Holiday essentials** (Kofferpacken) **and destinations** **People and passports** (links with who I am and dates) Jeder Mensch ist etwas Besonderes

The long-term plan shows clearly how certain topics are determined by the time of the year and cross-cultural opportunities that can be exploited (more on this in Chapter 9). For Spanish, it would be appropriate to introduce *el turrón* as a Christmas treat or maybe to celebrate any of the many regional feast days, for example San Isidro, San Ponç when covering dates and the calendar (and for French le poisson d'avril and le quatorze juillet, etc.). In italics we have shown the key story texts which can be covered, one each year starting from Year 2, and we discuss the use of stories in MFL in the next chapter on teaching language skills.

Conclusion

In this chapter we have suggested an approach to planning MFL using the *topic–language–resources* trichotomy which then needs to be further broken down into specific learning intentions and lesson objectives. We have emphasised the circular nature of planning, with localised circumstances (pupils, resources, capacity) shaping our learning goals. Furthermore, pupil performance will feed into and direct our ongoing planning, as it must within the constructivist framework of formative assessment (discussed in Chapter 7). Short-term and long-term planning, fitting together like a Russian doll, are essential in MFL – as with other areas of the curriculum – to ensure variety of resources, balance of activity, clear and focused direction and pupil progression.

Issues for reflection

- Look at an MFL scheme of work to which you have access. In what ways is it suitable or deficient for your pupils in terms of the national Framework?

- Do you see real opportunities for progression built into your MFL scheme of work? Is there a correlation with the progression of learning objectives listed in the Key Stage 2 Framework?

- Taking one of the learning objectives from the Key Stage 2 Framework, think about how this could be reached through an appropriate activity which is specific to the character of your pupils.

- Are there any dates or events in your school calendar which could fit naturally into MFL planning as a means for the children to model their skills?

Teaching the four skills – practical ideas and activities

THIS CHAPTER LEADS on from the previous 'groundwork' chapter on planning to focus more specifically on the classroom reality of teaching and learning. We suggest ways of presenting and practising language and how to engage pupils' interest through the practical use of resources and stimulating activities. While we acknowledge that listening and speaking skills are naturally given priority in primary MFL, we argue for integration, at the appropriate stage, of reading and writing to support aural and oral development in MFL as well as to reinforce generic conceptual skills, especially in literacy.

Key issues

- Planning must incorporate development of all four language skills (listening, speaking, reading, writing) as they reinforce one another in the foreign language and support first language cognitive development.

- Different skills should be emphasised at different developmental phases with the written form introduced last, in line with first language progression.

- Despite some anecdotal hostility to the inclusion of writing in primary MFL, the written form (both for pupil reading and for pupil writing) can play an important role in reinforcing oral and aural skills in MFL.

- Where skills are treated as transferable in MFL and cross-curricular links are made explicit, these, among other skills, contribute to developing phonic awareness in first language development.

Introduction

Since the introduction of the National Curriculum KS2 pupil progression has been delimited equally – though we acknowledge that MFL is not actually taught in equal distribution – across the four skills (Listening, Speaking, Reading and Writing) in line with the secondary curriculum and it is therefore useful when planning to consider how each skill can be developed. This skills division is of course somewhat arbitrary as most acts of communication are the result of combined competence but it remains true that different activities 'privilege' different skills and, for parity of opportunity across the range of different pupil learning styles as much as anything, it is beneficial to include a range of aural, visual and oral activities.

The current Key Stage 2 Framework has moved away from a four-skill model, using the neologism 'oracy' to cover the strand of 'listening, speaking and spoken interaction', a grouping which emphasises the interdependence of the skills:

> *Oracy (listening, speaking and spoken interaction) has a more prominent place in language learning than in most if not all other areas of the curriculum. In the early stages children will spend much of their time listening, speaking and interacting orally and will be given regular and frequent opportunities to listen to a good model of pronunciation.*
>
> **(Key Stage 2 Framework for Languages 2005: 7)**

When deciding what language to include in planning it may be useful to think of the teaching and learning process as following a pattern of *presentation* → *practice* → *production* (the 'three P's'), in other words the principle of reducing support to shift input from the teacher to the pupil. Of course, this process needs to be broken down into stages where pupil participation is 'scaffolded' to become increasingly autonomous. The 'three P's' sequence (presenting → practising → producing) has long served as a useful frame for introducing new language and for planning use of resources. We begin this chapter with a discussion of these stages.

Presenting, practising and producing new language

The first planning stage is deciding what is to be taught. The teacher might be guided here by the scheme of work or by the textbook or CD-ROM resource that they wish to use. Modelling language clearly and unambiguously is important in order for children to understand what is expected of them. Levels of perceived difficulty will depend on pedagogic decisions (the form of the lesson) but also on decisions about the language to be included (the content), for example the degree of lexical intercomprehension, the degree of personal and cultural resonance attached to the content. The following are some general considerations which may guide teachers' decisions about which new language to present and in which form. Let us take the example of introducing 'food vocabulary' in French:

- The number of items (this will depend on age and prior learning but could range from one to ten items of new vocabulary).

- Is the language to reflect the world of the children – the sort of food they might eat at home, for example samosa? Or, will the new words aim specifically at increasing cultural awareness by using more 'typical' French or Spanish foods? (This is a key question that we will consider further in Chapter 9.)

- How many of the words are cognates *(le chocolat)*, direct French borrowings from English *(le hamburger)*, direct English borrowings from French *(la quiche)* or 'false friends' *(les chips)*? Many words may already be familiar to pupils, in which case the French pronunciation becomes the key focus.

- It is often useful at the outset to think about how the vocabulary will be used in context because this may affect the form in which it is initially presented. For example if these words will be used *j'aime/je n'aime pas (les champignons, le poisson)*, etc., then it is appropriate to introduce the language with the gendered and numbered definite article *(le, la, les)*, but if pupils are going to follow up with *je mange, je bois, je prends (du thé, des frites)* then it would be useful to present the language with the partitive article *(du, de la, des)* in the first instance. While such decisions inform teacher planning there is, of course, no need to make this point overtly grammatical to pupils.

Once we have decided on a vocabulary list and its associated grammatical elements, we can think about how we will present the language. Traditionally items are drilled with pictures which can be on flashcards, OHTs, or by using downloaded images on the electronic whiteboard. Vocabulary topics such as food, as well as clothes, colours, etc., lend themselves perfectly to the use of authentic props (called 'realia'). But, again, elaborate props are not a prerequisite. Simple drawings on a whiteboard can suffice or, especially for action topics like sports and hobbies, mime is effective and involves the pupils in multi-sensory learning.

The important aspect is that the language is clearly 'modelled' by the teacher repeating several times before inviting pupils to repeat. Primary teachers are generally expert at this style of clear, unambiguous presentation. As the pupils repeat with the teacher and move on to answering simple questions this is the *practice* stage during which pupils are led to use the language in response to controlled visual and/or spoken cues. Here the teacher can vary the tone of voice and speed of delivery (loud and soft, slow and fast) to help pupils stay attentive. After drilling, many teachers then follow a sequence of three-stage questioning which operates on the principle of gradually withdrawing support leading to less teacher-led practice, first with the whole class and then focusing on individual pupils:

- *(Ne répondez pas si je me trompe)* C'est du lait [Pupils only repeat if the teacher's phrase matches the card s/he is holding]

- *C'est du pain ou de la viande?* [Multiple choice: pupils say which of the two they see]

- *Qu'est-ce que c'est?*

The time spent on 'practising' in this manner depends on the teacher's confidence that pupils have 'got' it. The trick is to revisit vocabulary frequently and to change styles of presentation to avoid monotony. Teachers will know when pupils have assimilated items at this stage by eliciting individualised responses to cues, which can be oral or otherwise (e.g. pointing to pictures), or by asking for simple translations or explanations from pupils.

Although we have included the 'What is it?' question here, we suggest that, beyond presentation drills, questioning should be more open to maximise inclusiveness through greater participation and to increase cognitive activity within the group by encouraging children to think of a range of possibilities. For example, if pupils have been learning classroom objects in Spanish, a teacher following the traditional question–answer format might then point to a chair and ask *¿Qué es?*. Some pupils will be able to remember and will answer correctly *una silla*, but if the question is phrased more openly as a cue *¿Qué ves en el aula?* (What can you see in the room?) followed by a demonstration of some possible responses, e.g. *veo papel, veo la puerta*, many more pupils will go on to give 'right' answers and still more pupils will be trying to think of more words. The more able pupils will pick up the cue first but all pupils will be included; even if they repeat previous responses they are still practising the language. With food items, the cue might be *Donne-moi en français le nom d'un plat/d'une boisson/d'un fruit* and so forth.

When pupils are able to correctly respond to cues, they are ready to use the language items more autonomously in the *production* stage. In reality they will still need guidance and support but this is the stage at which they are able to appropriate the language into their repertoire, taking 'ownership', by applying the language to a context. In the next chapter we look at some ways in which this can be done by embedding the language across the curriculum. Using our example of French words for food items, pupils can be asked to describe what they ate for dinner the previous evening (Year 6); enact a simple restaurant sketch; describe their favourite meal and, once the written form has been included, write a menu (see p. 127), a shopping list, a recipe, etc. All of these can be done in collaboration with other children in pairs and groups leading to cookery, display work, acting out a sketch, as well as drawing and labelling. One activity we have seen KS1 learners enjoy and which links to oral practice is drawing the food on a paper plate! The possibilities are endless but it is important to remember that the final expected range of outcomes (the 'learning intentions' discussed in the previous chapter) will shape initial decisions about the language we wish to cover in the sequence.

Teaching the four skills: resources and planning

Listening

Although it seems common sense to assume that children need to hear the new language before being expected to speak it, the way in which new language is presented is often underplayed. We talk of '*speaking* German or French' and seldom attribute equal value to '*understanding*'. Similarly, while we now allow children to hear words several times in the foreign language before asking them to reproduce them (following our understanding of *first* language acquisition), the time allowed between listening and reproducing remains often very limited and totally disproportionate with the vast input young children have in their mother tongue before being expected to produce an utterance. This period of receptive silence is Krashen's 'silent period' during which children are exposed to a vast amount of input without being under pressure to (re)produce language. Far from being a time of passive receptivity, language is actively assimilated at this stage through ongoing cognitive processing.

The process of 'parrot-fashion' reproduction of language is rooted in the behaviourist tradition whereby pupils will accurately repeat the modelled sounds through a drill of listening and repeating. While we would agree that this style of learning has an important role to play in memorising new vocabulary and providing a short-term entry to production, we would also emphasise that the quality and the style of the input is important in developing phonic awareness and listening skills. In other words, understanding elements of a foreign language is as important as being able to speak in the language. Although younger children, arguably, do have greater powers of mimicry, the behaviourist listen–repeat paradigm is not sufficient in itself (children actually not being parrots!) if the input is not scaffolded in some way to aid assimilation.

'Scaffolding' strategies in developing listening skills include visual support, speaking at different speeds, adopting exaggerated intonation, even using hand and body language (like an orchestral conductor) to stress salient informational elements or to draw attention to certain phonic features. There is much debate about using the written word as a support in aural comprehension. Many teachers we have spoken to in researching teachers' views for this book believe that this can lead pupils to mispronounce words because they apply English phonic patterns. However, we are convinced of the usefulness of the written word *as a support*, that is, not the sole means of presenting new language, and believe that it paves the way to developing literacy in MFL. We have seen many cases such as the one cited by Alison Hurrell (1999: 71) when her pupils were unable to understand the word *dangereux* despite her repeating it several times, saying it slowly, dividing up the syllables, etc. As soon as she started to write it on the board (d-a-n-g-e . . .)

the pupils understood immediately what she had been saying in French. Using the written word may also avoid pupils improvising (wrongly!) when they cannot understand what they are saying/singing, as illustrated by our example cited in the next chapter of singing 'Sunny semolina' instead of 'Sonnez la matine' in Frère Jacques.

It is also worth remembering that when pupils *do* mispronounce written words in a foreign language this is no more than they do when developing literacy in English where the patterns of written forms need to be learnt even though children are able to say the words, for example when early readers pronounce the 'k' in 'know'.

The time between initial input and pupil production of target language varies according to age, language content and, especially, individual preference. While most children will join in choral drilling within the safety of numbers many are reluctant to speak in the foreign language when they are not used to it. It is not helpful to rush or force this process as the different pupil modes of participation are highly individual, for example if some do not wish to speak the new language (yet) this reticence should be respected – Hurrell (1999: 71), borrowing Krashen and Terrell's (1983) legal metaphor, calls this the children's 'right to silence'. One scaffolding activity we have seen work – also used in English phonics development – is silently mouthing the words with exaggerated facial movements for pupils. We cite an example further on in this chapter of 'silent mouthing' as pairwork. This helps to increase confidence and to prepare pupils for when they are ready to speak. Pupils enjoy replicating the movements – in one school called 'mouth dancing' – and it raises phonic awareness of different mouth shapes in different languages.

Another strategy to familiarise pupils with foreign language sounds is for the teacher to use target language without necessarily requiring pupils to respond in the foreign language. This type of cross-linguistic dialogue is quite usual in bilingual families and still serves the purpose of normalising foreign language use and getting pupils used to different sounds. It is also a good way of checking pupils' comprehension!

While all use of the foreign language in the school will help develop listening/comprehension skills, focused skill-specific activities can include listening to taped native speakers giving information or engaged in dialogue. As pupils are being asked to listen to specific information they can be asked to complete a tickbox or gapfill worksheet such as in the example overleaf to focus their attention. Indeed, Lotto (Bingo), upon which this activity is based, is only a fun form of a 'listening exercise' but presented as a 'game' and so eternally popular.

Listening activity to practise food and drink vocabulary

Drawn on board

Script (read by teacher)

— *« Vous désirez? » demande le serveur.*

— *« Moi, un hamburger avec des frites, s'il vous plaît » répond Emilie.*

— *« Très bien. Et pour Monsieur? »*

— *« Un sandwich au jambon, s'il vous plaît » dit Loïc.*

— *« Et comme boisson? »*

— *« De l'eau, s'il vous plaît » ils répondent.*

Each child is given the following activity sheet:

Coche les plats et les boissoins que tu entends (Cross out the food and drink that you hear).

With the food items in this activity we can see how pupils are helped by the choice of cognates (except, arguably, *les frites*). Furthermore, pupils might be told that there are four items (three food items and one drink). The concept of drink can be conveyed by the teacher miming as s/he reads *'Et comme boisson?'*. Although *de l'eau* may be difficult to grasp, some pupils will be able to deduce by a process of elimination *(ce n'est pas 'coca-cola'!)*.

The visual on the board helps to set the scene and the teacher can point to each of the three characters as s/he reads their turn. The script can be read a few times. This activity lends itself to potential links to speaking practice as the pupils could be asked to give their answers in French and (older) children might even read the script.

Although not actually language, music and 'sound' in a broader sense constitute a valuable resource in evoking certain emotions and images which can be expressed through the target language, for example *Ce morceau de musique te fait penser à quelle couleur?*. In a similar way to the visual conceptualising described below, 'Foley score' sounds (involving props to make certain noises such as those heard in radio plays) can be great fun for story-telling (e.g. slow footsteps and a scream or a quickening horse gallop in the rain) and evoking images, for example *C'est quel animal? Il est comment?*. The key here is to enjoy different sounds, which is effectively what we are asking children to do with the foreign language.

In one school we visited recently a German teacher told us how she emphasised the *sounds* and *shapes* of words to great effect:

- With Year 2, we learn the story of Sleeping Beauty (Dornröschen) through the song. The children love the word 'böse' as in 'die böse Fee', the wicked fairy who casts the terrible spell on Dornröschen. It can be said in a very nasty way, and a lot of fun can be had with one half of the class chanting 'Die böse Fee!', while the other half responds 'Die gute Fee', with a totally different expression.

- Some of the words I introduce with the Year 4 food topic include 'lecker' and 'igitt-igitt' which mean 'yummy' and 'yuck' and can be great fun to play with in class. The children love the sounds.

- Sometimes we play with silent words too! 'Hör zu!' looks gorgeous when you're lip-reading! When we have learnt hör zu, schau her, steh auf, dreh' dich um and setz dich, we form them on our lips for a partner to read and respond to! If I ask the children how they know which one I was saying, they can describe the lip shape for it.

Speaking

Speaking and other means of communication

Oral competence in the foreign language is often seen as the ultimate goal of foreign language learning: to be able to *speak* 'fluently'; yet it is also the aspect of engagement with the foreign language which strikes the greatest terror into the hearts of many teachers and (especially secondary-level) pupils alike. This may be because speech production is, by its nature, *spontaneous* (we have less time to prepare what we want to say than when writing) and *interactive* (we speak *to* someone and they respond, so failure to exchange spoken turns successfully leads to *immediate* communication breakdown). These same characteristics apply equally of course to when we are communicating in our first language. The key difference is that we feel confident enough to be able to deal with communication breakdown or to manage the course of interaction towards a successful outcome because we are instinctively satisfied with the range of extralinguistic communicative strategies at our disposal (rephrasing, repeating, changing intonation, body language, etc.). This repertoire of extralinguistic strategies is gradually acquired in first language development through exposure and trial and error. Likewise, they are important skills in foreign language learning and should form an integral part of developing competence in speaking skills both through exposure (listening) and through explicit 'learning' or discussion of the characteristics of communicative competence in the foreign language. It is often surprising how much foreign language learners of all ages can successfully communicate with little strictly linguistic competence in the foreign language when driven by the momentum of real motivation to convey meaning. The desire to communicate using the target language and other communicative strategies without having recourse to English is to be promoted from the start to encourage good communicative habits in early learners for progression and, later, for secondary school.

When practising dialogues or presenting phrases to the class, children often like to do this through a 'foreign' character. This can be themselves with a foreign language pseudonym or might take the form of a puppet or a cuddly toy which becomes a foreign language 'friend' or 'alter ego'. Simple finger puppets are easy to make using card wrapped around the finger and decorated or a ping-pong ball with a hole cut in large enough for the finger. Sock puppets, simple glove puppets or even a spoon puppet (a face on the back of a wooden spoon with hair stuck on) are all easy and cheap to make. Figure 4.1 shows ingenious use of a flannel wash glove. The puppet is given a name, usually a name in the target language such as Stefan, Etienne or Juanita, and the children, who can become quite attached to their puppets, use the character of the puppet to express themselves in the target language or to explain things to. Obviously, the puppets do not 'speak' English! This stage of removal from their English language reality makes an enormous difference to the 'affective filter' of the pupils (this is Krashen's term for the screen of emotional and contextual factors which cause embarrassment or awkwardness and so can inhibit participation in language learning activities).

Using the target language

It is important that pupils are encouraged to use the target language in real contexts around the school and around the classroom but for this to happen they must feel

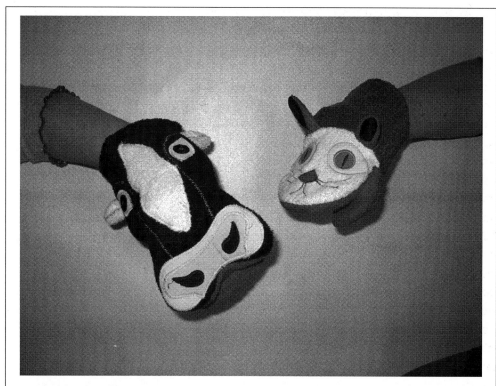

FIGURE 4.1 Wash glove puppets

safe and supported – 'it's OK to make mistakes, to repeat words, to mispronounce, etc., as that's in the nature of all communication'. Furthermore, pupils will be encouraged more to use the foreign language unself-consciously if they see that it is being used around them by teachers (and other members of staff!) for natural communication and in different contexts. We return therefore to our insistence on the need to have MFL embedded throughout the curriculum and the life of the school, starting if possible from KS1. If foreign language communication is exclusively experienced within the realm of a visiting specialist it is, by definition, perceived as segmented and detached from the real business of day-to-day classroom life – the so-called 'Spanish and vanish' problem inherent in depending solely on peripatetic specialists, however good.

We are not suggesting here that teachers interact all day in German or French – many would not wish to do so and/or would not feel able to do so. What we are suggesting is that the drip-feeding model of MFL provision which is already in place in many schools (in the form of greetings, register calling, etc.) is expanded to some teacher–teacher interaction and to some MFL delivery in new places (different areas of the curriculum, the lunch menu, assembly singing, etc.). Even young children often perceive *speaking* a foreign language as difficult – and express negative ideas such as 'French is hard to pronounce' (said to the authors by a seven-year-old London pupil) – but we are convinced that these ideas are often, albeit subliminally, 'learnt', given that we have also seen many examples of early learners adapting successfully to accurate phonic production of new sounds. Perceived 'difficulty', we would therefore argue, is a socially produced attitude. (We discuss in more detail issues surrounding the *choice* of one MFL over another in Chapter 1.)

One useful way to increase MFL for daily interactional purposes is to teach (and for teachers to use) key interactional phrases, for example (in Spanish) *sí, no, vale, de acuerdo, ¿Qué significa?, ¿Cómo se dice . . . ?, no sé, no entiendo, necesito . . ., bueno, bien.* This can constitute appropriate targets for class teachers' own continuing professional development (see Chapter 11).

Using images to create meaning

Images are used extensively in MFL. Throughout the book we cite many examples of flashcards, labelling pictures, drawing pictures from a text and so forth. The value of images is in the creation of new linguistic links in the target language. These new connections do not *replace* but build on and reconfigure existing associations. The use of young learners' creative imagination in the production and expression of mental images is already well established in the primary curriculum and can be tapped into to encourage the construction of new meanings through MFL. The type of activity described here draws on the pupils' own imaginations and so teacher resources and preparation are minimal yet the activity is a rich, dynamic and creative process.

Pupils are asked to 'imagine' a monster and to describe it mentally in the target language: how many heads does it have, what colour is it, what is it called, where does it live, etc.? As pupils envisage their own fantastic monster they can be led to answer certain questions but it is more interesting if they are left to describe freely as the association will be highly original. Pupils then share their mental images, maybe making comparative statements about their own and others' monsters using their own initial descriptions as an aide-mémoire. This activity allows pupils the time and space to plan what they will say and to seek help as they need it.

Another activity which helps sentence development as well as being creative and fun is to give pupils a simple sentence such as 'A man gets out of his car . . .' *(Un hombre baja . . . de su coche)* and ask them to insert an adverb or to add another phrase or to describe the man and the car, again using language that has been learnt or, indeed, asking for a new word. This type of text expansion is used a lot in literacy (creation of 'super sentences') and so meshes well but adds a further dimension in the foreign language as it increases awareness of difference in word order and may reveal more about language-specific conceptual imaging given that bilinguals often associate different images with the 'same' words in different languages (the intercultural implications here are discussed further in Chapter 9). This activity type is also flexible and allows for a range of differentiated outcomes, that is, there is no 'right' answer.

Speaking beyond word level

Within the context of specific development of MFL speaking as a skill there are many games, songs and role-plays that help proficiency and familiarise pupils with certain words and phrases. As with listening, these require some visual or aural support which may be pictorial, 'realia', spoken, etc. Examples of these resources are given throughout the book. One key issue, though, that we would like to raise here is, again, the importance of progression. New language is often presented in the form of vocabulary lists yet at some stage pupils need to move beyond word level to produce more complex phrases and to link these to make sentences. This stage of progression should not wait until secondary school. Primary teachers are expert at developing this awareness of sentence- and discourse-level sophistication in English so can easily apply it in MFL. In fact, the approaches used in literacy can be applied equally in MFL, for example adding adjectives to qualify nouns, then using connectives to add subordinate clauses, then building up to linking phrases with conjunctions either causally *(puisque, comme)* or temporally *(quand, alors)*. These can be introduced orally in drill form with musical rhythm as in the examples here:

- *Quand il fait beau*   *je joue au foot (dans le parc).*
- *Quand il fait du soleil*   *je fais une promenade.*
- *Quand il pleut*   *je regarde la télé.*

- J'ai sommeil   alors   je vais au lit.
- J'ai faim   alors   je mange un sandwich.
- J'ai chaud   alors   j'enlève mon pull.
- J'ai soif   alors   je bois de l'eau.

These activities use picture prompts (or mime) to piece together recently learnt phrases, but this type of sentence-level development is often best supported, at least in part, by the written form. This brings us to discussion of developing reading and writing skills in MFL.

Reading

Dispelling the myth

Some primary teachers still believe that MFL provision for early learners should focus exclusively on listening and speaking and that using written foreign language leads to:

- mispronunciation (pupils mispronounce as they read while they reproduce accurately without a written support)

- confusion with developing literacy in English (hindering first language development)
- demotivation (reading and writing are associated with 'boring schoolwork').

We have found no evidence to support these myths. On the contrary, we suggest that reading and writing skills support and reinforce speaking and listening skills. In most schools the written word (in foreign languages) is clearly in evidence around the school anyway, so we cannot assume that pupils will just make sense of it without structured guidance. We have seen many examples of skilful teaching using all four skills successfully. While pupils will inevitably mispronounce some new words as they see them (as they do in English), recognising different systems of phonic patterns will eventually raise awareness of sound links and will improve pronunciation. The Key Stage 2 Framework also makes explicit the mutually reinforcing link between developing 'literacy' in the MFL alongside oral and aural skills:

> *The literacy skills of reading and writing are supported by, and in turn reinforce, the development of oracy. They are likely to take on greater prominence as children become familiar with the relationship between sounds and letters/characters in the new language and apply this knowledge in reading and spelling.*

> **(Key Stage 2 Framework for Languages 2005: 8)**

Awareness of phonics in MFL

Here we cite Hurrell's suggested 'phonic clouds' concept (1999: 81) as one nice way of approaching reading from a phoneme-script perspective. Particular phonic groupings (which may be written as single letters or clusters) are suspended from the classroom ceiling in the form of a hanging mobile. Each time pupils encounter a new word with that sound in they can add a new 'cloud'. Here we look at how this can be done with the pronunciation of the Spanish phoneme /x/, written as *j* or as a soft *g* (when preceding *i* or *e*).

This can be done with phonemes that are always spelt the same as in the example (Figure 4.2) or with phonemes that are spelt differently (homophones). In French this can be especially useful because of the irregularity of the phoneme-script correspondence, for example /ε/ is found in *la tête, le verre, le crayon, le lait, la haie*. Homophones can also make for challenging, fun learning and surprising match up games (see Table 4.1).

In the same way that children learning to read English learn to appreciate that some letters in certain words are silent and that others are pronounced differently in different contexts, pupils learning a foreign language can make the same distinctions. The pronunciation of -*ough* is a classic example of this (as in through, thorough, though, bough, cough, tough, bought) and is particularly difficult for children having English as an additional language.

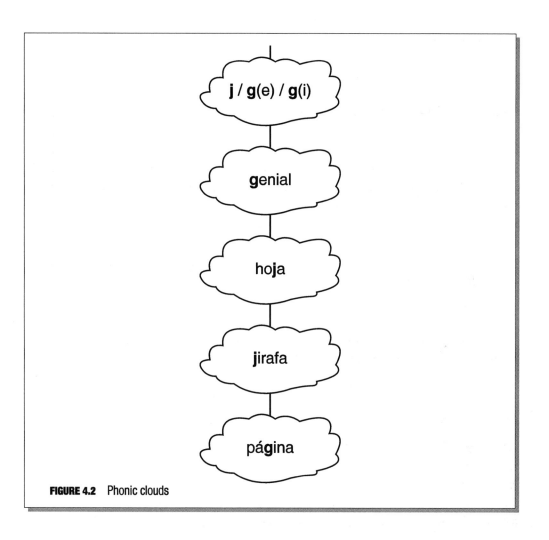

FIGURE 4.2 Phonic clouds

TABLE 4.1 Table of homophones

aile	ton
dans	camp
quand	elle
thon	dents

Getting started with reading

Almost all primary schools which have any engagement with MFL provision have used labelling as a minimal form of developing reading skills through familiarity with foreign language words. These are often posted around the school as laminated words (*la sala de profesores, la cantina, el vestíbulo*, etc.) and in the classroom (*el orde-nador, la mesa, la pizarra*, etc.). This is a good starting point (and pupils will enjoy creating such resources themselves as they start to take their first steps in writing in MFL), though the words risk becoming invisible if they are not *used* regularly in interaction. Similarly, the foreign language can be used (alone or with English) to label tasks that younger pupils are doing such as colouring in (see Figure 4.3).

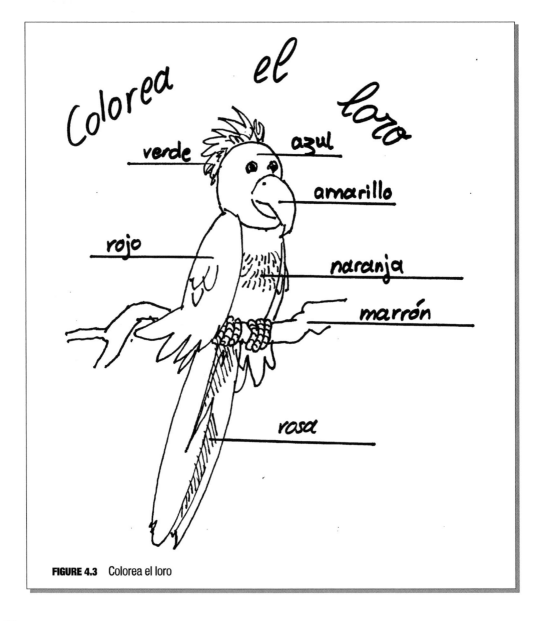

FIGURE 4.3 Colorea el loro

In the classroom books are an obvious reading resource. There is a range of MFL books available for early learners, although using the board, OHTs or electronic text can be a cheaper way of working from text as a class. Other alternatives are 'big books' for all to enjoy (the English big book can be adapted by covering English text with the foreign language text) and home-made story cards made for example by trainee teachers or even older pupils. The making of resources can be exploited as a valuable, collaborative activity which pupils enjoy and which gives them a stake in the process of their learning.

Text on the board (which includes here OHP and electronically projected text) can be used in many ways to support other skills, from reading a dialogue to text comprehension. We recently saw Year 3 beginners in Spanish using the following dialogue written on the board to consolidate what they had learnt orally. After a few lessons they were able to reel off the dialogue without the written support.

A	Hola
B	*Hola*
A	¿Cómo estás?
B	*Muy bien, gracias*
A	¿Cómo te llamas?
B	*Mi nombre es . . . . . .*
A	Adiós
B	*Adiós*

Simple texts can be retold orally in English (as a checking device) or interpreted pictorially. For example, KS2 pupils will enjoy illustrating the following text which consolidates language recently covered and they will be keen to focus on the detail:

Monsieur et Madame Viret habitent dans une maison rouge avec une grande porte jaune. Ils ont un beau jardin avec des fleurs et un pommier. M et Mme Viret ont deux enfants, Jeanne et Michel. Jeanne a dix ans et elle porte des lunettes. Michel est plus petit et il a les cheveux noirs et frisés. M Viret est gros mais sa femme est grande et mince. La famille a un gros chien qui s'appelle Minou. Minou est blanc avec des taches brunes sur le dos. Il a de petites jambes et une longue queue.

Aujourd'hui il fait du soleil alors M Viret porte des lunettes de soleil et Mme Viret porte un joli chapeau de paille.

The text could go on to describe more clothes, the car, nearby buildings, etc. This illustration activity works best if it is timed because pupils then focus on under-standing and using as many linguistic clues as possible rather than focusing on the detail of the drawing itself. Simpler descriptions would be appropriate for younger pupils, for example physical descriptions and clothes also work well when children are asked to draw an Identikit picture from the description given by a crime witness. The 'wanted' posters (see Figure 4.4) can then be displayed with the descriptions.

SE BUSCA

VIVO O MUERTO

FIGURE 4.4 Se busca: Vivo o muerto

An alternative reading skills task is to draw a simple picture on the board (such as that in Figure 4.5) and write some sentences next to it which pupils identify as true or false *(verdad o mentira)*. These can be presented in multiple choice pairs as in the example or not, depending on the level of support and easiness the teacher wants to allow for.

Reading in the target language, as well as being a valuable end in its own right, is also extremely useful for facilitating the development of other skills, as in listening, for example responding to questions in the target language or completing a gapfill task, or speaking, for example reading target language cue cards or other prompts. Being able to spell in the foreign language is a useful skill as pupils begin to write and it establishes 'good habits' by maximising use of the target language. However, learning the whole foreign alphabet might seem a little daunting at first (having only just learnt the alphabet in English) so it is a good idea to start by spelling out certain words as they are learnt (or as learnt words are revisited in their written form).

MFL linked to whole literacy development

David Wood (2004) reminds us of the importance of developing reading skills in the form of phoneme–script correspondence as a means of developing awareness of the very nature of language:

El chico está triste.
El chico está contento.
Hace frío.
Hace sol.
Come un helado.
Come un bocadillo.
Tiene su gato con él.
Tiene su perro con él.
Lleva gafas de sol.
Lleva un sombrero.

FIGURE 4.5

When we help children to learn to read, we are doing more than teaching a new and neutral 'code' for representing what they already do with and know about speech. Rather, we are introducing them to radically new ways of thinking about *language* itself.

(Wood 2004: 203)

If reading in MFL is ignored or sidelined then the understanding of language as 'more than a code' is inevitably blinkered to appreciation of first language conventions only. We see literacy development as a holistic, evolving process which includes appreciation of different media and supports as well as different levels of language used in different contexts. Developing MFL literacy forms a vital part of this process. To deny pupils access to MFL in its written form is to deny access to a rich source of literacy development and a valuable learning support as well as a new world of (inter)cultural signs. Reading and writing in MFL, with appropriate age-sensitive material, also provide extension and differentiation opportunities.

Writing

As familiarity with reading the foreign language increases, most children, who will already have writing skills in English, can be guided to progress to writing in the target language. Many of the conventional objections to writing in primary MFL are similar to those used to argue against developing reading skills in the foreign language, that is, that writing is a specific literacy skill which will inhibit motivation to learn in MFL by creating unfair divergence too early on between the more able who can manage and the less able who will struggle and therefore develop negative attitudes to MFL, treating it as yet another subject where difficulty in reading and writing is keeping them behind (see Sharpe 2001: 86–7). However, while we are sympathetic with this view, we believe that reading and writing in the MFL can provide valuable support for speaking and listening in terms of phonic awareness, as we have seen above, not least of all, being able to separate words by knowing where they start and end. Of course, we are not suggesting extensive writing tasks, nor that writing should have priority in MFL lessons. Each teacher will have their own view about how much writing is appropriate for their pupils and when it is appropriate to introduce this skill. Pupils who struggle with literacy will only be disaffected if they feel out of their depth with writing in an MFL so there is much potential for differentiation here. Indeed, if MFL is to be taken seriously as an integrated part of the curriculum, it would be artificial to exclude any written forms of the language in a school environment. Here we discuss a few ways which can lead pupils to begin writing in the foreign language.

A good introduction to writing is to exploit those words that pupils are most familiar with, for example colours and classroom items which are labelled. Gapping out letters, which is a good way to focus attention in reading, can lead on to pupils writing in the missing letter. For example, once pupils are familiar with the following dialogue, having practised it a lot orally and having read it several times over an extended period, many will be able to fill the gaps. In this example, the same letter is missing, but different letters could also be omitted, or even letters which make up a different word of their own, depending on the level of support desired:

> *¿Falta qué letra? ¡Escribela!*
> *Buen__s días. Me llam__ Alejandr__. Y tú ¿c__m__ te llamas?*

In the first instance, writing may be limited to copy-writing, for example for simple vocabulary or for labelling – though this may not be the easiest start to writing in the foreign language (see Hurrell 1999: 83–4 for a discussion of the pitfalls in copy-writing) – but it is important that there is progression which allows pupils some degree of autonomy and creativity in writing, as much as in other skills. Here we can move the principle of 'gapping out' onto sentence, then text level. The eventual goal, for older children, will be having the confidence to produce written work in the foreign language autonomously. Again, we are not suggesting extensive writing tasks, but short dialogues, menus, brief descriptions, etc. The knowledge each teacher has of his/her own pupils and their abilities remains the ultimate guide. Here we suggest a line of progression in writing, each level represents a more complex, less supported stage of skill development than the previous level. The stages are in no way prescriptive (indeed, many will contend that there is any such natural order) so the stages are naturally recurring and multi-directional and any tried and tested approaches can be revisited. We emphasise that pupils will already be familiar with the language. It is important that words are first presented orally to early learners, and then only exploited in their written form once they have been fully assimilated into pupils' repertoire. This helps to overcome the potential problem with mispronouncing the written form.

Progression in developing writing skills:

copy words
e.g. colours (as in the parrot colouring activity above); making labels for school furniture

gapfill letters into words
e.g. completing learnt phrases (example above); completing a partially completed crossword puzzle or wordsearch

copy short phrases
e.g. short dialogues; Christmas card greetings

gapfill words into short phrases
e.g. completing learnt songs with words gapped out

copy sentences
e.g. from the board or in dictation (traditional but can be fun!)

gapfill short phrases into sentences
e.g. description of topics such as daily routine; ordering food; talking about a hobby

'produce' words (using reference material such as a glossary and the teacher as necessary)
e.g. labelling
writing topic lists in games

produce short phrases
e.g answering questions in a listening activity
describing pictures; gapfilling phrases in a dialogue; finishing off sentences

produce sentences
e.g. answering questions about something (a text, a video or a picture); writing a fuller description; translating English sentences.

There are many good activity books which detail further activities to integrate writing into MFL learning. Also the Key Stage 2 Framework learning objectives for literacy combine reading and writing learning outcomes for KS2 pupils.

Exploiting narrative in MFL

In the long-term scheme of work in the previous chapter we showed key story texts which can be covered, one each year starting from Year 2. This taps into a principle which cuts across all of the four skills but which can be built up as skills competence progresses, namely that of listening to, recounting and inventing stories. Children enjoy stories in the foreign language in the same way they enjoy stories in English (and other mother tongues). Stories appeal to a basic cognitive style of making sense of the world through narrative. They are an excellent way to familiarise children with the sounds and rhythm of a foreign language and to encourage reading. Stories with which children are familiar may be better, at least to begin with. Detailed comprehension of the language is not as important as the children's enjoyment of the sounds of the language and, with the support of pictures, exaggerated tone of voice or gesture, they will concentrate to understand the storyline. As Cheater and Farren write, '[the children will be] captivated by the structure and shape of the tale, the sound of the voices, the rhythm and repetition of little-understood phrases' (2001: 51) in much the same way as in their first language. Stories naturally include many elements of repetition (think of the 'Who's been sleeping in my bed?' and 'Why, what big . . . you have?' routines) and this will help to reinforce the sound patterns to pupils, who will more than likely want to join in when they know the phrase that is coming. There are many traditional tales, such as those cited in our German scheme of work, which are available in many languages or even in bilingual editions.

Conclusion

While 'fun and games' are an important part of MFL and play a major role in motivating pupils, early learners also need to be challenged and to have their learning guided through clear stages of progression if initial motivation is to be maintained. We have suggested in this chapter that whole-child development through MFL means the integration of multi-sensory learning through different resources and activities and also through integration of all four language skills. The chapter features many practical suggestions for using resources and setting up activities to this end.

We do not believe that writing should be emphasised over speaking and listening in MFL – or even that it should be introduced in the early years – but nor do we advocate steadfastly ignoring the written word. Such hardline positions are not helpful. More important are an open mind and a willingness to use whatever support proves effective in helping pupils make meaning through MFL.

Similarly, while we recognise that some activities in MFL will be teacher-led 'transmission' type activities, for example, repeating together, phonetic drills and singing, we also urge teachers to ensure that pupils are encouraged at the 'production phase' to use the new language to create and construct their own meanings ('mistakes and all').

Issues for reflection

- Other than the activities suggested in this chapter, can you think of other first language literacy development strategies which might be integrated into your MFL teaching?

- Are there opportunities for reinforcing MFL learning through labelling classroom objects or having useful 'chunks' of language visible in the room or elsewhere in the school?

- Can you identify problems (of pronunciation or spelling, etc.) specific to your MFL which might need extra attention? Which helping strategies might be appropriate?, for example use of cognates, phonetic drilling through rhyme.

- Where pupils are taught by an MFL specialist is there adequate reinforcement of and reference to MFL learning made by the class teacher in literacy, numeracy and other areas of the curriculum?

5

Teaching approaches – differentiation, motivation and learning across the curriculum

THE ENORMOUS DEVELOPMENTAL changes that define primary teaching and learning necessitate a wide repertoire of age-sensitive teaching approaches, albeit one that will mesh effectively with later learning. This chapter will look at key issues in secondary language learning which primary teachers need to be aware of and then will go on to discuss different ways in which primary pupils can be involved in active MFL through content-based learning tasks using drama, games and a host of other activities which support whole-curriculum learning.

Key issues

- Developments in primary MFL need to mesh with developments in secondary MFL and so an awareness of the KS3 MFL curriculum is needed.

- Activities need to be tailored appropriately for different primary classes given the different, age-related motivations for particular learning styles.

- MFL has the potential to support and reinforce other areas of the primary curriculum.

- In order for MFL to be successfully embedded across the curriculum it must be seen as more than a discrete, skill-oriented subject. We advocate forms of 'content-based' language learning, which ensure new language is used meaningfully.

Introduction

The primary teacher is in a unique position to deliver MFL as a cross-curricular experience. Unlike her/his colleague in the secondary school, the primary teacher is already an expert in delivering whole-curriculum learning and has privileged access to the global experience of the pupils' perspective. These are major assets in the process of successfully embedding MFL across the curriculum. Of course, as with all innovation, support is needed for necessary basic skills and awareness of how to expand existing practice in new directions. This chapter aims to contribute to such support by first looking at the aims underpinning secondary MFL pedagogy – aims which earlier stage teachers need to be aware of – and by then considering how MFL is most effectively embedded in the curriculum by linking to other subjects as well as constituting its own specialist area. We will justify this position on the grounds of increased pupil motivation and meaningful use of language in context and will suggest several practical ways cross-curricular learning can be implemented.

MFL in the secondary school

MFL teachers in the secondary sector, like other secondary subject specialists, are frequently reproached for lack of awareness of the child's experience of school prior to Year 7. Various initiatives are now in place which to seek to redress this limitation in order to improve smooth progression, socially and pedagogically, between the two very different environments of primary and secondary (this transition is discussed further in Chapter 10). Similarly, it is essential that primary MFL teachers take into account curricular frameworks beyond KS2 in order to ensure continuity and so, in this chapter, we will consider some of the key changes which have affected secondary MFL teaching and learning in recent times and the impact of these on children learning primary MFL. For while primary teaching has its own distinctive characteristics, in many ways the delivery of MFL also shares many features in both primary and secondary. What, therefore, are these differences and how could they mesh?

Since the introduction of the National Curriculum in 1988 secondary MFL, in common with other curriculum subjects, has been characterised by increasing uniformity of content and style as national frameworks define pupils' progression through commonly scripted attainment level descriptors and a common Programme of Study. The current Key Stage 2 Framework for Languages offers another framework of learning objectives to complement the KS3 MFL framework. While both suggest given ladders of progression rather than prescriptive methods, they also espouse increasingly shared positions about what constitutes good practice. At Key Stages 4 and 5 there remain in England only three main examination boards offering MFL GCSE and AS/A-levels (OCR, EDEXCEL and AQA) and there remains little difference in format and content between the different boards' examination papers. So an increasingly uniform picture has emerged about what children need to learn in MFL and how this can be achieved. Furthermore, since 2004, MFL, while still compulsory at KS3, is no longer a core curriculum subject at KS4. Although it must still be offered as an 'entitlement subject' at KS4, this has effectively meant that secondary schools who have a strong track record in MFL have kept it compulsory and other schools whose achievement in MFL is low and whose pupils often feel disaffected with MFL, have removed the compulsion and, in some cases, have seen the MFL take-up at options plummet, with consequent effects on staffing numbers, staff morale, and the status of MFL within the school. Many writers and researchers feel that the curriculum content and ensuing teacher strategies may be, at least in part, at the root of this disaffection.

Focus on communicative language teaching

The current Key Stage 2 Framework for Languages has been designed to lead into the current secondary MFL curriculum. In terms of language content (development of intercultural competence is dealt with in Chapter 9) both reflect current thinking on *communicative language teaching*, but what does this really mean? To answer this question we need to consider the aims of the National Curriculum in terms of the communicative competence it sets out to equip pupils with. The content of the MFL National Curriculum (NC) for the secondary stage could be said to combine the following two aims:

– achieving functional competence (being able to do things – perform certain functions – with language)

– ability to use and apply grammar through knowledge and practice of linguistic features (sequenced according to a traditional hierarchy of 'difficulty', often starting with nouns and articles, then progressing to adjectives, then on to present tense, usually regular, verbs).

Let's look more closely at these aims. First, what is meant by functional (communicative) competence? What are the functions we expect children to be able to perform with the language they learn? The secondary NC's interpretation of communicative functional competence broadly aims to prepare pupils to:

1 talk about themselves/their own world (self, hobbies, family, pets, food, holidays, school, town, likes, dislikes)

2 get by in the target language culture (ordering food and drink, asking for directions, buying things).

Now, on a linguistic level, in order to be able to meet these communicative aims, children are taught words (including spelling, pronunciation and gender), then phrases and sentences (using given verbs), then texts (suggesting appropriate types of phrasal and sequential sequencing with connectives and adverbial markers). There is some difficulty with the mesh between these communicative and linguistic aims, however. Consider the following three points:

- Many functions can be performed with 'incorrect' or minimal language. Compare these sets of desired 'model' responses with alternatives:
    - *Quel âge as-tu?*
    - * *Dix – et tu?*
    - *(J'ai dix ans – et toi?)*
    - *Qu'est-ce que tu prends?*
    - * *Une coca-cola.*
    - *Un coca-cola.*
    - *Où habites-tu?*
    - * *Je habite with mon familie in un maison dans Redhill, à Surrey*
    - *(J'habite avec ma famille dans une maison à Redhill, dans le Surrey)*

We can see that the alternative phrases, though incorrect grammatically to differing degrees, achieve the communicative (information-conveying) function and would probably not cause comprehension difficulties to our legendary 'sympathetic native speaker'.

- Many of the 'getting by' functions in some texts and secondary syllabi are ill-suited to the real communicative needs of children, for example booking accommodation, going to the doctor unescorted, even hiring a car! and so are projected on to some imagined future of the child as an adult tourist. These situations are the legacy of an understanding of communicative needs (for adults!) identified through David Wilkins' seminal work on establishing 'threshold levels' of competence for the Council of Europe in the 1960s.

- Many functions require a more sophisticated linguistic repertoire than will have so far been provided. A classic example is when discussing jobs, e.g.
    - *Qu'est-ce qu'il fait dans la vie, ton père?*
    - *Il est . . . Miss, how do you say 'portfolio manager for a stocks and investments broker'?*

In this case, a quick-witted teacher might respond *Il est financier* or may have pre-empted the problem by only including a finite number of options; for example rather than asking this question, the teacher may point to a picture of a man working in an office and ask for the image to be matched to the previously taught item *employé de bureau*. Nevertheless, there will inevitably be another occasion when pupils will be frustrated as they attempt to produce some free language which is beyond their linguistic means and the teacher will need to juggle the planned learning objectives with the child's enthusiasm for wanting to express their 'truth', that is, to be genuinely communicative. The traditional 'ladder' of linguistic progression, therefore, only loosely, and somewhat artificially, corresponds to the communicative function being taught. It is important, therefore, to establish the link to and fro between new language being taught and the communicative context in which it is used, in other words, to make use of the language meaningful.

The KS3 Strategy for MFL and links to KS2

The MFL Key Stage 3 Strategy has gone some way to addressing this last issue as it has shifted the focus back onto technical language awareness rather than communicativeness *per se*. The KS3 Strategy is now embedded in most secondary MFL departments, to varying degrees, and builds on the frameworks established for the National Literacy Strategy and, later, for KS3 English. In fact, the KS3 MFL Framework would be readily recognisable to all primary teachers as it uses very similar language and concepts to those that they work with every day in the NLS, for example, the word-sentence-discourse level construct.

To what extent is the KS2 MFL Framework known in primary schools?

We found that most of the primary teachers we spoke to who were responsible for arranging their own MFL programme – either as language coordinators for the school or as class teachers acting independently to start up MFL with their class – were aware of the QCA's MFL framework and scheme of work. Many are using the scheme of work as a core reference but adapting it to suit their context to dovetail with other areas of the curriculum in their school day and to match their own choices about materials, suitability and usefulness. In our view, this is exactly how a framework should be used. At the time of writing the Key Stage 2 Framework for Languages was being rolled out so we are unable to comment on the effectiveness of its implementation.

To what extent is the KS3 Strategy for MFL known in primary schools?

Most of the primary teachers we have spoken to knew something about the *content* of the KS3 Strategy which has been rolled out to secondary schools. Some had heard about it and most 'expected there was something like that' and were even surprised that it was not (yet) more generally established. However, few were aware of the ethos behind the Strategy, itself not dissimilar to the aspirations of the Primary Literacy Strategy inasmuch as it aims to equip children with a greater metalinguistic awareness and increase analytic understanding of how language works. The 2005 Key Stage 2 Framework for MFL has introduced explicit links with the NLS by establishing literacy as one of the core strands in the MFL framework, thus harmonising first language and foreign language learning objectives and learning strategies, e.g.

Children should be taught to

L3.1 *recognise some familiar words in written form*

L3.2 *make links between some phonemes, rhymes and spellings, and read aloud familiar words*

(Key Stage 2 Framework for Languages 2005: 72)

There is much common ground between the ways in which the NLS is delivered and the possibilities for teaching MFL in the classroom; indeed, here we are arguing the case for mutual reinforcement. The following is an example of a lesson we saw recently combining explicit teaching of first language (English) literacy with MFL.

A Year 6 Literacy lesson observation

The teacher asked pupils to describe what a verb is. Most were able to answer that it was a 'doing word' or that it 'describes an action' and to give an example and to identify the verbs in sentences, first in present tense then in different tenses, then in compound forms.

The teacher had prepared some sentences on PowerPoint which had gaps for the children to fill in with different verbs. Some sentences offered limited possibilities, e.g.

– *Last night I _____ a football match on television. (watched)*

while others could be gapfilled with different choices

– *I _____ an ice cream on the beach. (ate/bought/dropped/had/fancied, etc.)*

Pupils were also able to do some gapfills in this way with Spanish sentences, though these were more restrictive in possible choices, like the first English sentence cited. Some pupils understood the sentence but had forgotten the Spanish vocabulary and said the word in English, e.g. 'play' instead of *juego* in

– *(Yo) _____ al fútbol todos los días*

Pupils were asked to describe the difference between a regular and irregular verb in English (*-ed* endings and irregular endings) and then to give certain verb paradigms, e.g. sing – sang – sung, eat – ate – eaten. Some pupils, though a small number, were able to give past participles in Spanish too and explain regular endings *-ado* and *-ido.*

Later, children were asked to go through the six persons of an English verb (I sing, you sing, he/she/it sings, we sing, you sing, they sing) and were able to say that all forms were the same except for the third person singular which takes an 's'. Then they chanted some Spanish verb tables. This in itself is not of 'high value' (Heafford 1990: 88, cited in Pachler and Field 2002: 54) but we were impressed that pupils were then able to answer 'OK, so what's the third person plural of *comer*?'. While some pupils struggled, pupils were asked to explain their answers and show on a verb table (arranged in two columns for singular and plural), for instance, that third person is the third one down and that 'singular is one person and plural is more than one'.

	↑ singular	↑ ↑ ↑ plural
1st person	I yo	we nosotros
2nd person	you tú	you vosotros
3rd person	he/she/it él/ella	they ellos/ellas

At another school where Literacy is also a central focus of the MFL provision, that is, knowledge *about* language is seen as a principal benefit of language learning, rather than aiming for linguistic competence in a given language (knowledge *of* a language), we saw in the pupils' exercise books several written 'rules' in boxes on verb conjugations, possessive adjectives and spellings, for example:

word endings	-sion in English	=	*-sione* in Italian
word endings	-tion in English	=	*-zione* in Italian

Other examples of how MFL can be taught in the style of existing curriculum delivery include the following.

A Year 4 Numeracy lesson observation

Numbers have always been one of the first things taught in MFL and many adults can still count automatically to 20 in at least one foreign language even without being able to say much more. However, numbers in the foreign language can be practised in many enjoyable ways and can then lead on to reinforce simple maths.

Pupils counted together numbers to 30 in French, first following the teacher's prompts, then chanting all together in time with the teacher, then individually around the room so that each pupil represented a number (to 24). As each pupil called out their number they stood up then sat down again. Afterwards, all odd numbers went to one end of the room *(les impairs, allez à côté de la porte)* and the even numbers next to the carpet area *(les pairs, allez à côté de la moquette)*. The teacher then called out some simple arithmetic sums and the pupils arranged themselves in lines of three accordingly, repeating their numbers, e.g. *trois plus cinq égalent huit; vingt-quatre moins dix égalent quatorze.* Pupils helped each other find the answers and thoroughly enjoyed the activity which lasted about ten minutes in total. The high level of involvement and physical interactivity leads this type of activity on to a higher level of 'value' from that of choral chanting.

Examples of songs as a cross-curricular link to Music based on Years 4, 5 and 6 lesson observations

Singing is a tried and tested way to familiarise pupils with the foreign language. Teachers who may not have a high level of proficiency feel 'safe' with the contained nature of the language in a song text and the rhythm and repetition help reinforce vocabulary, structure and phonic awareness.

We have seen many lessons including foreign language songs, especially French classics like *Frère Jacques, Sur le Pont d'Avignon* and *L'Alouette*. Songs like *L'Alouette* lend themselves naturally to specific areas of vocabulary so, unsurprisingly, we saw children pointing to their heads (tails and beaks!) while singing it. In the same school we saw the tune of *Frère Jacques* used to practise other phrases like *Quel âge as-tu? Quel âge as-tu? – J'ai huit ans, J'ai huit ans*, and the tune of *She'll be coming round the mountain* to practise animals and phrases of liking/disliking like *J'adore les serpents, oui, c'est vrai.* We even saw the theme tune of *East Enders* used to chant phrases of daily routine while pupils mimed actions:

Je me suis levé à sept heures

Je me suis lavé

Je me suis habillé

Puis j'ai pris mon petit déjeuner

Et je suis parti

Pour aller à l'école

Songs worked best where there was some support in the written form in the early stages but this remains a contentious issue. With very young children reading ability may be too low. One Year 4 class teacher on the South Coast told us she was reluctant to introduce the written form because she wanted the focus on oral practice and that seeing the words would confuse the children. However, without having some preparatory focus on pronunciation, many of the songs were confusing to some pupils and involvement was largely symbolic. Who else remembers learning *Frère Jacques* as a child but not really understanding what it was about? Both the authors confess to not having had a clue – instead of *Sonnez la matine* we both used to sing 'sunny semolina'!

These examples demonstrate how MFL can be integrated across the curriculum rather than, though preferably as well as, being treated as a separate, discrete subject. There are valid arguments for both approaches: subject-specific MFL sessions enable focused foreign language work for its own sake and thereby give MFL a certain status in the school and in the child's (and parents' and teachers') perception of MFL learning. It may also be argued that certain pedagogic approaches lend themselves specifically to MFL learning, for example comparative grammar work, however, as we have seen with the examples above, this also feeds into and reinforces Literacy. MFL is often seen as a 'special, 'distinctive' subject – possibly because the class teacher may be nervous about teaching it or because it may not be taught by the regular teacher – and often gets tagged on at different times as a 'bit of fun' or 'light relief' in the form of songs or a game. This distinctive status is a double-edged sword. In the short term, the 'gamey', 'something extra' attitude to MFL delivery may offer very positive associations with the subject (as fun or light relief from the 'serious' business of learning) yet, in the longer term, there is a danger that if it is only seen as a special 'appendage' to the main business of core subject learning then it can too easily be detached and eventually dropped without having any perceptual negative impact on 'normal' curricular development.

Different motivations

The rationale for introducing MFL to younger children, discussed in Chapter 1, also takes into account the different motivations for different age-specific teaching and learning approaches. As Keith Sharpe acknowledges,

> while it may be difficult to show clearly that young children are more efficient learners of foreign languages, it is perhaps less difficult to argue that on the whole they are easier for teachers to motivate ... Primary teachers tend to be skilled motivators, and the material they are working with is more plastic than if they were teaching older pupils

(Sharpe 2001: 35)

Primary school children also tend to be less self-conscious when presented with a new mode of communication. In Piagetian terms, they are less rigid in their perceptual understanding of the world than secondary-age pupils and this, coupled with more holistic curriculum delivery by the same class teacher, makes it an ideal time to embed foreign language awareness in their thinking.

It is broadly recognised by secondary school teachers of MFL that Year 7 pupils still enjoy 'child-like' activities such as singing, chanting and acting out and that they will participate in these with few inhibitions. They are still very playful and often seek to 'please' the teacher in a way familiar to primary teachers (this may, of course, be said of older pupils as well but the adolescence threshold discourages overt approval-seeking). By Year 9, often considered a difficult 'in-between' year, pupils are growing out of the activity-types which they enjoyed in Year 7 yet the linguistic resources available to them for free discursive language production remains inadequate at KS4. This means that communication in MFL lessons can be restricted to highly-structured mechanistic exchanges (such as scripted role-plays) which leads to frustration and low motivation.

Although the underlying motivating factors may be universal (competitiveness, positive feedback, fun) and apply equally to the secondary context, the primary teacher is able to capitalise on younger children's relative lack of inhibition and greater focus on pre-puberty physicality through games and drama activities. The benefits of integrating games in MFL learning seem evident:

- The enjoyment factor is paramount. If children are motivated they will focus their energy into the learning process and give the activity their whole attention. In an already heavily burdened curriculum, pupils are positively disposed towards a subject which entails fun and games.

- Pupils understand the principles of games and will usually be familiar with the format in English of the game to be played in the target language. Time is not therefore wasted on learning the 'form' of pedagogic conventions and pupils instinctively focus on the language being used.

- The routine and repetition element of games both allows the teacher to feel comfortable if they are not very secure with using new target language and, more importantly, lends itself to reinforcing specific target language phrases and vocabulary without seeming to pupils like a boring drill.

- As the pupils are focused on the outcome of the game, this is real 'task-based' learning which leads to increased fluency and confidence in the target language.

There are hundreds of these types of activities listed in publications new and old but here are a few to give a flavour:

Fête déguisée: To familiarise children with clothes vocabulary, colours and sizes. Children dress up from a fancy dress box or this can be done on a non-uniform day. Children are given a couple of minutes to look carefully at what classmates are wearing then they stand back to back (or blindfolded) and try to remember what their partner (or another pupil chosen by name) is wearing:

- *Tu portes un chapeau rouge*
- *Tu portes une casquette bleue et blanche*

A handout with labelled pictures and a colour chart would provide support at the beginning if required.

Un défilé de mode: On the same theme, older children can plan a fashion show with catwalk commentaries in the target language. This can be great fun for assemblies.

Numbers: Old favourites to familiarise pupils with numbers are the games of *Lotto* (on improvised bingo cards) and *Ring the Number* whereby two children from the different teams stand on a mark then rush to circle the number on the board called out by the teacher. Teams can have different-coloured marker pens (les Bleus, les Verts) and this can now be done on an interactive whiteboard.

Directions: Pupils 'guide' a blindfolded classmate around the room or hall by giving directions in the target language.

Tongue-twisters: Some writers (e.g. Lee) think tongue-twisters should be avoided as they 'set learners a needlessly difficult task (which) even native speakers of the languages find hard to say' (Lee 1971: 83) but, while we agree that they are better presented in a simplified form, we think pupils may find them amusing and they can aid pronunciation and phonic awareness when the phonemes being practised are referred to at other times. As with other figurative expressions they can be written on the wall and children will enjoy illustrating them, e.g. *Le chasseur sachant chasser chasse sans son chien!*

Mime: Pupils guess what the teacher or a classmate is doing, e.g. *estás comiendo; estás jugando al fútbol.* The action can also be done in slow motion *(a cámara lenta).*

Find a partner: Any variation of the idea of pupils moving around to find a partner with the same birth-month, the same star-sign, the same telephone number or favourite sport (from a cue card), will offer opportunities for maximum participation in speaking practice.

While these activities are fun and effectively consolidate new lexical and structural input they are not an end in themselves. It is important to ensure that pupils are *stretched* in the foreign language and that progression is built in. For example, the phrases practised in the mime game can then be used in a circular story, orally, with other elements brought in, for example adjectives, other vocabulary, and this might culminate in a piece of writing in the target language for older KS2 children (from pictures or a gapped writing frame). In this way language practised through games, drama and physical activities feeds into other areas of the curriculum. Although this seems ambitious – maybe even controversial – such a process of 'embedding' is a key feature of the Key Stage 2 Framework and indeed offers many potential possibilities for differentiation.

Focus on content versus skill

Where MFL is given its own regular slot in the timetable the question arises about the nature of the content as well as how much time should be allocated. The traditional view in the secondary school of MFL teaching as developing a technical *skill* rather than focusing on the *content* of what is actually taught has sometimes resulted in a narrow definition of what MFL is for. As discussed above, the skills-focused communicative function has led to disaffection among older, secondary pupils who often feel that the level of content is undemanding (or childish) whereas the subject is 'technically' difficult, requiring application of complex rules, memorisation of lists of words, grasping new grammatical concepts. This reported discrepancy looms large in Jeff Lee's research (1998) which underpinned the KS3 Strategy for MFL with its renewed focus on making the technical 'language work' interesting and achievable. In the same vein, many pupils complain that the MFL work they do in the secondary school is less fun or more difficult than what they did at primary school where memories of foreign language learning are of playing games, singing songs, acting out scenes and drawing displays. One Year 7 secondary pupil in London told us: 'It [MFL] was more fun at [primary school] with Miss [primary teacher]. We used to get to sing and do clapping and that. With Miss [secondary teacher] we do more writing and it's more difficult.'

It is difficult to know whether pupils like the one quoted here would indeed truly enjoy the same style of teaching they remember enjoying at primary school or if, rather, they are simply expressing nostalgia for a memory, couched in cosiness, of their former lives as younger children. Indeed Lee's research (1998) showed that a more likely source of disaffection is that the content of the secondary MFL curriculum is too undemanding (while, at the same time, still perceived as 'technically' difficult). It is hoped that once MFL has been taught to all primary children then the secondary curriculum can 'shift up' a gear in terms of content given that all children will have a command of the basics by Year 7 thereby paving the way for more 'meaty' age-appropriate content at Key Stages 3 and 4. It could be argued that this would present a case against diversification (away from French predominance) but, as we state elsewhere in the book, the gains made by language learning at primary do not constitute measurable stocks of knowledge specific to a given language – a lexico-phrasal bank – so much as an openness to different modes of communication through developing a repertoire of effective language learning strategies (pattern recognition, phonic awareness) and positive attitudes to the experience.

The imbalance between content- and skills-learning in MFL needs to be addressed in both secondary and primary schools if MFL learning is to be seen as a vibrant, meaningful and *integrated* part of the curriculum. In many other countries – such as with the *sections européennes* in French secondary schools – the most effective way of both increasing foreign language proficiency and developing a wider, pragmatic awareness beyond purely linguistic skills, has been found by using foreign language as a medium to teach other areas of the curriculum, that is to use a foreign language to learn content, rather than consciously practising it as a skill. This 'immersion' method is the extreme end of what content-based language learning can mean.

Foreign-language medium schools have existed since the advent of compulsory education. They are usually fee-paying and attract large numbers of expatriate, mother-tongue children or children from 'international' families, all of which are factors which weigh heavily in favour of linguistic diversity and openness to language learning. More recently, mainstream state education has used the idea of foreign-language medium education to develop a variety of projects to encourage the use of foreign languages across the curriculum. However, we are not suggesting here that pupils should be immersed in MFL across the curriculum and that other subjects should be taught exclusively in a foreign language but that MFL should be seen as an integrated element of the mainstream curriculum. Instead of focusing on foreign language competence as a discrete skill, the most effective way of cultivating this skill is recognised as *using* a foreign language as a means of *developing* (i.e. extending) content learning of different subjects. In this light, the focus shifts from the *means* to the *end* and foreign language becomes a vehicle for learning about the world. This places the emphasis on the content (the substance of what is being learnt) rather than the form (the lexico-grammatical structures) which are used to convey the meaning.

The ways in which this has been achieved are diverse and depend largely on institutional and practical limitations as well as scepticism about the broader benefits, particularly with relation to fears of hindering first language development (after all, national exams in 'content-subjects' are still taken exclusively in first language). However, to reiterate, we are not suggesting that the MFL replace English as the medium for most classroom teaching – even if there were staffing and resources available – but that adapted forms of content-based language learning both reinforce MFL learning and the English-medium learning of different subjects. Let us look briefly at which forms adapted content-based learning may take.

Integrating content-based language learning into the curriculum

No one doubts that elements of foreign language learning in its traditional guise (the skills-oriented language lesson) still has a place. On the contrary, content-based learning, if anything, brings into focus a specific set of objectives which need the same degree of planned lexical and structural 'scaffolding' (progressively and recursively planned exploitation) which the communicative approach in the MFL lesson espouses. The difference with the integration of content-based learning is that communicative outcomes are tied to immediate learning needs, enabling students to realise this need to achieve short-term completion of tasks and to gain knowledge accepted as part of intellectual development in the school context. It should be noted, though, that conventional, skills-oriented (functional) language teaching, with its aims to equip students for foreign travel/outside contact through linguistic and intercultural preparation for anticipated encounters with the other, remains as valid as ever. Content-based learning does not aim to replace this type of learning but to extend it and imbue the learning process with more direct meaning-making. Content-based learning enables the foreign language to be experienced as a necessary skill rather than as a discrete subject for study like, for example, learning to play the piano.

One of the main obstacles to implementing content-based learning in its 'strong' form is of course the lack of truly effective bilinguals (or native speakers) working in our schools, and neither of course are these necessarily the best teachers in any case! Added to this are concerns that pressures to meet curriculum requirements and to adapt English-language materials will only obstruct delivery of the National Curriculum. However, content-based language learning can also be applied in a 'weaker' form whereby different elements of other subjects are delivered in the foreign language. This is a manageable aim which can both add richness to the whole curriculum and reinforce the vitality of the language learning process. In this way, MFL is embedded across the curriculum.

The primary school environment lends itself perfectly to this style of language teaching as, unlike in the secondary school, the primary teacher has a profound understanding of the whole curriculum and how the different disciplines mesh together. The primary school teacher can either therefore integrate the foreign language into an area of the curriculum that suits their own skills and linguistic comfort zone or, where they are working with an MFL specialist, they can work together with the MFL teacher to plan cross-curricular input. The following two examples illustrate how MFL can be taught in this way. The first looks at how another area of the curriculum can be taught by the regular class teacher using MFL and the second how the regular class teacher can work in collaboration with the MFL specialist to ensure delivery of meaningful, content-based language learning.

Example of the regular class teacher using MFL to link to art and literacy

After completing a story book in Literacy and having exploited this in English in the usual way (e.g. comprehension questions, storyboarding, creative writing) pupils then imagined a follow-up scene from the story for a 'what-happened-next' scenario and designed an illustration using paint and other craft materials, some for a poster and others for a 3D display. These scenes were then labelled in the foreign language and speech bubbles were filled in with some simple foreign language dialogue.

Increasing numbers of children's books are translated into different languages so, although it may not be desirable to use the unabridged foreign language text as such, these can be used to help the teacher with phrases and vocabulary specific to the story. Like many of the suggestions in this book, this works even better when there is a link to another school in the target language country so that the children's efforts can be appreciated by native speakers of their age (see Chapters 8 and 9 for more about school links).

Example of cooperation with an MFL specialist to link MFL to geography, art and ICT

The following work module was planned between a Year 5 class teacher and a peripatetic MFL special-ist (though anybody else with foreign language capacity connected to the school could help, possibly a native-speaker parent or assistant who is able to bring a confidence with the language as well as cultural knowledge which may be beyond the scope of the regular class teacher). The specialist talked to the pupils in simplified French about a town in France that she knew quite well. (She had spent a year there as a student but a native speaker could equally describe their town or region of origin.) The specialist used props (a map, posters, postcards and a model of the town's castle) to explain aspects of the town's geography and history. Using simple questions and encouraged by the regular class teacher the specialist began to ask pupils questions about their own town or region, for example:

– *A Nantes, il y a un grand château célèbre. Voici une image de ce château. Il est beau, non? Est-ce qu'il y a un château aussi à Bristol?*

For some questions, the specialist and the class teacher had prepared dialogue (though the preparation was unknown to pupils) and this encouraged children and also provided them with some information they did not know, e.g.

– *A Nantes, il y a environ deux cent mille habitants* (writing the number on the board). *Et ici, à Bristol, il y a combien d'habitants?*
– (class teacher replies) *Il y a trois cent cinquante mille habitants à Bristol, Madame.*

After plenty of supported oral practice in this way the pupils were able to use French to prepare a display and a presentation about their own town or region. Working together with the specialist allowed the regular teacher to focus on the organisational aspects of setting up the project work and the specialist was able to give spontaneous linguistic support to both pupils and the class teacher.

The key benefit in adopting this style of approach is that it stretches the pupils in their MFL learning and lifts MFL to a position of real communication where pupils are actually 'making meaning' and developing concepts in the target language. The language learning and practice strategies entailed in the preparation of materials and the presentation aspect of the project chime with many of those suggested in the Key Stage 2 Framework and such an approach represents a simple and effective assessment opportunity.

Conclusion

In this chapter, we have seen how the 'communicative' approach adopted in most secondary schools and endorsed by the National Curriculum could be more motivating if preliminary work covered at primary stages enabled older children to engage with more age-appropriate content-based material. We have highlighted the increasing uniformity of national learning frameworks across the curriculum and throughout the various Key Stages, a uniformity which aims at cohesion and a holistic learning experience. We have argued the case for MFL being thus embedded across the curriculum through links with other subject areas. The primary teacher, as a naturally 'skilled motivator' and whole-curriculum expert, is in an excellent position to oversee this type of innovation and we have given some snapshot examples based on our research in schools of how this may be effectively achieved.

Issues for reflection

- In your school, or a school you know, which activities in MFL seem to most motivate pupils of different ages?
- If your pupils do have an allocated MFL slot, how naturally cross-curricular are the activities, for example links to music, PE, literacy, citizenship, numeracy?
- How might you enhance pupil learning during these activities?
- Do you think that the activities your pupils do in MFL are progressively challenging in terms of content?
- What opportunities are there to extend pupil learning in different subjects by using MFL?

Learner strategies and preferences – overcoming the 'tricky bits'

LANGUAGE LEARNING IN primary schools is allocated a limited amount of time in primary MFL classrooms. We will show in this chapter the interaction taking place and how it can potentially be enhanced in this environment in view of the time constraint.

Time constraints pose a twofold challenge for teachers: in order to maximise the given time for primary MFL, teachers need to focus firstly on the learning process and secondly on the most effective learning and learner strategies. In addition, pupils often know instinctively how they best learn, and develop their preferred learning styles. They are also aware of what they themselves find difficult to learn in primary MFL and describe as 'tricky bits'. Dialogue between teachers and pupils in the primary MFL classroom about learning and, when appropriate, on learning strategies, can lay the foundation for pupils to find and develop their own learning solutions and thus enhance the pupils' 'learning to learn' capability.

Key issues

- Primary MFL, although a vulnerable subject due to time constraints, provides opportunities for learning to be maximised in MFL lessons.

- Time on task and wait time are mutually reinforcing and crucial to effective MFL learning.

- Pupils need to be involved fully in the primary MFL learning process; when invited to articulate their thoughts, pupils can develop, apply and extend their range of learning strategies.

- Strategy training, readily built into MFL lessons, can help pupils extend their repertoire.

- Knowing how to learn a foreign language can help children to become more effective strategy users and ultimately lifelong language learners.

Introduction – all about learning in the primary MFL classroom

It is useful for primary MFL teachers to be aware of relevant learning and language learning theories. Extensive literature on these topics exists and it is not the purpose of this chapter to pick over this terrain in detail. However, we will briefly refer to some of the more pertinent learning theories and apply them to primary MFL.

Piaget's well-known and influential educational theory of cognitive development suggests that this development is supported by child-centred pedagogy and initiated by experimentation on the child's surroundings, often termed 'discovery learning'. Piaget also introduced a scale of cognitive development, according to which all children pass through four stages at different ages. Pupils at Key Stage 2, aged 7 to 11, are deemed to be at the stage of concrete operations; younger pupils at Foundation Level and Key Stage 1 learners, are in the pre-operational stage. These categories imply that all teachers need to plan an appropriate type of learning experience and also formulate strategies enabling pupils to make a transition to a higher cognitive level.

The rigid age allocation or pigeon-holing of cognitive thinking has been criticised by many, as has the neglect of factors such as the influence of the teacher and other social influences. Within Piaget's theory this lack of a social dimension has been particularly challenged. Other aspects of his approach, such as sensitivity to the age allocation as a starting point when considering learning experiences and planning for progression, have been incorporated into the more recent theory of social constructivism. One of the prime initiators of this school of thinking was the Russian psychologist Lev Vygotsky. Vygotsky developed the concept of the zone of proximal development (ZPD) that distinguishes between what a learner can achieve when working alone and what a learner can achieve when guided by a more proficient other. This concept has gained considerable credence among educationalists, not least because it reflects the basic model of the teacher–pupil relationship and the intended result of their cooperation in a learning outcome. It emphasises that the intellectual level at which a learning experience is to be pitched has to be within the grasp of the learner. That way, teachers can ensure there is what Piaget called 'cognitive matching', and set an appropriate level of learning for pupils to progress to and enable them to feel challenged. The ZPD also describes the value-added of collaborating as a kind of pooling together in a qualitatively enriching dialogue where one participant is not necessarily more proficient than the other.

Primary MFL teachers in particular should not set the intellectual level of a learning experience too low as disinterest may result. We have seen this in the cases of some Year 6 classes where the MFL input was scarcely any different from that which the pupils had covered in earlier years, including at Key Stage 1. This could also be observed in Year 7 at secondary school where the input often covers the same ground; as one Year 7 pupil observed: 'I couldn't believe it when our French teacher started doing numbers one to ten with us as we had done up to a hundred at primary school.'

When the concept of the ZPD is applied to a learning situation, learning can be accelerated through teacher scaffolding of pupil learning. The latter, a metaphor coined by Jerome Bruner to describe Vygotsky's teacher intervention, is achieved through verbal advice or support activities to help pupils to facilitate their understanding, and by cutting out any potential 'waste' time. The ZPD embraces wholeheartedly the influences on learning and justifies the crucial role of the teacher as the main but not exclusive scaffolder, a role that can also be undertaken by pupils themselves as they work collaboratively to challenge and support each other.

Social constructivism also perceives learning as a social act, taking place within the individual, between individuals and in the wider context of the community. Social constructivism highlights the importance of speech and language and the intrapersonal dimension of the learning process as Light and Littleton (1999: 92) point out: 'This view of cognition challenges our traditional conceptions of development and learning. It invites us to reject a conception of the developmental process as the creation of the autonomous thinker ... in its place is a view of learning as intersubjective and dialogical.'

On the basis of the social constructivist approach Lave and Wenger (1991) developed their Situated Cognition theory and they, similarly, define learning as a social process that cannot be decontextualised from a real-life environment whereby learners are connected by what they call joint participation in a community of practice. The pupils are, according to this theory, members of several communities: at school, at home, with friends and at various extracurricular clubs or groups. The MFL classroom with its rituals and routines is one such community, and a concept we find useful as a foundation on which to base ongoing primary MFL pedagogical developments. A 'classroom community', a term coined by Behrman (2002), is established when the teacher sets tasks that reflect real-life scenarios to ensure contextualised learning. Learning can then be understood as an interactive process taking place between pupils that is facilitated by teachers as they 'scaffold' pupils' learning. This they do to a lesser extent as time passes, thus enabling pupils to become independent learners and asserting effective primary MFL teaching and learning as interactive and authentic in itself in the classroom. This perspective also fits into a formative and constructive assessment framework (see Chapter 7) that provides pupils with a 'scaffolded' way to improve and progress, an approach that is a key to learning socially in the classroom community.

Language teaching is not restricted to the interaction in the classroom, as Macaro (2001: 1) points out: 'language learning involves much more than teachers and learners simply interacting'. Teachers should seek ways, Macaro goes on to say, to offer practical suggestions as to how pupils can learn better. In the following sections we discuss how learners of primary MFL can develop strategies enabling them to be as successful as possible, for it is those learners with the widest range of strategies who are certainly the most effective. Since strategy is a broad term used in various fields and areas, we will define its specific use within the context of education, more specifically in primary MFL.

Strategies, strategies, strategies

In general, a learning strategy can be seen, according to O'Malley and Chamot (1990: 1), as 'the special thoughts or behaviours that individuals use to help them comprehend, learn, or retain new information'. Once these skills are acquired, the learner can, as Oxford (1990: 8) states, improve and vary these behaviours and also apply them to new learning contexts: 'specific actions taken by the learner to make learning easier, faster, more enjoyable, more self-directed, more effective, and more transferable to new situations'. Learning strategies thus defined can be understood as techniques enabling the individual to absorb, organise and retain information, that is, as a set of skills that can be transferred to other areas. With reference to language learning, Grenfell and Harris (1999: 22) stress the habitual and individual nature of the learning process when they define the learning strategy quite simply as: 'a set of habits or practices which learners may adopt in approaching the learning of a second language'.

Learning strategies have been further subdivided in the following way with, at the macro level, general learning strategies comprising all techniques required for all kinds of learning, such as metacognitive strategies (planning and self-evaluation) and some cognitive strategies such as resourcing, rehearsal or repeating. At the meso level, language learning strategies are said to relate to all strategies used to cope with language learning generally and, at the micro level, there is a further sub-division concerned with second and/or foreign language learning. These levels should not be seen as hierarchical but as operating on a zigzag basis. O'Malley and Chamot (1990) also introduce the dimension of social and affective strategies.

There is scope for developing the construct of our young learners as self-reflective agents with some measure of control and insight into their own learning processes (there are examples of this later in this chapter), although the role of the teacher is essential in helping to orientate and harness the strategies to promote greater learning efficiency.

In the literature, the terms learner strategy and learning strategy are sometimes used interchangeably. Macaro (2001: 19–20) particularly emphasises the fact that the term 'learner strategies' captures more effectively the learner as active participant in the learning process. This interpretation of the term 'learner strategies' resonates more with our view of the foreign language learner as active human agency.

With limited time for MFL learning, an enthusiastic and joyous learner response to the teaching context is not sufficient; pupils need to be active participants in their own learning. The resurgence of interest in learner/learning strategies is reflected in current discourses on MFL teaching and learning, the popularity of the 'learning to learn' (L2L) agenda that refers to meta-awareness. The promotion of personalised learning is also important for primary MFL teachers and something we need to promote as part of effective differentiated provision, particularly when time for teaching and learning MFL comes at such a premium.

Wait time and waiting time

One of the obstacles when incorporating the learning of a foreign language into the primary curriculum has been the lack of space in the primary curriculum – 'already full to bursting' (Jones 2005: 4), a sentiment echoed by many headteachers in recent years. It is desirable that children learn as effectively as possible and that good use of learning time is made in all subjects, however it is especially important that the time allocated for primary MFL be well used given its vulnerable status as an entitlement subject in the curriculum.

Drawing on his extensive research into educational effectiveness, and cited in Edelenbos and Johnstone (1997: 79–80), Bert Creemers identified five characteristics that determined effective teaching. The first of these, relevant to our discussion here, is the distinction between 'time for learning', in the sense of opportunities for learning, and 'time on task', meaning maximising such opportunities. MFL has often been the subject to be squeezed out when there are other pressures, abandoned temporarily, or reduced to a 10-minute learning slot which is some way below what is required to ensure sustainable learning (see DfES 2004 Report). The 'time on task' is, as Edelenbos and Johnstone (p. 80) assert, a variable of key importance yet difficult to measure since 'what really counts is [the] unobservable mental activity rather than [the] observable physical activity'. In a similar vein, Cullingford (1995: 16) defines 'time on task' as 'those moments when children are actually engaged with the work, rather than getting up to find a pen, talking to a neighbour, dreaming, playing with a pencil, or just waiting for the teacher to give an instruction. This latter time can be described as "waiting".'

'Waiting time' should in no way be confused with the concept of 'wait time' (see Chapter 7 on assessment) which refers to the extended time teachers are advised to wait to allow pupils to think about a response. In such a scenario pupils are in fact on task. Cullingford refers to research studies indicating that children spent a disturbingly high proportion of time – sometimes as much as 75 per cent – in the school day on 'waiting time'. Our observations of primary MFL lessons would indicate a considerable amount of activity; indeed the pace of lessons generally is energetic, if not at times frenetic, although activity in itself is not synonymous with learning.

A typical, well-paced language lesson includes a high amount of task-oriented use of the foreign language, such as asking for and going to find a pencil. Simple instructions in the target language like this should be part of the foreign language lesson and can then become part of the whole-school drip-feed approach at any point in any lesson.

Pupils are faced with a considerable amount of information and language input and they need to take in, organise and attempt to retain new language items in their long-term memory in the short time span of a primary MFL lesson. The questions arising from this are: how do young learners cope and what are the possible implications for teaching techniques? At this stage, we will present the results of discussions undertaken by 12 teachers with pupils about their learning styles and consider the implications on teaching.

Learner strategies and 'tricky bits'

In the first part of our survey teachers invited pupils to describe aspects they found difficult in their MFL learning and, if possible, give reasons. They then asked them to identify and explain what they considered easy aspects of learning a foreign language. The pupils were invited to express in their own terms strategies they used to learn, after the teachers had explained to them the authors' interest in knowing about how they coped with, as one pupil memorably put it, the 'tricky bits'. It became evident that the pupils, like the teaching staff taking part in the survey, were aware of the *time restraint* on their learning time. This applies also to schools where primary MFL learning was guaranteed a weekly slot in the curriculum, and yet pupils felt it still contrasted with other subjects that appear more regularly. In the inimitable style of youngsters, some Year 6 pupils expressed their concern about this restraint and impact on their learning:

'Because when we go out to play we forget our German and we have to remember it for a week.'

'It is a lot to take in in one lesson, and then remember for the next lesson – in a week's time.'

These two statements are representative of the vast majority of pupils in our sample – nearly all the pupils interviewed commented on the difficulty of *remembering* their MFL input. Interestingly, Scottish primary school children were found to be able to memorise lengthy plays and to produce them with good pronunciation. The DfES 2004 Report took that into account and recommended that primary schools not only plan a dedicated weekly slot for MFL but make provision for continuous drip-feed across the curriculum. Implementing the recommendation would allow time for revisiting and for consolidation, thus ensuring that the learning input can be processed from short-term to long-term memory.

Pupils are able to and indeed have identified complicated parts or 'tricky bits' in MFL learning, and we found a remarkable consensus among the children. In Table 6.1 we group the statements pupils made into the following categories: memory, pace and pronunciation.

TABLE 6.1 'Tricky bits' in MFL learning

Difficult aspect	Pupil statement
Memory	
Learning long/really hard words/lots of words	'Sometimes there are too many words to take in that you can never really remember them.'
A whole sentence	'It overloads your brain.'
Genders	'It is hard to remember which words go in which group' (the authors noted some imaginative phonetic spellings from pupils such as maskeling [for masculine] and new to [for neuter]).
Pace	
Having to take in too much	'Once we finish one topic we go straight onto another one and we forget the last topic and then we sometimes get asked about the last topic and we can't remember.'
Pronunciation	
Different and new sounds	'Getting your mouth round pronunciation – because it's a sound I have to teach my mouth from scratch'; 'Because the words are complicated and aren't in the English language so we aren't used to them'; 'Letters that look the same as English but are pronounced differently'.

The data in Table 6.1 reflect the importance the pupils interviewed attribute to the act of 'remembering'. It is vital if the children are to be able to recycle and manipulate language at later stages in their learning to acquire competence with respect to learning strategies from an early stage onwards. Young learners can and do devise their own means of helping them to remember vocabulary and phrases in the target language as the descriptions in Table 6.2 show.

Developing independent learning capability

Such statements show that pupils can identify how to successfully transfer new input to long-term memory on the basis of repetition, and emphasise the importance of developing listening skills. Without exception, all children at all levels identified language items such as numbers and colours as 'easy to learn' because of constant repetition and practice. As one Year 3 child put it: 'I can always remember how to say hello and goodbye, colours, animals and counting'; and in the colourful language of a Year 5 pupil 'I remember numbers and colours because the teacher is always yappering about these in French'.

TABLE 6.2 Language learning strategies

Auditory–vocabulary-related techniques	
Word association	'If it sounds like another word then use that word to remember it'; 'Good morning, good afternoon and good evening all start with the same word – buenos días, buenas tardes, buenas noches'.
Constant repetition	'It helps if we say them over and over again'; 'Say them over in our heads and out loud and sometimes with actions'; 'We practise saying them over and over again with different voices and we also chant'.
Mnemonics	'Pfeifen – whistle – sounds at the start like you're trying to whistle.'
Visualisation	'I try to remember the pictures and remember how to say the words by closing my eyes'; 'Sometimes seeing the word helps'.
Songs and rhymes	'We make up a rhyme and keep repeating it.'
The written word	
Writing it down	'Writing it down helps because then we can look in our exercise books if we can't remember things.'
Modelling on teacher and other pupils	
Lip-reading from our teacher	'We lip-read from our teacher to get how she makes the sounds'; 'You can visualise the mouth-movements when it is your turn to say it'; 'I try to imitate the accent as well as possible, make it sound funny'.
Reading body language	'We look at the way Miss uses her lips so we can read her lips and look at the actions she uses as she talks.'
Listening and saying/copying	'We pass a microphone [a toy echo mike] round the class so everyone can try and pronounce the words correctly. You hear it over and over again which makes it easier to learn'; 'I try and say the words out loud so I can remember'.
Teamwork and communication skills (social competence)	
Working collaboratively for mutual reinforcement	'Say the words with a friend so you both get it into your head.'
Word and object association (kinaesthetic)	
Finger puppets and toys as memory joggers by association	'We use finger puppets that help us remember'; We like holding objects while saying the words'.
Writing	
Sentence and text construction	'Break down the word for the right spelling'; 'Make small kinds of phrases and build them up'; 'Write a draft and check the teacher's key words sheet'; 'Write words you're unsure about, spelling it how you think it sounds'.

Psychological	
Feeling relaxed	'Chant the words, practise the pronunciation and enjoy it!'; 'Just listen to the sounds, everything is for a reason, don't be shy, ask questions and if we do well the teacher will be in a good mood and do fun activities'.
Ask for help	'We ask for help if we are struggling with any pronunciation or remembering any words'; 'I say I've forgotten or ask the teacher what it was'.
Intuition	'You've got to feel the language'.
Use of reference material: independent learning (metacognitive strategies)	
Using a dictionary, glossary, word-list or the Internet	'Google can find a word you do not know'; 'Looking things up on a computer'.

In a relaxed non-threatening MFL classroom atmosphere, pupils try to improve their strategies by modelling themselves on peers and teachers. In such an environment children will also feel secure enough to seek clarification and to practise 'strange' sounds within the group. It is noticeable that the pupils interviewed were aware of and able to extend their learning as their statements with respect to means for independent learning show. These in particular point to the importance of the ability to ask questions and apply strategies to obtain information. Independent learning depends to some extent on sustaining inquisitiveness and developing research skills. A test for independent learning would be to ask pupils to explain their findings in their own words to peers as evidence of understanding. Thus the foundation of research skills can be laid in primary education.

Teachers can benefit from such knowledge of their pupils' perceptions of their own learner strategies. This knowledge can provide the basis for a joint exploration of the subject. The statements are clear reminders for teachers that relate to common sense pedagogy such as the need to constantly spiral back to structures and vocabulary over the course of learning and to limit the amount of input at any one time to enable the children to 'remember' what they learn.

Enabling pupils to cope with the 'tricky bits'

Talking *about* learning, developing awareness of language (AOL) provides pupils with an opportunity to acquire a metalanguage in primary MFL and to be able to identify their strengths and weaknesses as part of a formative framework of learning (see Chapter 7 on assessment). Harris (1997: 21) suggests that strategy training can be implemented by establishing the learning needs and areas of concern with the pupils, considering what strategies could be used, deciding how to teach the strategies and drawing up success criteria for strategy learning. This approach could easily be incorporated into regular lesson planning and, crucially, give pupils some ownership of the learning process. Teachers who discuss learning needs and 'areas of concern' with their pupils, can, as a result, include support strategies into their lessons. Table 6.3 provides examples of support strategies provided by one teacher using target language German.

TABLE 6.3 Auditory–vocabulary-related techniques

Mnemonics	Comments from teachers who encourage mnemonics:
	'I encourage them to use their own meaningful mnemonics, e.g. lesen – sounds like lazy and I read when I'm feeling lazy; basteln – the start of the word sounds like basket full of handicraft equipment, glue, wool, etc.; schreiben – Year 4 made a link with Ancient Egyptian scribes'.
	' "Schere" was proving difficult with some Year 5s till they came up with Alan Shearer – "Schere", the footballer. I am not sure what scissors have to do with football but the children used it a lot, doing a pretend football kick if a partner forgot "Schere".'
Tunes, songs and raps These are well-known means to support memory and listening skills	'Tunes are unbelievably powerful. Hast du Geschwister? Chanted to a "ner ner-ner ner ner" tune becomes suddenly memorable, rather than tricky for Year 3s.'
	Even a more complex question like 'Wie ist das Wetter heute?' can in the words of this teacher be 'a doddle even for Year 2 if it is sung'. This teacher states that she puts a lot of things to tunes and uses tunes for individual needs 'if a child is struggling to recall something, the tune sung quietly to them will often unlock what they are searching for'.
	Another teacher suggests teaching nouns such as 'drinks Orangensaft, Apfelsaft and Milch as a three-part round.'
Pronunciation	'I like to show them that German words taste good and some words provoke a kind of tasty reaction among the children. These words include möchte, Bluse (the lovely lip shape here), Federmäppchen, zwölf, Orangenmarmelade (the sheer length of it), Hör zu! – my Year 2s find they taste lovely together!' 'We came across the word "Leberknödel" which the children thought sounded delicious, more than what the word actually means (liver dumplings!).'
	'In my class we have pronunciation games where the children have to define their own noises and come up with ways to remember pronunciation. One pair suggested they could remember how to say Erdbeereis as Ardbearice and Chips as Ships. Then as a class we come up with a "hot tip" about pronunciation rules.'
	'We break down words into smaller bits – ra-dier-gum-mi (pencil rubber) – then, put them together again, like Humpty Dumpty' (see Figure 6.1).
Visuals and object associated	'Just put the finger puppet on and away they go.'

FIGURE 6.1   'Humpty Dumpty' word learning strategy

The idea of a challenge is an excellent learning tool and a very powerful motivational strategy (see also Chapter 5), as most children respond to learning challenges. Some Year 3 children in the survey embraced this philosophy when they urged children learning languages to 'put on your thinking cap and switch on your brain'.

The concept of challenge also resonates with one of the fundamental tenets of the popular Critical Skills approach which positions itself around a learning approach that is challenge-led and that seeks to engage learners in a collaborative effort to meet those challenges. This approach can be incorporated into primary MFL lessons as in the following examples.

Focusing on gender: 'Children some time ago were challenged to learn then recall the correct genders of food items. A week later, they came up with *Honig* being masculine, because bears like honey and fierce bears are boys.'

Focusing on vocabulary by associating word with object: 'I asked the children to work in groups and to put the vocabulary together from the unit into decorative dodecahedrons that I then hung from the ceiling for them to admire and to use as a kind of reference.'

Learning books

We acknowledge the strong views that are held, and not just by primary MFL teachers, about the place and the role of the written word. This is discussed further in Chapter 4. At this point, we simply report that many primary MFL teachers do provide some kind of exercise book or folder in which children keep worksheets, puzzles and personal information in the target language and that exposure to the written word is in fact considerable. Some colleagues make extensive use of such books with older pupils and encourage the children to do mind maps of new input for example, and to make their own notes and drawings about their learning as a kind of personal reflection so as to help them learn in their own way.

Recognising difference and extending the learner's repertoire

While there is evidence in both pupils' and teachers' comments and observations that listening is the predominant skill, it is important to stress that language learning activities chosen for lessons should ideally address all skills since visual, kinaesthetic and auditory learning styles vary between individuals. Indeed, Shaw and Hawes (1998: 61) assert that 'Each person has a learning style as unique as their signature or fingerprint.' It would be impossible to teach a class of pupils on the basis of each individual learning style but most pupils will respond to an approach where their needs are being met at least some of the time. It may be necessary for those children who have a strong preference in any way, to pay closer attention to the requirements of their personal learning style and use materials to match this style in order to optimise their learning. The primary MFL teacher might also take the opportunity to strengthen and build up other learning styles; for dyslexics, who rely to a great extent on auditory techniques, it might well be important to encourage development of their writing skills.

In recent years there has been a growing discourse on the gender-specific character of certain learning styles and boys' preference for certain school subjects. The peculiarly British obsession with categorising behaviours and identifying gender-led tendencies in education has meant many gross simplifications of anecdotal wisdoms about what boys and girls are like as learners. Research findings are contradictory. For example, it is often believed that boys have a preference for a kinaesthetic style of learning and enjoy a lot of interaction and speaking practice, yet other research points to a preference for a more traditional didactic style because of its ordered and routine-based nature (Barton 2002b).

The advent of the National Curriculum in the late 1980s obliged both sexes to study an equal range of subjects. Girls generally did well at traditional 'male' subjects such as maths and sciences yet boys did not do well at traditional 'female' subjects which included MFL. However, these statistics only tell half the truth. More recent research into boys' 'underachievement', mainly in secondary schools, acknowledges that the term is an oversimplification masking more complex categories of learner than 'boys' and 'girls'.

Much of the gender-divide discussion centring around learner styles suggests that boys respond best to the following teaching and learning styles:

- clear explanations
- positive and immediate feedback
- fun, dynamic teaching
- knowing where they are going with the task set.

There has been considerable investment in highlighting these preferences in professional development training and in educational literature, yet it is hard to imagine that these elements of 'good practice' do not apply in equal measure to girls. If girls are more conscientious in writing and prepared to persevere with longer tasks, does this not simply indicate a greater capacity to comply? If so, we believe the differences are more likely to be rooted in social expectation and learnt ways of being rather than reflecting innate biological and cognitive differences. Indeed, differences which are based on assumptions about gender persist in the way teachers interact with pupils including types of reprimand and the nature of feedback. For example, boys are more frequently reprimanded but the reprimand relates more to inattentiveness and misbehaviour whereas girls receive more positive feedback but reprimand to girls, though less frequent, tends to relate to (academic) task performance and so error is treated more seriously by girls (Wood 2004: 287).

The use of 'competition', 'affirmative male role models' and inclusion of 'topics of interest to boys' (sport, cars, etc.), which are among the strategies often proposed to engage boys' interests, should surely form part of any balanced, holistic curriculum planning. We believe the key, especially with early learners where the gender divide has not yet become a self-conscious issue, is to deploy a wide range of styles and to be mindful of individual preferences to avoid stultifying stereotypes, for example that all boys are clamorous and have short attention spans and that girls are naturally compliant stoics. In fact, when asked which activity types they preferred in MFL 'more self-confident girls tended to select activities similar to those chosen by the boys' (Barton 2002b: 280).

Gardner's multiple intelligences (MI)

Research into cognitive processes, and short- and long-term memory, have gone hand in hand with exploring different ways of storing and retrieving information. Preferences of information storage and retrieval are often referred to as cognitive styles. In his seminal book, *Frames of Mind* (second edition 1997), the Harvard Professor Howard Gardner put forward the theory of the existence of seven, non-related forms of intelligence, the combination of which releases full human potential. While we do not wish to reify this approach, it is clearly identifiable in PSHE in many primary schools where each child is encouraged to identify her/his strengths. The children's self-esteem is developed through the assertion and celebration of the fact that each of them is 'smart' in some way.

Teachers need to take into account preferences in thinking and learning by developing and providing a range of activities that will appeal to, strengthen and extend preferences. Perhaps unintentionally, many of the 'intelligences' are regularly targeted in primary MFL lessons, especially verbal-linguistic, visual, musical and kinaesthetic. In Table 6.4 we show how each 'intelligence' can be matched to activities used in MFL lessons. We also integrate the structure of an individual Year 6 lesson taught by a specialist primary MFL teacher showing the intelligences she identified in the order they were addressed during the lesson:

The teacher structuring her lesson around the theory of intelligences in one language lesson observed a positive response by the pupils to the variety of activities offered to them:

'I found this method of teaching particularly effective as it motivates the children and results in fun and interesting learning.'

She pointed out a missed opportunity in that she could have included interpersonal intelligence in the form of peer assessment.

Although the teacher has described her lesson on the basis of the identification of the multiple intelligences, the lesson could also be said to be effective on such other grounds as interactive learning and the variety of activities taking place, and a fun and a relaxed atmosphere. It is also feasible that fun and relaxed atmosphere are interlinked with the various activities appealing to the learners and, with good timing, keeping them on task.

Care must be taken, as with respect to all theories, not to adopt the idea of different cognitive learning styles blindly or to accept these on an over-positivistic basis. It is worth noting that Gardner himself has expressed 'unease' about the way his multiple intelligence theory, which he said was never intended as 'a blueprint for learning', has been interpreted in classrooms: 'Much of it was a mishmash of practices – left brain and right brain contrasts, sensory learning styles, neuro-linguistic programming and multiple intelligences approaches, all mixed with

TABLE 6.4 Multiple intelligences and MFL interpretations in a lesson

Intelligence	MFL applications	Sample lesson
Verbal-linguistic	Brainstorming, listening, speaking, reading, writing, word games	I began the lesson by asking the class to repeat the words for items of clothing in German after me.
Intrapersonal	Personalised and differentiated tasks; homework, self-evaluation, building self-esteem	I then split the class into teams and held a competition to see who could be the first to put on the item of clothing I called out.
Kinaesthetic	Drama, mime, role-play, dance, hands-on learning, making and creating things	
Visual and spatial	Art work, construction, concept maps, flashcards, posters, colour-coding	I asked the class to draw a picture of themselves wearing the items of clothing taught in the lesson, labelling each item in German.
Musical	Songs, chants, rhymes, rhythms, raps, drills, awareness of sounds	Music can be a powerful aid to learning and can be used to create an optimal learning state and to boost attention and memory and so I played a tape of German children's songs while they were doing this.
Interpersonal	Pair and group work, peer tutoring and assessment, team games, project work	Teamwork.
Logical and mathematical	Pattern identification, hypothesising, experimenting, word play	Lots of playing with sounds.

dazzling promiscuity' (*Education Guardian*, 31 May 2005). Theories will always need to pass the test of being tried out in a real-life context as it is only when they pass the test in an everyday classroom environment that they can be integrated into lessons. The children's performance will provide evidence of which parts of a theory can be successfully applied and aspects that need to be challenged or simply discarded. Strategic competence cannot be developed on the basis of a theory alone; rather it relies partially on the teacher's freedom to think and experiment creatively, building on the learners' previously acquired strategies. The acquisition of strategic competence can only occur when pupils are offered a variety of activities presented in mixed styles, and preferably guided by aspects of the four skills (see Chapter 4), and when the pupils are invited to reflect on their experiences in their role as learners and on their potential. John White, writing about the MI theory in the Institute of Education journal *Ioelife* (White 2005: 9), warns that 'Putting children into boxes that have not been proved to exist may end up restricting the education they receive, leading teachers to overly rigid views of individual pupils' potentialities, and what is worse, a new type of stereotyping.' Teachers need to always bear in mind children's potential for growth in other areas, and that intelligences are multiple, plastic and learnable.

Conclusion

While it may appear a gargantuan leap from those first ineffably enthusiastic steps of learning a foreign language in the primary school to becoming a strategically competent lifelong language learner, it is at the primary stage of learning that foundation stones are laid. A very good starting point is to understand that what pupils see and hear is understood in terms of what they already know. We found a remarkable synchronicity between the pupils' perceptions about learning and the views of their teachers and we urge teachers to talk to their pupils about learning on a regular basis in an attempt to demystify learning and to make the learning journey a shared and fully transparent one, for this is the essence of learning to learn. We have emphasised the need to engage pupils fully in their learning and for teachers to encourage independent learning where possible. Unpublished research into pupils' learner strategies across subjects at KS3 by the Assessment Group at King's College London identified 23 themes. Of these, the themes that we think are important for primary MFL and that should straddle the KS2 to KS3 MFL learning continuum include:

- setting learning targets and understanding what is needed to achieve these;
- acting on one's own initiative;
- self-assessing one's own learning;
- asking questions and searching for answers;
- looking for patterns;
- making connections between different things;
- building on previous learning;
- remembering what has been learned;
- working collaboratively in order to learn;
- being able to explain one's own learning;
- having the confidence to persevere with one's own learning;
- taking pleasure in learning.

The Key Stage 2 Framework acknowledges the importance of 'Knowledge About Language' and of 'Language Learning Strategies' by including them as the 'cross-cutting' strands in the Framework. Commenting on the former, the authors of the Framework assert that

> *Knowledge about language supports children in communicating effectively in speech and writing. It helps them to apply their prior knowledge, both to understand and to generate new language.*
>
> **(KS2 Framework for Languages 2005: 9)**

Commenting on language learning strategies, the Framework states that:

> *An important aim of language learning in KS2 is to familiarise children with strategies which they can apply to the learning of any language ... By selecting and using different strategies, children develop awareness of how they learn and the ability to use specific strategies for particular tasks.*
>
> **(KS2 Framework for Languages 2005: 9)**

This is a reflection, albeit slightly differently worded, of what the children themselves have reported and this bodes well for these aspects of the Framework.

There are case studies and vignettes of teaching and learning with comments from children and teachers in this chapter and indeed throughout this book that provide evidence that this is what happens in metacognitive primary MFL classrooms where a culture of classroom community provides that magic buzz of fun, interaction, enquiry and purposeful learning. In such a learning environment 'tricky bits' are challenges not problems, as demonstrated by a little Year 4 boy who wrote that he tried to remember words 'by breaking them down into "cilobols" ' (*sic*), and this from a child who, according to his teacher, could not yet tie up his shoelaces.

Issues for reflection

- Which theories of learning do you identify with and how do these influence your MFL teaching?
- Consider how is it possible to create a community of learning in the MFL classroom? Which routines and rituals are important?
- Which styles of learning have you identified in the MFL classroom and how can these be best catered for and extended?
- What would you identify as 'tricky bits' in learning MFL for pupils, and why?

7

Assessment and monitoring progress: How am I doing? What have I achieved? How can I progress?

Manageable and sensitive ways of dealing with assessment and the monitoring of progress in primary MFL will be explored in this chapter, bearing in mind the need to respond to the diverse needs of learners, and taking into account statutory requirements and expectations. The chapter considers ways of recording progress and acknowledges the debate and concern of some teachers about whether there should be any kind of assessment at all in primary MFL. The emphasis will be on assessment for learning defined by Black and Wiliam (1998: 2) as 'All activities undertaken by teachers, and by the students themselves, which provide information to be used as feedback to modify the teaching and learning activities in which they are engaged.' This does not dispense with elements of summative assessment, simply described by Black and Wiliam as 'any assessment made at the end of a period of learning to evaluate the level of understanding or competence'. Assessment will be considered as an aid to learning, and the development of self-learning and pupil autonomy in some aspects of their language learning, thereby sowing the seeds of lifelong language learning capability.

Key issues

- To test or not to test, that is a question to consider.
- Assessment is an integral part of the learning and teaching loop.
- Useful feedback to help plan for progression is provided by assessment data.

- Since formative assessment has become well embedded in the primary school, especially in the core subjects, it would be useful to develop further formative practices in primary MFL.

- We should consider how summative assessment can be useful as stops on the roadmap of language learning and how it meshes inextricably with formative assessment.

- Teachers need to monitor and record assessment data in order to have a track record of pupils' progress.

- Excluding reading and writing in the teaching provision does not rule out assessment of other skills, attitudes, etc.

- Assessment is an important part of primary MFL provision and gives it parity of experience and status.

Introduction

Assessment is an absolutely integral part of teaching and the learning process. Some classes and teachers might meet this statement with disquiet. This is probably due to a misunderstanding of the concept of assessment, resulting in an image of just one of its aspects, probably tests of one kind or another. Tests often cause apprehension and anxiety because of the high stakes involved, such as indelible and unchangeable grades, and league tables which can blot the copybooks of the children, teachers and the schools concerned.

Formative assessment and the benefits it can bring is being strongly promoted at the present time. Indeed it is well embedded in primary practice across the board, especially in literacy, with which primary MFL has inextricable links. We strongly assert that primary MFL learning should be located within a formative assessment framework that focuses on establishing what the children can do and offers feedback as to how they can improve and progress. Progression in learning is a major issue in the establishment of quality and enduring primary MFL provision.

Although Black and Wiliam's seminal 'Black Box' work on formative assessment takes care to point out that the use of formative assessment is not a 'magic bullet' for education, the improvement it can have on learning in the classroom, as their research proved, is significant and measurable. Jones' ongoing research with the King's College Assessment Group found classroom practice where teachers really did find that their efforts made a difference, as a Year 6 teacher commented: 'It is making a real difference to pupils' learning. They comment on it themselves.'

What then had she been doing? Many of the techniques offered by Black et al. (2003) are simple and easy to incorporate into the classroom and into primary MFL. This

Year 6 teacher had made sure the children were clear about the learning intentions and success criteria for each German lesson she taught, discussing strategies for learning, for example, how to get the right pronunciation by thinking about the rules of German pronunciation, giving them time to think and, above all, making the learning worthwhile and important in the eyes of the pupils. An erroneous perception by some colleagues that primary MFL is all about throwing soft toys around the classroom is that primary MFL itself might be seen as, in the memorable words of Patricia Driscoll, Primary MFL expert at Canterbury Christ Church University, a 'fluffy bunny' subject, devoid of the rigours of other subjects. In this respect, an appropriate assessment framework is helpful in establishing the necessary rigour.

Pedagogically, we would contend that it is important to evaluate, value and validate what the children have been learning and are able to do in the foreign language. In addition, every other area of the primary curriculum is assessed and we need parity for the children and to accentuate the importance of primary MFL.

To test or not to test: is that the question?

Some teachers, a small but vociferous minority, hold strong feelings that assessment has no place, at least no formal place, in the teaching and learning of primary MFL. This is represented in the following assertions:

'MFL must not be an assessed subject but be seen as free to enjoy, incorporating drama, music, art and the other creative subjects.'

'I hope a national assessment scheme would not detract from our motivation – that children enjoy language learning and develop positive attitudes.'

These statements from two primary teachers suggest that the 'specialness' of primary MFL identified by nearly all teachers of the subject would be spoilt if the heavy hand of testing were to come down on the subject. Testing is perceived as squeezing out the joy and motivation that is currently unbridled by, for example, national testing requirements. While primary MFL has the status of 'entitlement', it is unlikely that such a formal assessment burden would be imposed. However, it would be useful for the primary community to keep a watchful eye as inspection arrangements are amended over the years, since primary MFL provision, including assessment of learning, is likely to attract an inspection agenda, especially if primary MFL is proposed by the school as a strength in its self-evaluation. While the Ofsted Inspection Report of November 2003 on primary MFL Initial Teacher Training provision was very encouraging overall, assessment of pupil learning was identified as a weakness. The report mentioned that some trainee teachers did not know how to assess or record data, were unfamiliar with formative assessment, and that some trainees eschewed the need to assess at all.

There is, by contrast, a groundswell of opinion that primary MFL *needs* to be assessed for positive reasons to do with validation, recognition, feedback, progression and for the purposes of liaison with secondary colleagues. This chapter emphasises the fundamental principles of an assessment for learning approach that focuses on helping young learners to learn how to learn foreign languages as effectively as possible.

A learning-centred perspective to assessment

Any discussion of assessment is inextricably linked to the process of learning, for, as Drummond (1993: 15) asserts:

> It is a child's learning that must be the subject of teachers' most energetic care and attention – not their lesson plans or schemes of work, or their rich and stimulating provision – but the learning that results from everything they do (and do not do) in schools and classrooms. The process of assessing children's learning – by looking closely at it and striving to understand it – is the only safeguard against children's failure, the only certain guarantee of children's progress and development.

Indeed, it is important that assessment is seen as an essential part of the whole teaching cycle and that a teacher's assessments should inform teaching plans in a seamless way, and not be perceived as bolt-on or peripheral. On the contrary, feedback from the learning process through appropriate and sensitive assessment is an entitlement for all pupils, as expressed cogently in the Scottish Guidelines for 5–14 in primary MFL:

> Pupils have an entitlement to a coherent, progressive learning experience that develops understanding and skills and it is important that pupils, teachers and parents should learn in a sensitive yet systematic way what it is that the learners are actually able to do as they progress from one year to another. Assessing, set in the context of effective learning and teaching and taking account of the five key activities of teaching, planning, recording, reporting and evaluating, will provide vital feedback that will inform subsequent learning and teaching.
>
> (SOIED 2000: 5)

This would provide the 'confidence factor', highlighted throughout this book, and that was identified in the research undertaken by colleagues in Scotland when defining guidelines for teachers and managers of primary MFL. As Alison Hurrell of the University of Aberdeen and a member of the team, reports in a private communication: 'When we were working on the guidelines, we were always very conscious that primary teachers lacked confidence in their ability to assess MFL competence and also felt that by assessing the children somehow the essence of what they were doing would be altered, i.e. no more fun!'.

The 'fun factor', we are suggesting, will not be hampered by context-sensitive assessment and teachers should not hesitate to 'junk', redesign or create assessments suitable for their pupils that are in accord with their teaching approach and content of learning. In fact the 'confidence factor' can help to ensure that the 'fun factor' keeps a prominent place in assessment. One primary teacher, for example, reported that she was unhappy with the LA suggested tickbox-style test designed to be administered at the end of a unit of teaching but she lacked the confidence to decide what to do otherwise. Then, in the light of the fact that so many children 'scored' poorly and seemed to be demoralised, she finally decided to dispense with the test and devise her own in conjunction with her secondary colleague. Teachers, too, are on a learning curve when it comes to developing teaching and assessment strategies appropriate to primary MFL, as is always the case, incidentally, when a new subject is being developed. It is an important stage in the development of the community of primary MFL practice, a community that needs to embrace increasingly formative practices as part of its developing expertise.

Formative and/or summative assessment

The two approaches to assessment, formative and summative, are often contrasted and the former privileged enormously to the detriment of summative assessment. This has probably been in part due to the previous dominance of summative assessment and the often negative impact on pupils whose every effort has been graded, not always in a way that provides encouragement. Indeed, summative assessments can and should be useful both as part of a formative framework and as part of the learning process. As Black *et al.* write: 'The challenge is to achieve a more positive relationship between the two' (2003: 55–6). The key issue, then, is to find, select and create worthwhile activities and tasks that will enhance assessment as learning, and that will provide an opportunity for pupils to demonstrate their knowledge. Teachers will need to be clear about the criteria for success and share these with the pupils, just as is the case in literacy and numeracy learning with the now ubiquitous WALT (what we are learning today) and WILF (what I am looking for) learning intentions and success criteria respectively, anthropomorphised as dogs, owls or other creatures in the primary classroom on wall posters for the pupils to share.

One primary colleague mentioned that she has a wealth of what has been designed as teaching materials and in view of a dearth of purpose-designed assessment materials she simply designates some of them to be used as assessment activities in the lesson. Table 7.1 is designed to give just a flavour of the myriad possibilities that teachers are using as part of their formative practice repertoire that includes some summative assessment. There are many other possible variations on these themes.

Most of the techniques are self-explanatory but we detail three of them which may not be completely obvious to the uninitiated. Each technique focuses on motivating children, getting them to think, establishing a challenge and providing feedback.

TABLE 7.1 Examples of assessment techniques

Application of assessment	Practical examples
Peer assessment	■ One-to-one peer assessment of speaking, writing or drawing in response to a target language stimulus ■ Two stars and a wish ■ Group peer review of a spoken effort, e.g. a role-play or a walkie-talkie phone conversation between two pupils ■ Peer assessment of audio or video-taped pupil efforts ■ Stop and swap work
Self-assessment	■ Quick recap 'test yourself' ■ Self-assessment of taped oral work ■ Critical review of written attempt against shared criteria ■ Portfolio collection of selected good work or, e.g., personal CD-ROM folio ■ Assessment of progress over time, e.g. ticklists, comments and targets ■ Traffic lighting to indicate understanding ■ Thumbs up, across or down for same purpose
Pupil reflexivity	■ Extended wait time ■ 'Stop and think' spots in lessons ■ Pupil learning diary activities ■ Problem-solving skills approach, e.g. setting a language learning challenge for the lesson ■ Class reflection ■ Mind mapping™/spider diagram techniques ■ Traffic lighting own work, e.g. with coloured pencils, with coloured sticky dots, etc. ■ Thinking homework/independent learning task
Teacher assessment that is compatible	■ Two stars and a wish ■ Competitions, songs and games with an assessment aim ■ Listen and point/mime/tick ■ Read and draw ■ Qualitative comments and targets ■ Token collection

Two stars and a wish is a very simple technique that requires the identification of (at least) two aspects of positive feedback, the two stars. This represents successful output, what has worked, good effort and so on. The second part is the identification of a wish, an aspect to develop or that can be improved in some way. It is very important that as well as identifying stars and wishes, the children understand how they might develop their work. It is just as important for children to know the success criteria of the star element so that they can transfer their skills and knowledge on future occasions. The following are examples of star and wish feedback given by three Year 4 pupils to a peer following an oral role-play activity in which the latter had been playing a role:

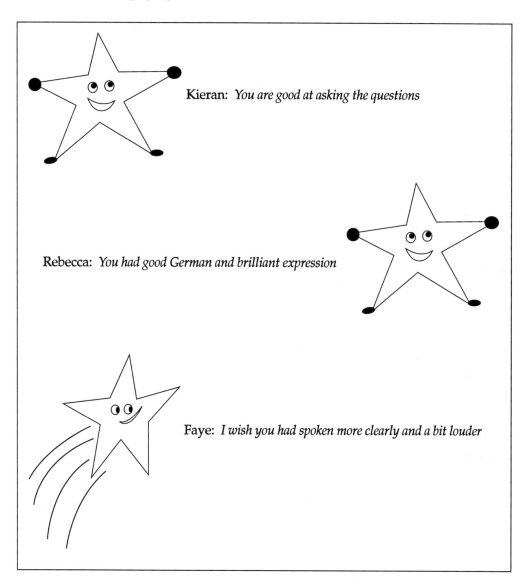

Kieran: *You are good at asking the questions*

Rebecca: *You had good German and brilliant expression*

Faye: *I wish you had spoken more clearly and a bit louder*

These are good examples of how children can easily learn how to focus and, by giving positive feedback to their peers, help to create a classroom culture of support for their own learning.

Collecting tokens is an activity whereby children attempt to acquire tokens (small pieces of coloured card, for example, or tiddly winks) for good responses. This can be done with any of the skills and for any defined effort but is a quick and useful way to assess speaking as a token can be handed out immediately following a response.

At the end of a lesson, week or learning cycle, pupils, who keep their own tally of tokens, inform the teacher of how many tokens they have, and – this is very important – for what. They can thus have a very tangible idea of how they are progressing. It can be made into a group competition but it can also be a private, individual activity. Pupils could be encouraged to self-nominate or nominate their peers for a token.

Traffic lighting, a very widespread practice within the repertoire of activities for assessment for learning, is where pupils assess their own understanding by mimicking the traffic-light system, in terms of no understanding, semi understanding and full understanding (red, amber, green). It is a simple and effective procedure that has been in use for some time in core subjects. Our research findings indicate a wealth of teacher appropriation and interpretation (which is how it should be), with teachers using giant traffic lights they have made and asking pupils to respond, or pupils making their own mini traffic lights, and even more privately, using coloured dots or other shapes in their language diaries or booklets they might use to record aspects of their MFL learning. This gives immediate feedback to the teacher who can then reiterate points and plan the next learning step. Our research has also indicated that over time some teachers have moved to a thumbs up, across, down situation (see Figure 7.1) since it has been noticed that some children dislike using the red light even in a classroom culture that does not penalise 'not knowing' but, on the contrary, seeks to develop the children's confidence in being able to be honest in their self-assessment as a precursor to being able to move forward. Thumbs down or across are perhaps less intimidating and more child-friendly than those glaring lights. When 'traffic lighting' of whatever kind is accompanied by use of target language expressions such as the fun phrases in Spanish – ¡bomba! (wicked!) and ¡fatal! (terrible) – then it can be seen that assessment can easily become a platform for extended target language use.

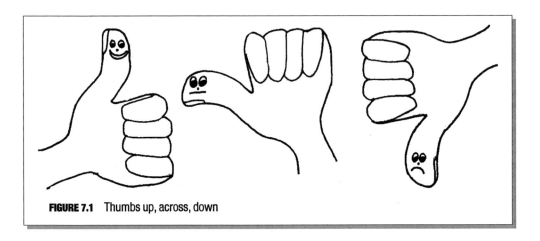

FIGURE 7.1 Thumbs up, across, down

Teachers can adapt such techniques and devise many others of their own. The important issue is to ensure that they are comfortable with such techniques and can use them purposefully for the benefit of progressing children's learning. Pupils also need to feel comfortable, for example with self and peer assessment. They need time to develop confidence in these roles and benefit from rehearsing the techniques and discussing success criteria as Jones' research shows.

In the following example, teacher A, a primary MFL Advanced Skills Teacher who teaches science and maths as well as German throughout the school, and who features in the first case study later in this chapter, had been working with her Year 6 pupils on role-plays deriving from a topic on school equipment.

'The role-play recently was based on the idea of expressing 'I can't, I need . . .'

'Lesen!'
'Ich kann nicht lesen! Ich brauche ein Buch!'

Prior to the role-play, the children had learnt the following verbs relating to the topic of school equipment:

'lesen, schreiben, zeichnen, rechnen, malen, turnen, basteln'

The children were also familiar with these nouns based on the school theme:

'Bleistift, Spitzer, Malkasten, Pinsel, Füller, Radiergummi, Schultasche, Schere, Buch, Heft, Lineal, Federmäppchen, Turnzeug, Farbstifte, Filzstifte'

The teacher's objectives were:

- clear, accurate German-sounding pronunciation;
- good recall of vocabulary learnt;
- correct use of 'einen, eine, ein'.

She instructed them to play a board game. If a child landed on a 'magic button', the group had to choose a verb they wanted to boss them to do (e.g. Basteln!). The child had to reply with 'Ich kann nicht basteln. Ich brauche ein(e)(n) . . .', choosing an appropriate noun.

The children were reasonably familiar with the idea of commenting on each other's work as their comments show:

Hannah to Robert:	*You speak with a really good German sound, but sometimes forget to stay in German* (he lapsed into English for counting his dice moves!).
Robert to Beth:	*You remember the words very well, but need to do the 'r' sound better* (referring to the guttural German 'r').
Jack to Keir:	*I really like your clear pronunciation.*

Lisa to Siena:	*I think you're amazingly quick at learning new words.*
Becky to Ellie:	*You're good at remembering the words. You have good pronunciation. Make sure you say what you mean. (She said one thing, but meant another (noun), on one occasion.)*
Alex to Graeme:	*With your pronunciation, it's hard to tell if you're German or English, but you need to put a bit more effort into your 'r' sound.*
Graeme to Alex:	*What you said made good sense. You say your words very clearly.*
Ben to Emily and Robyn:	*You're very clear.*
Ben to Jack:	*I like the way if you get it wrong, that you go back and correct yourself.*
Robyn to Ben:	*You say your words really clear, and you say 'well done' to others.*
Robyn to Jack:	*You keep forgetting vocabulary. You need to learn 'pencil'.*

It is interesting to note how the pupils appear to like 'playing teacher'; Alex's comment to Graeme is a classic in this respect, a perfect take-off of a typical teacher comment! Also noteworthy is the fact that the children find a great many 'star' comments and are able to make criticisms in a non-threatening but direct way in the inimitable style of children.

Whatever peer assessment and other modes of assessment are undertaken in the primary MFL classroom, it needs to be consistent with the whole-school assessment framework. The next section features two case studies of practice that works in two different contexts, the first a primary school in the North of England and the second in Scotland. This underlines the need to plan assessment that is coherent and appropriate to the age range, the primary MFL teaching arrangements and the whole-school assessment ethos.

Case studies: assessment scenarios

Case Study 1

In this first case study, the teacher teaches German throughout the school from Year 1 through to Year 6. She describes the whole-school assessment approach herself and points out the main aspects of assessment in the context of her school.

Ongoing assessment

'I feel when I am teaching primary MFL I am almost constantly assessing . . . have they grasped that? . . . are they ready for the next bit? . . . do they need more on that? . . . is

child X really confident? . . . can I partner them in a role-play with child Y? . . . who needs help? . . . is that pronunciation as good as it could be?

That sort of assessment goes on minute by minute, lesson by lesson. Then at the end of a unit, an end activity will often be useful to assess them . . . maybe a game, e.g. a card game, or a role-play, or some other performance. I'm keen to know if they can recall vocabulary learnt, use structures well, use authentic-sounding pronunciation, be keen, be confident to speak out, etc. Sometimes I just store the information from that in my head – sorry, not very official! – sometimes the class teacher will make written notes. The class teachers are "in" on all MFL lessons in school, learning alongside the children.'

Assessment post-lesson collaboration with colleagues

On one occasion, this teacher sent the following letter to all teachers.

To all class teachers:

In the run-up to report writing, may I invite you to use some time during German classes to make some informal written notes on the children in your class?

Which children:

- Listen attentively?
- Are keen to participate in songs and rhymes?
- Are keen to 'show' simple role-plays?
- Have a good recall of vocabulary?
- Pick up new structures easily?
- Speak clearly, with a good German accent?
- Really enjoy German lessons?
- Etc., etc.

I'll be very interested in the observations you make and I hope they'll make individual report writing for MFL much easier for you, when the time comes!

Attached is a class list but you may of course prefer to use your own class list.

Thank you!

'I find I need them to help me do this kind of assessment, because in concentrated 20/30 minute slots, I'm so deeply involved in the lesson (only speaking and listening, so teacher is all-singing, all-dancing!), it's hard to step back and make written comments, plus I am working with 180 children across the school in just 2 hours 40 minutes a week, dashing from class to class (plus science, maths and literacy).'

Assessment data to be sent to secondary schools

'The feedback is useful for me to pace lessons appropriately, to identify children who I can stretch, and those I have to be more "careful" with; and for the class teacher it builds up another perspective in which to see their children. Our special needs children, e.g. severe to moderate learning difficulties, can surprise us all in MFL, maybe because there's no written work involved. With many other children, MFL observations usually conform, or otherwise, to general academic ability.

To secondary schools I send information about what areas have been covered in MFL, but as yet no individual MFL comments, though all children get a brief comment on their report each year.'

Record keeping

'At Key Stage 1 I spend a brief 20 minutes weekly in the classes. I never feel I know the children as well as I'd like and am very often guided by the classroom teacher, with whom I tend to have a natter after the session. I wouldn't really assess them at KS1 in areas other than: Do they respond with enthusiasm? Do they join in? Are they keen to show their finger puppet role-play to the class? Are they "with me"? The class teachers who know the children really well make the best links between MFL and other areas. Though, having said that, when we have finished our numbers to 10 topic and colours, I do get them in pairs to place coloured mutli-link on numbered squares, listening to my instructions . . . but I don't keep a written record of those who could/couldn't, because I am more keen that they feel proud that they could!'

Case Study 2

Teacher B, a teaching head who teaches French to her own mixed-age top junior class in a Scottish primary school, identifies many advantages and assessment techniques in her practice and believes that assessment ensures all children are achieving their potential. Free from the severe time constraint that teacher A has, teacher B is able to focus more on the assessment criteria themselves.

'Using formative assessment techniques allows the teacher and pupil to see where they are in their learning and where they are aiming to go. Children remain motivated and enthusiastic to learn.

Assessment criteria

'With younger pupils, most of the assessment is through observation, listening and visual techniques. Our French teaching in the younger classes is done purely through talking and listening, although stories are read and children are exposed to words, we do not assess reading and writing until the last two years of primary school.

We encourage self-assessment in all classes. With young children they can use the traffic-light system to show how well they feel they understand. Older pupils may colour a checklist of vocabulary using the same colours, or simply give themselves a score out of ten for how well they feel they performed in a particular exercise.'

Assessing older pupils and the four skills

'With the top two classes, we assess all four aspects of learning a foreign language. To assess talking we use dictaphones, tape recorders, video recorders and walkie-talkies. Children especially enjoy using walkie-talkies for conversations. This encourages them to learn to question as well as respond. Listening is assessed using tapes giving instructions and directions. We also use story and question sessions and teacher-led questioning and instruction sessions. We use Big Books for reading and also have sets of the same books in small readers. Children work in groups and pairs to read to each other. Flashcards are used to introduce new reading words after the children have learned to pronounce them.

Writing is usually done as an ongoing assessment of French jotters. Occasionally we will carry out a writing task for assessment purposes, but these activities are always well supported with flashcards, word walls, posters, etc. It's like teaching Primary 1/Reception children to write. You need to provide as many words as they need until they get used to using specific language.'

Recording

'Pupils like to know how they are doing and are motivated to reach targets. Assessment techniques allow the teacher to see if pupils are retaining key vocab and able to use it in the correct context. Teachers can also quickly determine which children have good pronunciation and which need more help. We have a pupil profile for each child and record any key events in their learning. Written assessments can be kept in the pupil's folder to refer back to when necessary. During day-to-day assessment, we discuss learning with the children and also record any problems or successes. These then form the basis for reports to parents and for discussion at parents' nights and help the teacher to plan the next steps required in the French lessons.

As children learn new vocabulary, they are able to participate more and more although it is important to constantly revise topics as children will soon forget vocab that they are not exposed to on a regular basis. Self-assessment checklists for older pupils also let them see how their understanding of French is growing.'

Common concerns

In the above case studies, it can be seen how aspects of formative and summative assessment blend seamlessly, albeit in different learning and teaching environments. While the first case study deals with time constraints, the second focuses more on means and recording. Feedback for the teacher is paramount and thus assessment provides an opportunity to find out children's difficulties and gives some idea about how effective the lessons are. Primary MFL lessons are a rich source of diagnostic assessment material as evidence can be gathered during any lesson, and observations of pupil work, behaviour and questioning the pupil about what they are doing can be done in a relaxed manner. Areas of strength and weakness can be identified and the information gleaned used for the purposes of differentiation. At appropriate stages, assessment data are used for 'feed forward' for secondary colleagues and as feedback for parents.

There is a noticeable concern for the well-being of pupils in the primary MFL classroom, especially the younger pupils. While much emphasis is put on the 'fun factor' by many teachers, MFL learning is potentially intimidating given its 'strangeness' in terms of unfamiliar sounds and spellings and the whole concept of 'otherness', hence the priority that both teachers give to the children feeling comfortable with their learning and assessment.

There are differences of emphasis as to which skills are assessed, reflecting the different teaching programmes and teacher belief on these issues. It is a topic to which we now turn for general comment, given its continuing controversial status.

What skills should be assessed?

While some teachers stick doggedly to their belief that primary MFL learning should be almost exclusively oral and aural, others introduce reading and writing to differing degrees and at various stages. This will clearly be mirrored in the choice of assessment activity. The Qualifications and Curriculum Agency (QCA) scheme of work, the National Curriculum guidelines for MFL at Key Stage 2 and the Key Stage 2 Framework for Languages lend themselves to the easy extrapolation of assessment objectives and activities and have huge potential for formative practices.

From the Framework, for example, the following Year 3 oracy learning outcome could be assessed in role-plays using the 'two stars and a wish' strategy: 'Understand conventions such as taking turns to speak, valuing the contribution of others'. Year 4 literacy outcomes of being able to 'Read and understand some of the main points from a text' (e.g. a pizza recipe) and 'Write words, phrases and a few sentences using a model' (e.g. a poster for a French-speaking country) could be peer-assessed using agreed and clearly explained criteria. The 'thumb tool' (thumb signals and facial expressions) is advocated in one of the Year 5 oracy teaching activities (O 5.2) to develop 'simple opinions when using familiar vocabulary about food, animals and places', alongside spoken expressions (e.g. 'c'est super'). In this way, teaching, learning and assessment blend together seamlessly.

Examples of assessment activities to match attainment target levels

The National Curriculum guidelines postulate four levels for each of the four attainment targets (ATs) which lend themselves to 'assess as you go' through the levels. For AT 1, for example, level 1 expects pupils to be able to understand commands, short sentences and questions. A simple assessment as well as a practice activity would be to 'listen and mime'. This could be organised as a self or peer assessment as well as a general check for the teacher.

For AT 2, level 4 expects pupils to be able to take part in simple structured conversations of at least three or four expressions, supported by visual or other clues, with grammatical accuracy and good pronunciation. We have seen teachers identify with the children specific points to look for (a whole-class exercise) before engaging in peer assessment of the performed conversations.

Level 3 of AT 3 expects pupils to show they understand short texts and dialogues made up of familiar language. The teacher could make reading cards with a range of differentiated exercises for both consolidation and assessment, two for the price of one!

Level 2 of AT 4 expects pupils to hand write or word process items such as simple signs and instructions. Learning and assessment activities might include a 'listen, stop, think and write' task, or a version of Blockbusters requiring children to write text into the game diamond shapes on the overhead projector or interactive whiteboard (IWB).

This is perhaps the moment to mention again the issue of the written word. Rather than 'writing or no writing', the issue is really how the written word is introduced, how much and when, to enable the pupils to make the necessary phoneme–grapheme correspondence without which they will not be able to progress beyond a certain point (see Chapter 4 for further discussion on writing). The inclusion of reading and writing vastly extends the range of assessment opportunities and the possibilities for differentiated learning. It can be seen from the AT 4 example that the teacher should be able to record assessment data quickly and often with the help of the pupils themselves through self-recording.

Recording progress and achievement

We have ascertained some reluctance on the part of primary MFL teachers to record data other than brief summative comments on end of year reports, which is nonetheless a very widespread practice. As Liz Scott, Primary teacher in Argyll and Bute and Professional Services Officer, Scottish CILT, working on the development of AfL in MFL, commented: 'They avoid it strenuously for fear of being evaluated on the data.'

However, this fear can be overcome when teachers work together and Liz reports that, deriving from the deliberations of a working party, teachers have devised a bank of reporting comments to help them write annual reports, and that teachers also use a checklist of comments based on the Scottish Primary MFL Guidelines 5–14. She identified one teacher who has created a coding system based on level descriptors that refer to criteria such as learning phrases and grammar, oral response, interest level and pronunciation, in the case of P6 class level pupils in Scotland.

The overcrowded primary curriculum tends to leave little time for MFL learning as we stressed at the beginning of the book but, as can be seen in the case studies, both teachers show in their comments ways to work within this constraint. The collaborative efforts of the Scottish teachers also show imaginative and quite simple ways of recording progress data effectively. There is in fact a variety of practices that we have found that are not time-consuming and that give ongoing evidence of general progress over time. These include variations on the following:

- lesson logs in pre-printed boxes in which teachers note down items covered in the lesson with brief comments, and notes on any individuals as necessary;

- class lists, one used per lesson, which are annotated against any number of children with comments;

- grids that combine pupils' names on one axis and topics covered/skills demonstrated on another; teachers tick or colour-code boxes on the grid;

- comments in pupils' language diaries, notebooks or jotters;

- focus group monitoring;

- an annual or biennial report on progress.

The ubiquitous annual report is important as it at least gives parity of subject reporting and a glimpse for parents/carers into what the child has covered and or achieved in their foreign language learning. Furthermore, the final report is one that is usually passed on to the secondary school if nothing else, and along with other details of the primary foreign language learning provision, needs to contain essential transfer information to secondary colleagues, an issue further discussed in Chapter 10.

Many teachers promote the use of a portfolio as a method of continuously recording achievement. The European Language Portfolio (ELP), part of the Council of Europe's Common European Framework on learning, teaching and assessment (see Council of Europe 2001), is perhaps the best known example. This portfolio is an attractive specimen, with a variety of sections for pupils to record what languages they know and how they are progressing, thus providing tangible evidence of achievement as pupils add to it. Teachers need to be aware of the dual function of the portfolio, pedagogic and reporting. Kohonen (2004: 5) distinguishes the functions thus:

> The pedagogic function . . . emphasises the process aspect of language learning: helping the students to identify their learning aims, to make action plans, to reflect, monitor and modify the processes and to evaluate the outcomes through self-assessment and reflection. The

reporting function . . . on the other hand, is concerned with the product aspect of foreign language learning: providing a record of their language skills and cultural experiences by relating their communicative skills to . . . levels.

These thoughts may seem fairly sophisticated but are easily adaptable and begin with simple 'can do' lists that are much in use by primary MFL teachers. MFL has a particular role to play in language awareness training in that it enables children to be reflective and self-monitoring and the portfolio can be a very helpful tool for promoting these processes on the route to more learner autonomy. The recording of achievement is both relatively straightforward for teachers and provides an element of ownership for pupils. Such information provides important feedback about where children are on the 'climbing frame' of foreign language learning.

Issues of progression and continuity

The Languages Ladder Steps to Success™, the national recognition scheme for languages with accredited national certification, is potentially a mode of assessment that offers primary MFL teachers an assessment framework that validates and provides opportunities for 'when you are ready' assessment, by giving learners of all ages and all levels of ability a chance to measure their achievements in languages against a single grading system. The creation of the Languages Ladder takes forward a key recommendation of the Nuffield Inquiry – the establishment of a national standards framework for languages – and fulfils one of three overarching objectives of the Government's National Languages Strategy for England – to introduce a recognition system. The Key Stage 2 Framework specifies learning expectations and outcomes very simply, which as the authors of the document assert

> *provide the basis for self-evaluation as well as guiding informal teacher assessment, which can be linked to the levels of the Languages Ladder'.*
>
> **(Key Stage 2 Framework for Languages 2005: 12)**

The Languages Ladder uses 'can do' statements to measure learners' ability in the four main skills (reading, writing, speaking, listening) at three stages (Breakthrough, Preliminary and Intermediate). Within each stage are small steps leading to grades which can be awarded by a teacher in the classroom. For example, someone with Breakthrough Grade 1 speaking would state 'I can say/repeat a few words and short simple phrases'. Advanced, Proficiency and Mastery stages will be introduced in the future. The scheme encompasses primary, secondary and adult learners and is available in Chinese, French, German, Italian, Japanese, Panjabi, Spanish and Urdu, and many other languages are in the pipeline. Each skill area can be assessed separately, thus providing maximum flexibility as well as short-term motivational goals to encourage language learning. Linked to the Ladder are qualifications provided through the Asset Languages assessment scheme. This offers a combination of teacher and external assessment and will count towards schools' performance table scores.

The Ladder is redolent of the Graded Objectives in Modern Languages (GOML) framework first mooted in the late 1970s. It generated a whole new perspective on assessment and introduced into courses and into MFL departments in schools the idea of graduated and individualised assessment. It is an approach that underpins the general thrust of differentiated rates of progress and meshes well with the government initiative that has promoted personalised learning plans for all children. The laddering concept is a useful one and also an analogy for the crucial concept of progression. This concept has effectively been built into the 'badge' scheme of one London borough that has devised bronze, silver and gold standards for children to work towards at their own pace. It is a concept that is meaningful to teachers and children alike.

It is to be welcomed that we no longer talk of a primary–secondary divide but a '7–14 continuum of learning' (Jones 2005: 3). Primary MFL has initiated some good practice in this respect but it is still something of a weak link. It works well when primary and secondary teachers spend time in each other's classrooms and when they jointly make plans on the basis of what is useful to both sides. Clearly, useful assessment data are needed about what children have covered and how secondary colleagues can build on this, issues that are explored in Chapter 10.

Conclusion

Many primary MFL colleagues with whom the issues of assessment have been discussed are in agreement that this is an issue in need of some development. Teachers accept that they need to be aware of, indeed have evidence, albeit often stored in their own mental 'memory sticks', of the children's achievement and progress, but there is some reluctance to record assessment data, and certainly a dearth of recording instruments. It would be wrong for teachers to expect and rely on a set of ready-made assessment instruments from whatever source since there is the danger this would lead to a fixation with the instrument and the 'teaching to the test' syndrome. Teachers need to identify and create assessment opportunities as part of their own planning, teaching and learning cycle. There are simple, non-time-consuming ways of assessing and recording that fit with what teachers already do in other subjects as has been described in this chapter. Primary teachers are very skilled at what Torrance and Pryor call 'naturalistic teacher assessment – monitoring the performance of the class as a whole, being broadly satisfied that particular groups and individuals are moving at the pace one would expect' (1998: 35). They argue that while this monitoring is useful, assessment 'is more to do with the quality of teacher–pupil interaction and the feedback provided by teachers during the course of such interactions'. This means reacting to children's feedback about their learning and interacting in such a way that enhances the dialogical nature of assessment.

Assessment when understood and interpreted as a positive, enjoyable and challenging force for learning within a classroom culture that is supportive and that provides a stream of constructive feedback and think time is not in conflict with the MFL teacher's desire to be creative. Much of what teachers and pupils do in the primary MFL classroom can be described as assessment; for example tasks, quizzes, questions, pair- and group work and homework tasks all prompt learners to demonstrate their knowledge and provide opportunities for the pupils to reflect on their learning. Formative assessment is a good tool for making the shift in the classroom from passive recipience by the pupils to metacognition and the development of learning and thinking skills. Primary schools are hives of activity in this respect, acutely attuned to the importance of children's need for thinking time with attention currently focused on the development of thinking skills and critical skills. Thinking time is privileged in a metacognitive environment and can embrace the construct of 'wait time', a valuable and simple tool that, through extended wait time, gives more pupils more time to 'stop and think' about a suitable response. The pupils can also exchange thoughts, share ideas and challenge each other, providing opportunity for the teacher to move around the MFL classroom while pupils are on task and make observations and, if necessary, ask questions about what they are doing and why.

Assessment, then, we assert, is part of the entitlement to quality interactive primary MFL teaching and learning. As one teacher pointed out: 'We need to assess in the broadest sense, otherwise they [the children] may as well learn from a set of TV programmes where the TV delivers, but does not respond to the learning resulting from the delivery!' An assessment framework for primary MFL should, on the contrary, be very responsive and serve as a tool flexible enough to cater for different school environments.

Issues for reflection

- Should we assess all four skills and to what extent and at what stage is it appropriate to do so?
- How could and should assessment in MFL mesh with and reflect the whole-school assessment aims and policy?
- How can we train pupils to become skilled at peer and self-assessment?
- How do we find time in MFL lessons for pupils to have 'stop and think' time?
- How would you create a climate of trust in your classroom? To what extent is this a whole-school issue?
- What would be issues concerning the assessment of primary MFL for you as regards an Ofsted inspection?

8

New technologies – making the most of ICT

NO DISCUSSION OF curriculum innovation would be complete without an exploration of how integrated new technologies can bolster pupil learning, providing motivation and opportunity at different levels. This chapter will look at recent developments in ICT (Information and Communications Technology) with illustrations of how, for example, the interactive whiteboard and the Internet can be used to add value to primary MFL learning while enhancing ICT skills. Examples of how to exploit fully learning opportunities using ICT will be discussed.

Key issues

- ICT can allow for more individualised and differentiated language practice.
- The teacher is the single most important factor in determining the success of ICT's contribution to learning in the primary school.
- ICT offers teachers a wide range of possibilities to create a range of multimedia resources which can be tailored to the specific learning needs and preferences of their pupils.
- ICT offers greater flexibility in the creation and exploitation of resources, both for the teacher and for pupils, allowing more varied modes of participation and appealing to a broader range of cognitive processing styles.
- Access to information and the potential for forging new personal links through the Internet and other new technologies have led to a redefinition of cultural and linguistically bound identities.

Introduction

Children in many countries grow up today familiar with the keyboard and the computer screen in a way that would have been unimaginable a couple of generations ago. Not only is the ever evolving hardware of new technologies a ubiquitous reality in the twenty-first century but the means to retrieve and process the information which it conveys have a dramatic impact on the way we think, the way we communicate with each other and the way we identify ourselves and others. Given that the information revolution is inherently dealing with formative issues of processing information and developing skills it is unsurprising that education has represented a forerunning field in the development and application of new technologies. In schools, ICT also represents one of the clearest examples of how cross-curricular learning is achievable, desirable and, given the requirements of our current 'learning society', necessary.

The UK is at the forefront of integrating ICT skills in schools. We are, for example, the only European country to have installed interactive whiteboards on a massive scale and to have made ICT a National Curriculum requirement at both primary and secondary levels. The government has invested millions of pounds in developing ICT for education (£700m for 2005–06 in England alone!) and primary schools are currently entitled to substantial funding through the E-learning credits (eLCs) system. This money can be used for new hardware and software as well as for professional development.

In terms of references to materials and to sources of information, given that website addresses are notoriously subject to change we have not listed many specific websites in this chapter. Our aim here is to discuss pedagogical approaches and ways in which ICT can be integrated into individual, group and whole-class work in MFL, rather than to list specific ICT resources, though several are cited that we have seen in practice adding value to primary MFL. A wealth of commercial material does exist, as software and on the Internet, both in the form of target language resources (authentic and adapted) and as 'how to use' guides for teachers. Lists of such websites are easily found by searching the Internet or by consulting any one of the many educational ICT publications available, some of which are listed in our bibliography. The Curriculumonline website (www.curriculumonline.org.uk) is a key reference as it lists all the approved educational software and other ICT resources. Another indispensable source of information for UK schools is BECTA (the British Educational Communications and Technology Agency) (www.becta.org.uk). It should be noted that we are broadly confining our discussion here to computer use, though of course we acknowledge that the term ICT can encompass all technological resources, including the more traditional OHP, audio tapes, film and video. Opportunities for exploiting these more established and familiar resources are covered throughout the book.

Integrating development of ICT and MFL skills

ICT and MFL have a lot in common. Firstly, along with music and PE, they are often considered to be skills-based subjects though, in fact, this label underplays the complexity (and transferability) of the cognitive processes involved. They are also among the subjects which many believe children show an aptitude for (or not!). In other words, they are both subjects which tend to invoke strong reactions from teachers and parents – beliefs which are often passed on subliminally to children – about being either able to 'do' it or not and, by allusion, from the teachers' perspective, being competent to teach the subjects or not. However, in a similar vein to MFL, we believe that ICT learning is best delivered when it is both embedded across the curriculum – thereby treated as a matter of course by different staff members – *and* when it is taught as a separate subject. As a separately taught subject ICT benefits from specialist, focused input which both supports pupils and expands teachers' competence and self-confidence within the context of continuing professional development. As discussed in Chapter 5, this holistic, cross-curricular approach allows both MFL and ICT to be used as instrumental means in creating new meanings and new *forms* of knowledge. This represents another major area of common ground between the two. In the case of MFL, these 'new meanings' are extensions and reconfigurations of linguistically- and culturally-bound first language concepts, that is, both in terms of language awareness such as we have highlighted with links to first language literacy and other cross-curricular links and also in terms of broader (inter)cultural understanding (as discussed in Chapter 9). In a similar way, though not the same, in ICT the child learns to mediate knowledge further and his/her worldview through new sources of information and new forms of sound/image/word manipulation, thereby going beyond (and reconciling) the traditional divisions between spoken and written media, verbal and mathematical processing, linear and kinaesthetic learning styles and so on. The following is an example of how a teacher uses ICT to enhance research skills and intercultural learning through MFL.

For upper KS2 I have used a website (www.the-voyage.com) for an online advent calendar in the run-up to Christmas. For upper KS2, already competent to navigate a website, this is a great way to compare Christmas traditions in Britain and Germany. It's more practical than travelling to Germany (!) and more fun for the children than me just recounting my personal experiences to them. I listed a few items on the board which I wanted them to find out more about (such as Lebkuchen, or Barbaratag), and then let them explore the site in pairs, finding out about Christmas traditions in a fun way, which they really enjoy. Motivation is high; the quality of the site and quality of its information is high. Afterwards there is a chance to share and discuss what they have discovered, share surprises, and sort out any possible misunderstandings. Many children have Internet access at home and took the web address with them, so they could continue to open up the days of the advent calendar in the run-up to Christmas, hopefully also teaching their parents some new things!

The role of the teacher

One of the greatest assets of new technologies is their capacity to facilitate more individualised styles and rates of learning. While all primary teachers do instinctively differentiate and adapt their approach to suit individual pupils' needs, there is only one teacher for up to 30 children and so they cannot physically replicate the tireless individual attention given by computers to each child. Of course, this does not undermine in any way the role of the teacher. We believe that good teaching remains paramount, over and above any resource, including ICT, but that teachers today recognise the importance of using computers as 'electronic assistants', reference banks, audio-visual posts and much more. We have spoken to some teachers who are not yet fully confident with what ICT has to offer. One such teacher told us that she feels 'the children know more about computers than I do'. This is a widely held belief but should not deter teachers. While it is true that many children show greater confidence with computers than adults, often using computers at home and at school without inhibition, they often perform very limited functions such as playing games or looking up particular websites. Our task as teachers is, as it always has been, to teach children a range of skills and ways of seeing the world by using whatever cultural material and resources are available. In the past, these were the spoken word, books, writing, drawing, etc., and these continue but to the list is added electronically processing information. If pupils do have greater technical skills then the children can be encouraged to take the lead and teachers can learn from them. In this way the learning becomes a two-way process whereby skills and content are brought together. However, even older children continue to need thorough guidance and direction when using ICT, so the role of the teacher is not as 'facilitator' on the sidelines but very much as 'teacher' directing, shaping and running the show! ICT also provides welcome opportunities for collaboration with the school's ICT coordinator, with other teachers and with teaching assistants.

Extensive research investigating the impact of ICT in both primary and secondary schools (Watson 1993; Wegeriff 1996; Cox and Webb 2004), has confirmed that the role of the teacher is the single most important factor in determining the success of ICT's contribution to learning. In 1993 Watson (1993: 7.3.2.1) reported, in the first government-funded ImpacT report, that 'effective use of I(C)T was supported by individual teachers' understanding of, and willingness to experiment with, the underlying philosophy of the software being considered for use by the pupils'. Yet over a decade later subsequent research (Cox and Webb 2004) has shown that the regular use of ICT by teachers is still limited to a few select resources in specific subjects for a narrow range of topics. Among the reasons for this – apart from limited resources, timetabling constraints and insufficient training – was believed to be teachers' beliefs about the real benefits of using ICT and their confidence as users. It is clear, therefore, that teachers will only use ICT once they are genuinely persuaded of the benefits. Ironically, this conviction often emerges from the act of engaging. We do not advocate using ICT for the sake of it but where teachers appreciate that it is an enhancement. As one teacher told us:

> *'I firmly believe there's no point using ICT unless it is better than what you're doing already (a fancy projected image of a teddy is not a patch on the real thing, which you can hug when it's your turn!); and teachers need to ensure that the ICT skills required by the children in the language learning situation are well within their capabilities, or the ICT learning swamps the language learning.'*

Below we outline what we consider to be major current uses and benefits of using ICT but we recognise that it is only through using new technologies in a safe and supported context that teachers can appropriate the benefits of ICT in their own practice.

Whole-class learning

ICT plays an important role, as an additional resource, in engaging pupils in the presentation and practice of language in MFL. The use of presentation software such as PowerPoint need not replace more traditional resources such as OHTs, realia and flashcards but can be added to the repertoire of bright, attractive visuals. It is obviously convenient for the teacher to use electronic visuals inasmuch as, once they have been prepared (either downloaded or created), they do not require storage space, do not wear and can be easily updated and adapted. In the long run, they save teachers time.

As well as pictures, text can be manipulated on the 'big screen' for whole-class participation in any of the ways discussed below. As pupils are introduced to written words and then sentences in MFL, text can be gapped, highlighted and presented in different visual forms, including with motion (moving text) and with sound accompaniment, which all contribute to multi-sensory processing and will aid memorisation and the construction of meaning through appealing to different cognitive styles. Any of the activities suggested in the skills sections in Chapter 4 can be developed and given extra depth when presented electronically because of the increased scope for different font characters, sizes, colours as well as mixed media and the capacity to make children's participation with the cues on the screen spontaneously interactive. This is especially true when the whiteboard is electronically interactive. Indeed, the use of the interactive whiteboard goes beyond the transfer of traditional resources to an electronic medium.

The interactive whiteboard

The interactive whiteboard (IWB) is now well established in UK schools. The IWB can be used in 'real time' or to present material which the teacher or pupils might have prepared earlier. One of the most exciting features is the ability to store handwritten thoughts and comments of the pupils and to recall them for a later lesson. In 'real time' pupils can take a very active part in the lesson by using the IWB to display their work to others or to investigate materials on the Internet, downloading and saving it in conjunction with their own ideas and comments. The IWB has all the features of a stand-alone computer connected to the Internet with a large bank of educational software, but what it has in addition is the capacity to display games, texts, graphics, PowerPoint presentations to the whole class. Therefore, whereas individual or group computer work can be very beneficial, the IWB enables teachers to excel in their whole-class teaching skills at the same time as promoting confidence and communication skills among all their pupils. The following shows how a teacher in the South of England uses the IWB and mini-whiteboards to reinforce MFL learning through numeracy.

During my Year 4 Numeracy lessons I try to incorporate French where appropriate, an ideal opportunity for this is during the mental starter. To reinforce number bond work I load up the 'Virtual Dice' web page (provided by Birmingham Grid for Learning) on the class SMART board and select the 10-sided dice. By clicking the dice it generates numbers between one and ten randomly. I ask a child to say the generated number out loud in French, e.g. *deux*, and the rest of the class will then write the corresponding number to ten (i.e. 8) on their mini-whiteboards and one child will be chosen to say the word aloud in French. This is really a quick-fire session where the children have to think on their feet to find the number and the French word.

Individualised learning and group work using ICT

Working on the computer as play in MFL

Many CD-ROMS and web-based activities increase levels of interactivity and appeal to different learning styles because they are multi-sensory, leading the child to follow pictorial, written and/or auditory cues. Many of these practice activities are in the form of competitive games, often giving scores, which children enjoy playing on their own (to beat their own best score) or with partners or in teams. These games appeal to a basic instinct – *arguably* stronger in boys! – and follow the principles of amusement arcade or home video games.

When the software is attractively designed the competitive, game element of the activities allows fairly mundane drills to pass as fun. These are ideal for practising vocabulary items and, later, word and text gapfilling and arranging in correct order. The computer never gets impatient or tired of repeating the same words and so is ideal for practice drills. There are, of course, many interesting and exciting educational ICT games which involve role-playing and decision-making games based on specific scenarios where children can work in teams to plan strategies. For example, using computer-based modelling, children can build up a categorisation of specific vocabularies and learn about different forms of words such as nouns, adverbs, etc. A program like *Métro* enables children to learn the French terms relating to using the Paris Métro: at each stage of entering the Métro station, buying a ticket, choosing the right line, etc., the pupils have to select the correct French word (from a choice of several) and are rewarded by moving on a station (on a map on the screen) until they reach their destination.

Individual or group work on the computer encourages pupils to take risks in ways that they would be less likely to on paper, or orally. Feedback is instant, either from the circulating teacher or from the computer itself. MFL-specific software often has levels of difficulty to choose from and often gives 'clues' upon request. A child who may be reticent about answering incorrectly in front of the whole class or even to the teacher will not mind being corrected by the computer. When using a Word document spellcheck can be switched to the target language so that misspellings will be highlighted instantly. The opportunities for unlimited redrafting and improvement change the way a child approaches the task, encouraging experimentation and creativity. An idea for self-assessment is to temporarily store the various stages of redrafting in a separate file so that children can later retrospectively analyse the steps they took towards the final outcome (task completion), analysing and tracking their own progress.

Text manipulation

Even at a very simple level of word recognition, ICT will enable children to manipulate target language in its written form in a safe, experimental way. This is especially valuable for new writers who are still struggling to form letters on paper:

> The ability to make changes in computer-generated text without leaving any trace of previous errors or misunderstandings enables learners to
>
> ■ draft
> ■ evaluate
> ■ revise
>
> The use of these three skills promotes cognitive activity involving complex linguistic processing which is likely to reinforce grammar, syntax and choice of vocabulary because of the level of cognitive activity engendered.
>
> (Dugard and Hewer 2003: 23)

The advantages of manipulating text on screen rather than on paper are now widely vaunted, for example writing on a screen appeals to a wider range of learning styles including kinaesthetic; electronic text can be moved around the screen; children can make different word shapes; different fonts for different types of text can be used (e.g. a menu versus a postcard or even a verb versus a noun). Here, we can see how generic ICT software can be used to full effect in MFL, that is, as well as subject-specific software. Colour can be used for describing a colour or to show gender or other word categories. Underlining, bold typeface and boxes can all be used to highlight and differentiate particular words and word groups. Using authoring software (e.g. see the Curriculumonline site mentioned above) teachers can tailor-make specific exercises to match work recently covered in class, or indeed to match their pupils' learning preferences. These allow given vocabulary lists or other sets of words or phrases to be automatically turned into exercises and quizzes. ICT activities using sound files can also be created to accompany word-processed text and Hyperlinks to sound files which can be downloaded off the Internet.

Children with visual and/or auditory impairments will find manipulating text using ICT particularly advantageous because of the myriad possibilities for extra support, from sound to text enlargement. Even using a non-white background screen to read from can help to reduce the glare and brightness for light-sensitive pupils.

Presentation skills

Children will enjoy using the computer to make MFL displays and as props for presentation to the class. Examples of this we have seen are scanned and digital photos of family and pets which are then labelled (*mi hermana, Lucy, 8 años. mi gato, Bonnie*) and simple menu designs:

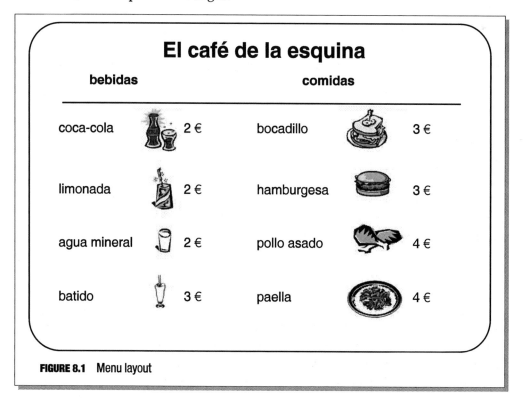

FIGURE 8.1 Menu layout

The awareness that the computer can be used creatively in this way to produce smart, original presentation styles raises the value of MFL and helps equip pupils with necessary skills for later learning (and, eventually, professional life!). Children's work on presentations and displays provides a clear example of why the teacher's focused planning is important for ICT. If clear guidelines are not set then pupils may spend disproportionate time and energy on 'form', for example playing with fonts and page layout, above 'content' (the language focus). It may be a good idea to work on the content while in class and then set the display format as work to do at home or in an art or ICT lesson. The point is that computers can do many of the low-value tasks such as copy-writing and drawing grids. These activities do, of course, have value while children are learning to draw, write, etc., but in MFL the *focus* should be on using the target language – this is cross-curricular learning at its best – as ICT in the MFL lesson is a support medium rather than an end in itself.

Collaborative learning with ICT

Computer-produced work (for presentation or other investigative projects which are discussed below) presents a good opportunity for collaborative learning. Pupils enjoy the opportunity to work in a semi-autonomous way and the individual and group work facilitated by ICT provides variety in the pace and style of MFL learning, typically an intensively teacher-led subject. Pupils with greater technical skills can be teamed up with pupils who are more linguistically able, and again possibly with pupils who particularly enjoy designing or presenting, depending on the task being set. Each pupil then has the opportunity to contribute to the group output and to scaffold each other's learning (learning through Vygotsky's 'zone of proximal development' discussed in Chapter 6) in a valuable and enriching way. Research has long since shown the benefits of such cooperative group work. For example, Loveless (1996: 147) cited American research which compared pupil progress in using ICT for group work between groups who knew they would be assessed as a collective group with those who knew they would be assessed for their individual contribution to the group output. Those working cooperatively rather than in competition with other group members achieved greater success. Examples of such collaborative outputs that we have seen in primary schools are:

- using databases for recording survey data in French *(le sondage)* on how classmates come to school, who has pets and which type, the colour of pupils' hair and eyes, etc.;
- using clip art to produce an illustrated class timetable in German;
- using desktop publishing to prepare a multilingual poster advertising a school event, with individual pupils assigned to specific design tasks.

Creating resources

Teachers creating multimedia resources themselves

For teachers whose technical expertise goes beyond that of regular end-users and who feel comfortable handling relatively easy-to-use software, or for those who have the necessary technical support, it makes sense to create personalised resources, either from scratch or by adapting free resources found on the Internet.

An authoring tool like HotPotatoes, which is free to most users, is easy to master, flexible and allows a wide range of activities to be developed such as multiple choice and short answer quizzes, jumbled sentences, matching and gapfill exercises. An example we have seen at a school in East Anglia is the creation of a multimedia crossword puzzle. The advantage compared to its traditional paper equivalent lies in the fact that the definitions can be based on sounds (or images) and not just on writing. The necessary images or sounds were obtained from free educational databases but drawings could also be made by children and then scanned and built in. Sounds can be recorded by an MFL specialist or by a native speaker, for example an assistant or parent, thus avoiding legal problems of copyright. Another great advantage of HotPotatoes is that once the teacher has created the activities they are saved in the form of web pages, which can be put on the web or given to pupils on a disk or CD-ROM. No special software is needed to do the exercises as they will run on any web browser software (such as MS Internet Explorer). Using these sorts of software programs schools can work collaboratively in a network to create joint websites through which they share resources and software.

Karaoke, an activity that involves singing songs to music with the lyrics scrolling out on a screen in front of the singer, is now universally popular and offers children the opportunity to practise target language with elements of performance and written support. We have seen it used to great effect by a teacher who had used software (in this case MAGpie) to synchronise video and subtitles. This offers an excellent way to introduce children to the written word in MFL and to work on phonetics at the same time (by highlighting elements of the words of the song).

This level of involvement in the creation of multimedia resources will require some coordinated training and at least some of this training should be subject focused, for those who are not familiar with the necessary software. But teachers can also acquire the necessary skills by taking part in collaborative projects with colleagues or seeking appropriate training courses as part of their CPD (see Chapter 11). We have spoken to many teachers who admitted that they were extremely reticent about using ICT – even sceptical about its benefits – but that, once they had gained in confidence and technical know-how, they were amazed at how much fun they and the children had working with MFL and multimedia.

Creating resources collaboratively and exchanging ideas

There is a lot of potential to forge electronic links between teachers and to share ideas about resources and good practice in MFL teaching. Random searches will throw up many excellent ideas for resources, even lesson plans, as well as official websites such as NACELL. Indeed, since finding the time is an issue for all teachers, the LA adviser and/or the primary MFL support structure (e.g. coordinator or assistant) might well take on the responsibility for providing an illustrative list. The potential for pupil links is discussed below, but for staff, national and international coopera-tive projects offer a way of sharing ideas and building links which may lead to future collaborations at all levels: professional development, pupil links, whole-school twinning, even personal friendships can emerge from such partnerships – MFL plays a key role in establishing such social networks. As well as teachers in school, there is scope for integrating this type of exchange in initial teacher training pro-grammes, which is precisely what we have done with two types of link between King's College London and primary teacher trainees at the IUFM de Paris – we cite this as an example of active practice in initial teacher training.

First, French and English student teachers communicated via videoconferencing about a range of professional topics, from different national developments in MFL to broader whole-school issues such as ways of teaching literacy, involving parents in school life, special needs education, etc. The exchanges were held in both languages so there were clear linguistic benefits but, also, trainees were led to think about different ways of educating and the degree to which assumed practices are often culturally determined.

The following year, we went a step further with another type of exchange, this time based on regular e-mail communication again around different topics but with a stronger focus on MFL resources for early learners. The correspondence led to the cre-ation of a simple multimedia resource centred around the theme of 'Red Nose Day' and its associated language and cultural characteristics. While this web-based resource was created principally for French primary school children learning English, the collaboration gave UK trainees opportunities to practise their French by e-mail and to develop technical know-how by providing input at each stage of the resource design.

The Internet: a window on the world

The Internet as a source of information for teachers

For teachers of MFL, the Internet represents a rich source of information on several levels. As mentioned above, it has become a well-established forum for exchanging ideas about resources, views about teaching MFL, lesson plans. Within the context of professional development, the Internet keeps teachers informed of latest devel-opments concerning subject teacher and broader educational issues and offers links to professional bodies, e.g. NACELL, CILT – the National Centre for Languages, ALL (Association for Language Learning). Many sites have messageboards where teachers can seek technical advice about the use of ICT or professional support for MFL teaching or indeed make any specific requests to colleagues in cyberspace. The messageboards, usually informative and often great fun, illustrate the sense of camaraderie and the spirit of mutual support and understanding which emerge from sharing thoughts and experiences within a 'community of practice' (discussed in Chapter 11).

The Internet has revolutionised access to ready-made resources for language learning and teaching. Many are free and just need to be downloaded and some are sold online. Often, however, resources will need to be adapted to suit specific learning contexts. We suggest that the Internet works well as a pool of inspiring ideas for teachers to create their own material as well as a bank of ready-made resources.

Children using the Internet

The Internet offers great potential for children to develop investigation skills. In primary MFL this is naturally restricted by pupils' limited knowledge of the foreign language, especially in the written form. Furthermore, as with Internet use across the curriculum, early learners will need very clear signposting when doing Internet searches. Quite apart from the possibility of accessing inappropriate sites which have slipped through the filter, too much time can be wasted on fruitless searches if children are not led to specific websites which have been selected beforehand by the teacher. Once specific websites have been chosen and vetted it is generally advisable to list them on the school intranet site.

Official tourist board websites are a good, authentic source of target language in use and provide a stock of cultural knowledge which is often presented in simple tabular form which is ideal for cross-curricular exploitation. An example of this is to look up town population numbers for an English town and a French town. Pupils' actual use of the target language here is very limited but they are nonetheless engaging with an authentic French language website which is a confidence boost and leads pupils to pick out and retrieve specific information from a text: a valuable information skill put to use in a genuinely communicative context. Other research tasks that are appropriate for primary children include finding the capital of Spain, finding the names of two rivers in France, changing a sum of pounds sterling to euros or another currency using a currency converter website. Information retrieval activities of these sorts are advocated in the Key Stage 2 Framework for Languages as a key Literacy objective:

L5.1 Children should be taught to re-read frequently a variety of short texts, e.g. e-mail messages and texts from the Internet

(Key Stage 2 Framework for Languages 2005: 73)

For some activities, especially with younger children, the target language use in such activities will be minimal, maybe just focusing on one or two key words, but the value in cultural learning and developing information and thinking skills within a cross-curricular context is enormous (this is the broader definition of MFL for which we make a plea in Chapter 5).

Twinning and virtual exchanges

New technologies have opened up several ways of corresponding with partner schools and have led to possibilities for redefining our relationship with the world. While school trips abroad continue to have immense value in terms of linguistic, cultural and personal developmental gains, ICT can open new pathways for children to engage with one another across nations, forging new types of identity within a global dimension. The social and psychological benefits of involving the school in international projects are discussed in greater detail in the next chapter, but here we suggest practical ways to approach virtually-managed projects and exchanges.

Exchanging information over the web

Some teachers have told us that they did not believe e-mail exchanges were appropriate for primary school pupils because of the emphasis on writing in the target language. While we would suggest that KS2 pupils can, in fact, handle an exchange by each partner writing in his/her mother tongue, we accept that other forms of exchange which are less text-based and so privilege oral and aural skills development work best with early learners. Some of the options available do require a certain degree of technical handling and many teachers will need ICT support in the early stages. However, as we have said above, the initial effort and extra time needed to develop know-how pay real dividends in terms of adding value to the children's experience of MFL.

The exchange of sound files is highly motivating. Children use simple phrases to tell their partners about an ordinary day at school for them or about a celebration that takes place in their country, etc. In terms of technical requirements, the use of a piece of sound editing software – such as 'Audacity', which is free – to record sounds is very simple since it follows the same principle as a video recorder. The sound files can then be attached to e-mails or posted on a web page. Pictures can also be added.

Children from different partner schools in continental Europe or elsewhere can also digitally film their school environment and comment on it orally, using a digital camcorder. This type of presentation will appeal enormously to children of the same age who share the same interests and concerns. The digital film thus produced can be integrated to a web page for easy access. Of course, any film put on the web that shows children must have parental consent forms signed. Moreover, the website can be restricted to limited user-access only for increased security. Technology facilitates this type of exchange inasmuch as it is faster in terms of transmission and compatibility of format, unlike, for example, video-tapes. The technical requirements are: the use of a digital camcorder, the retrieval of the video on a computer, the editing if necessary, and then the integration of the video onto a web page and the upload to a server.

Far from being out of reach of teachers, similar projects have already been carried out. For example, a project entitled 'I'm ten years old and I live in . . .' consisted of children from different target language countries making some web pages in their own language about agreed themes, like the means of transport for getting to school, food, etc. All the information was then gathered onto a single website, and this gave rise to very interesting comparisons leading to increased intercultural and linguistic awareness. Originally, the objective was to motivate children to develop ICT and writing skills by taking part in a project the content of which could be shared with other children but the cross-curricular dimension is obvious as children were encouraged to work on other subject issues such as geography. From the MFL perspective the website provided authentic material to develop oral comprehension and oral production, triggered by the sound files or the images. The technical requirements here are: the know-how to make web pages, including work on integrating image and sound. There are many websites (such as the European Schools Net site), as well as the embassy cultural and educational departments, which can help schools find partner contacts abroad. EU-funded Comenius projects also facilitate school networking.

Videoconferencing

Videoconferencing has been used by schools in different countries to share information about their schoolwork and to learn about each other's language and culture. The main advantage of videoconferencing projects lies in the fact that they emphasise oral and synchronous communication. Although the necessary equipment is still expensive if installing high quality videoconferencing systems, costs will decrease as conferencing via the web becomes more accessible. The latter already exists but its technical quality may be problematic. Indeed, it is important that any exchange with partners in the foreign language is not hindered by added comprehension difficulties caused by poor technical quality, so good sound quality is an essential criterion when setting up this type of face-to-face exchange. The quality of web videoconferencing, as well as its ease of use, is bound to improve in the years to come and we should keep this option in mind since such projects undoubtedly represent a considerable asset for the pupils involved, as we have seen where successful exchanges have taken place.

A project that we have seen using videoconferencing involved Year 5 children in their second year of learning Spanish linking to a Year 4 school in Spain where children were in their second year of learning English. The simple, well-prepared exchanges revolved around the following themes:

- Individual presentations
- Learning a song
- Questions and guessing based on images of animals.

The children were thrilled to be in face-to-face contact with native speakers of their own age. As well as the linguistic benefits, the cultural dimension was also very much present. Indeed, the Spanish children told their UK friends that they thought their school uniforms were funny! Clearly, there is a lot of potential for following up the issues raised in these exchanges in other subjects.

One of the key advantages of videoconferencing is that it combines sound and images in real time, which helps in terms of the motivation to communicate in a realistic exchange. Before taking part in such a project, teachers need to consider the following points, quite apart from the technical issues related to setting up the exchange in the first place (which can, of course, be dealt with by a technician):

- It is important to find a reliable partner and to make sure that the partnership is fair on both parties (depending on what the objectives are for each). The British Council can help find suitable partner schools (www.globalgateway.org.uk).

- No matter how smoothly the real-time exchanges seem to go, they require minute preparation. Pupils at this stage of learning – and even older children – cannot use the target language spontaneously and will need thorough preparation for the exchanges. This preparation includes coordination with the other teacher beforehand as well.

- Logistically, it might be advisable to have children working together and presenting in pairs, i.e. two at each end. Mutual support then operates when necessary and this is less stressful at the beginning for children who might feel insecure speaking to the camera.

Videoconferencing represents an apex in terms of communication between children of different mother tongues. In fact, it could be what all the other ICT/MFL activities lead to and it endows such activities with meaning since it results in children's concrete use of the foreign language in a real communicative context and in real time. In practical terms, there are obstacles which may delay its use for many, but other new technologies which facilitate high levels of authentic communication between pupils, such as e-mail and messageboards, are already accessible to all.

Conclusion

In this chapter we have considered the important and dynamic role of ICT in primary MFL teaching and learning. ICT offers much more than a new way of presenting traditional resources, though its highly efficient function as on-hand illustrator, support assistant, marker, display board, storage cupboard, etc., is not to be underestimated. Engagement with ICT also leads to new ways of engaging with the foreign language and culture and can provide new ways of learning – even new forms of knowledge – through increasing pupil ownership of the learning process (autonomy) and allowing greater levels of differentiated participation, for example in whole-class formative assessment.

We have looked at how ICT can support the teacher as a pedagogic resource in whole-class teaching and how it can be a powerful learning medium for pupils. We have suggested specific activities based on our observations in school but these can only give a flavour as the rate of change in ICT is increasingly fast and we believe that each localised context must appropriate ICT to suit the specific purposes of different teachers and pupils. One principal theme that remains perennial, however, is the role of the teacher in primary MFL and this is equally important when integrating ICT use. As extensive research, cited in the chapter, has indicated, the attitudes of the teacher and the teacher's willingness to experiment with and to engage with ICT are crucial factors in ensuring the effective deployment of new technologies.

Issues for reflection

- How confident are you with ICT? List when and for what purposes you use ICT at school.
- Are you exploiting the potential offered by ICT in MFL? If not, why do you think that is and who can help?
- How can you increase your personal use of ICT in the primary MFL classroom (increased facilities, professional development training, peer support, etc.)?
- Is there a colleague in school (ICT coordinator or MFL specialist) who can help you exploit ICT more fully in delivering MFL (e.g. through joint planning, writing a development action plan, team teaching, etc.)?
- Do you think an electronic link with a school in France/Germany/Spain, etc., would be feasible and beneficial for your pupils or for a whole-school link?

Cultural learning – opening the classroom door and broadening horizons

IN THIS CHAPTER we will examine the vital role of primary MFL in 'opening the classroom door' to encourage pupils to look beyond their own physical and psychological borders, both by forging different types of international links and by celebrating difference. Case studies and examples of materials will suggest ways in which pupils can be led to reflect on their own language use and cultural norms and to enjoy and value other linguistic and cultural experiences. We look at how patterns and practices in EAL language support for purposes of integration might dovetail with the expansion of MFL early learning and how the often untapped linguistic and cultural resource of increasing numbers of bi- and multilingual pupils can enrich intercultural learning. We also look at how MFL can help achieve curriculum goals for Citizenship.

Key issues

- MFL has a key role to play in broadening pupils' cultural horizons.

- Intercultural learning can take place both by extending the scope of how we interpret language teaching and, ultimately, by forging links with children from different countries.

- Including historical, context-specific developments of a language enriches the language learning experience and lifts it above abstracted technical coding of words and sentences.

- Difference is all around us and is to be celebrated. In any primary classroom there is a rich and varied diversity of cultural and linguistic heritage which can be exploited to support language and intercultural learning.

- There are also universal experiences and global challenges which can be linked to the primary MFL curriculum in order to forge overlapping, shared identities based on inclusiveness and common goals.
- MFL encourages a broader concept of citizenship, extending beyond political and geographical boundaries.

Introduction

Cultural enrichment has long been seen as a key benefit of language learning and 'intercultural understanding' has now been listed as a key objective in the Key Stage 2 Framework for primary modern languages:

> *Language competence and intercultural understanding are an essential part of being a citizen. Children develop a greater understanding of their own lives in the context of exploring the lives of others. They learn to look at things from another's perspective, giving them insight into the people, culture and traditions of other cultures. Children become more aware of the similarities and differences between peoples, their daily lives, beliefs and values. There are many opportunities to link this strand closely with work in other subjects.*

> **(Key Stage 2 Framework for Languages 2005: 8)**

In this chapter we look at how 'culture' can be defined in the primary MFL classroom and how we can systematically integrate elements of intercultural learning as we develop pupils' language competence. We emphasise the importance of examining cultural differences through looking at the lives of children of the same age living in different countries and the habits, symbols, rituals and artefacts that constitute their cultural life. We also believe it is essential that our pupils examine their own environment and recognise their own cultural experience. Accepting difference has never been more important given our task of preparing children for a fast-changing world of cultural mixing and global communication where the need to adapt to changing circumstances and different social contexts is essential. In many schools, especially in urban areas, children live with cultural difference all around them and this experience is to be celebrated, indeed MFL builds on this diversity and embraces difference. In other schools, where the ethnic and cultural make-up of a school population seems fairly homogeneous, intercultural awareness is all the more important as it opens the door on the differences 'out there' which pupils will one day confront.

Assessing the role of 'culture' in primary MFL

Throughout this book we emphasise the multidimensional role of teaching and learning modern languages. We believe that learning languages is so much more than developing a technical, linguistic skill. The social and cognitive processes involved in language learning do support other curriculum subjects but also enhance whole-child development as language and culture intersect. We embrace a broad vision of MFL and believe that it is only where language learning is narrowly defined as a technical skill that pupil disaffection results. Rather, MFL can be viewed as a study of culture – and cultures – where language is a cultural code which embodies specific world-views and historically shaped behaviours and preferences. In fact, it is somewhat unfortunate that, by definition, the name MFL suggests a language-only focus. It might be better to have a subject name with a wider focus to take into account the cultural dimension, for example, we can envisage MFL being rebranded as *International studies, French studies, European studies, Languages and culture* or some other such epithet. While language study remains the key staple in MFL, it is essential that language is viewed as an evolving social practice which is rooted in a cultural community of speakers with specific historical and geopolitical identities. To divorce these cultural aspects from the study of a language can only be reductive and, ultimately, alienating.

It is through the study of and interaction with 'the other' that children become aware of their own 'cultural' selves. In schools where there is little ethnic diversity, MFL and other such educational experiences have the potential to steer children away from a restrictive monocultural/monolingual view of the world. In areas where there is already ethnic diversity in the school, intercultural learning can encourage children to embrace variety and to be flexible in their burgeoning world-view.

Claire Kramsch (1993), who has written extensively on the intercultural dimension in language learning, suggests the metaphor of a 'third space' occupied by the language learner, that is, the 'in-between' space between two languages and cultures. MFL teaching is situated in this metaphoric third space as it seeks to bridge the known and the unfamiliar through language and intercultural learning. More recently, some writers have argued against this 'third space' concept as it implies that cultures are solid immutable entities which can be distinguished from each other rather than a complex system of processes which overlap and, possibly, conflict as different world-views might not neatly mesh. We hold with this latter view as we acknowledge that intercultural learning is anything but straightforward, however for teaching purposes we believe it is useful to conceive of cultural learning as having certain, discrete phases:

1 Starting point: using pupils' knowledge of and assessment of first language culture.

2 Interaction with the new culture and language (the input phase).

3 A phase of comparison between 1 and 2.

4 A reassessment of the initial position 1.

These four phases provide a useful teacher checklist when integrating intercultural work in language teaching and learning. Let us now turn to the parallel processes expressed as pupil learning objectives which are seen as requisite skills in developing intercultural competence.

Developing intercultural competence

The word 'intercultural' emphasises that cultural learning is about linking or reconciling different start and end points, that is, it is more than just learning about how things are done differently 'over there'. Developing intercultural competence in primary language contexts requires developing a set of skills in the same way we aim to develop children's thinking skills and language skills. Michael Byram lists the following four *savoirs* to describe the skills used in intercultural projects. They relate to the four phases of planning we have listed above, though Byram is writing specifically about preparing for intercultural *exchanges*, either real or virtual. Such exchanges or visits are an ideal goal to work towards but are not always possible and the absence of genuine interaction with foreign native speakers should not be seen as a bar on effective intercultural work:

Savoir être: an ability to abandon ethnocentric attitudes towards and perceptions of other cultures, and to see and develop an understanding of the differences and relationships between one's own and a foreign culture; this involves affective and cognitive change in learners.

Savoir ap   dr an ability to observe, collect data and analyse how people of anothe   age and culture perceive and experience their world, what beliefs, values a   meanings they share about it; this involves practical skills and a readiness to decentre and take a different perspective.

Savoirs: the knowledge of aspects of a culture, a system of reference points fami'   · to natives of the culture, which helps the natives to share beliefs, values and meanings, and to communicate without making explicit those shared assumptions.

Savoir faire: the ability to draw upon the other three savoirs and integrate them in real time interaction with people of a specific language and culture.

(Byram 1997: 38)

Many of the children we spoke to when writing this book answered the question 'Why do you think it's important to learn a foreign language?' with replies such as 'So that we can buy food when we go on holiday', 'Because my uncle's got a house in Spain'. While these answers are perfectly legitimate and we have no reason to dispute that learning a foreign language for such purely instrumental purposes is anything but well grounded, we believe that motivation to learn language(s) needs to be understood in much broader terms, both from the perspective of those who implement MFL provision and from the pupils' point of view. For a start, if MFL learning is only understood as connected to concrete, instrumental outcomes then it becomes increasingly difficult to justify its presence in the UK curriculum in the face of global English use. After all, we may tell children that they need to use Spanish to buy an ice-cream on holiday, but this message is often incompatible with their own experience given that English is widely understood and used within the tourist industry with which they come into contact when on holiday with the family. Similarly, we may tell children that having competence in foreign languages will improve their job prospects in the future, but most of the adults that they know fare well enough in the UK labour market without using French or German and so there is another discrepancy between the reasons given to imbue MFL learning with value and the experience and world knowledge of the child.

Furthermore, such an instrumental view encourages attachment to a particular language and its spatially situated usefulness, for example French for use in France and Italian for use in Italy. In this book we are arguing for a broader definition of MFL learning as language and cultural awareness with the development of transferable skills and strategies. If MFL needs to justify its presence at all in the curriculum we suggest that its *raison d'être* as a vital school subject is grounded in two bold, yet overlapping, strands (see Chapter 1 for a discussion of the rationale for early language learning). First to be cited are the cognitive benefits and skills associated with learning a new language (discussed in Chapter 5) but equally important is the developing awareness of language as a socially-constituted practice, a cultural behaviour.

Which 'culture'?

The term 'culture' is often used to denote a fixed or clearly-defined entity – a community seen from the outside which we associate with certain sets of practices, particular languages, types of food, housing and so forth. This has important implications for the intercultural dimension of language teaching, for it raises the question: which 'culture' are we to assume a language embodies? Brian Street, an anthropologist turned educationalist renowned for his pioneering work on literacy as a social practice, claimed that 'culture is a verb' (Street 1993) to emphasise the fluid, transient nature of what we call 'culture'. Street reminds us that 'the storage and transmission of both language and cultural knowledge . . . appear to involve a number of processes that are not captured by the study of language alone' (1993: 42).

Let us consider for a moment what type of culture we are referring to when speaking about teaching it in an MFL context. Firstly, we could distinguish between 'Culture' with a capital 'C' and 'culture' meaning the day-to-day habits and customs of the target language community, although, in fact this becomes something of a false dichotomy because the two are linked in the way we perceive ourselves as belonging to a nation. In the former category, we are speaking about the historical, national emblems of a country or language community, such as famous writers, philosophers, saints, artists, explorers, etc., but also national events which are still commemorated, for example the Gunpowder Plot, the French Revolution and the more recent Reunification of Germany are all remembered with national celebrations or holidays. These historical events and famous figures are often a source of traditional national pride and, in time, become woven into the grand narrative of a nation which binds together a collective consciousness and forges the notion of a shared identity. Within this definition of culture, exploring different ways of celebrating shared and different feast days in the calendar can provide a stimulating and enjoyable springboard for looking at difference. The following is an example of effective intercultural language learning with a Year 1 class, combining the excitement of games and holidays with the enjoyment of singing (and universal love of chocolate).

Year 1 Topic: Easter

Just before the Easter holidays, and following a topic on colours, I hide some mini chocolate eggs round the classroom before the children arrive, enough for one for each child. When the German class begins, I say an Easter rhyme to the children ('*In dem grünen Gras sitzt ein kleiner Has', legt ein rotes Ei, und du bist frei!*'). I ask the children if they can hear any words they know? (colours, cognates). I show the children an image of the scene in the rhyme, with a removable bunny, which reveals a red egg! We practise saying the rhyme together, with my cardboard bunny acting out the scene. I explain to the children that this rhyme is used sometimes by children in playgrounds, to decide who is going to be 'on' in a chasing game, and that we are going to use it to decide who can go looking for chocolate eggs in the classroom! I talk about how German children celebrate Easter and tell them of the tradition in Germany of the *Osterhase*, hiding eggs in the garden, or in the woods, or in the flat where they live. The children sit in a large circle on the carpet, and join in with the rhyme, as I point to each child using the rhythm of the rhyme. Whichever child I point to on the word *frei* gets up and goes to look for a chocolate egg hidden in the classroom. We agree they will put their egg on the carpet in front of them until the game is finished, so it is easy to see which children are still waiting for their turn (nobody gets two turns!). I think it is important for young children to know traditional rhymes that would be familiar to German children of a similar age. The children soon pick up the rhyme (well, we do repeat it about 30 times!) and join in with me, though occasionally a few of them 'forget' to join in because their thoughts are overwhelmed by whether or not it will be their turn next!

This type of activity resonates with Byram's *savoirs* inasmuch as this enjoyable game is allowing the children an insight into a (slightly) different cultural practice so that their system of reference points, in this case in relation to Easter, is broadened. It also fits clearly with many of the 'intercultural understanding' learning objectives described in the Key Stage 2 Framework for Languages, e.g.

By the end of Year 3 children should be able to:

Recognise a children's song, rhyme or poem well known to native speakers.

By the end of Year 4 children should be able to:

Know about similar celebrations in other countries.

(Key Stage 2 Framework for Languages 2005: 75)

In our second definition of 'culture', we are referring to daily habits and routines such as eating habits and ways of dressing. Even in a global world, many of us cling to what we consider essential elements of our shared culture and continue to ritualise aspects of our Englishness or Frenchness. Let us take, by way of an example, eating habits. Although few British people actually eat fish and chips more than occasionally we may feel that there is something comfortingly 'British' about this dish, as if it really were part of a shared cultural understanding and more than a serving of fatty fried fish and potato which only fairly recently came to be regarded as a 'national dish'. In fact, many such 'traditions' which bind us to a sense of shared origin are of recent date, many consciously constructed to give an illusion of long-standing tradition. One example of this, described in Hobsbawm and Ranger's (1983) *The Invention of Tradition*, is the 'ancient' tradition of Scottish clan tartans which, upon closer inspection, can be deconstructed as a romantic myth invented in the nineteenth century.

It is useful to keep this relativism in mind when introducing 'Culture' and 'culture' in MFL lessons. Indeed, teaching children about where our customs and the iconography that constitutes our Britishness originated represents useful, important work on understanding identities. If we ignore the historico-geographic dimension when discussing difference(s) then young pupils only see the end point of a complex chain of localised circumstances and so view different habits or beliefs as innate characteristics rather than behaviours and viewpoints developed over time to deal with specific contexts. Younger children naturally have a keen curiosity and a flexible, adaptable mind and it is this *souplesse d'esprit* which makes them such good intercultural language learners. As they develop a more centred sense of self and position in the world with relation to their own cultural context, it is important to encourage ongoing reflexivity so that children think about their own immediate experience and maintain openness and flexibility to new ideas. This reflexivity is an important opening-up phase when embarking on intercultural work, leading pupils to examine the specificity of their own beliefs and practices. We have seen some wonderful examples of this type of intercultural study woven into MFL learning and other areas of the curriculum.

At a Roman Catholic primary school in East Anglia, where prayers were often said in Italian, the staff had an open, really rather 'progressive' attitude to the geographic origins of the school's faith. For example, the school was named after an Italian saint and children performed, in assembly, a sketch portraying one of the legends of the saint's life (St Francis talking to the wolf and to the townspeople) in 'original version' by using simplified Italian with a side-of-stage narrator interpreting, e.g.

- San Francesco: È vero che vuoi uccidere la gente del villaggio?
  St Francis: Is it true that you have tried to kill the townspeople?

- Il lupo: Sì, Signore
  The wolf: Yes, Sir.

- San Francesco: Perché?
  St Francis: Why?

- Il lupo: Perché ho fame
  The wolf: Because I'm hungry.

There was also a map display in the hall showing where the saint had lived and where key events in his life, such as his conversion, had taken place.

At the same school there was an art wall featuring 'images of Jesus', including an early Byzantine Christ, an Italianate Renaissance Jesus, an Ethiopan black Jesus, the blue-eyed white Christ of a Hollywood film. Although not necessarily linked to the teaching of Italian (the principal foreign language taught in this school) this display, prepared by pupils, was a clear demonstration of how interpretation is culturally subjective. This important intercultural project allowed pupils to understand how widely shared beliefs – in this case the Christian faith – are also experienced differently at an immediate, local level. The Key Stage 2 Framework identifies as a key objective that children should be able to recognise how symbols, products, objects, can be representative of specific cultures (Key Stage 2 Framework 2005: 75) and this has been achieved in this example by supporting both the faith-based ethos of the school and its mission to be fully inclusive and to acknowledge difference. The headteacher of this school also regularly invites speakers of different faiths to speak in assemblies as she believes that pupils 'living in a multicultural, multi-faith world have to learn to get along with other people who might not have had the same cultural and religious background as them'. She added 'they often realise that many faiths are actually saying the same thing, spreading the same message'. This headteacher, like many others we have spoken to, recognises the key role that MFL has to play in this kind of education, whether it be called 'spiritual' or 'cultural', which aims to broaden the child's view of the world and to engender interest in and tolerance of difference.

Similarly, although Spanish is increasingly the language of choice in primary schools, the historical and geographical lineage of the language is often omitted so that it is taught only as representative of a modern holiday destination (beaches and tapas!). While this aspect of Spanish appeals to both pupils and parents and so increases motivation to learn, it is a pity not to capitalise on this motivation by exploiting the opportunity to broaden pupils' understanding of what constitutes Spanish culture. One school we visited in the East Midlands, where Spanish had been 'voted' the school MFL by parents and pupils, had set about engaging with Spanish language and culture by integrating Spanish culture in this broad sense across the curriculum, especially the important Moorish influence on Spanish language, food and architecture (see below).

Durante la época de expansión del islam los árabes introdujeron muchas cosas en España (estabán en España del año 711 hasta 1492). Así que quedan muchas palabras de origen árabe en español, por ejemplo

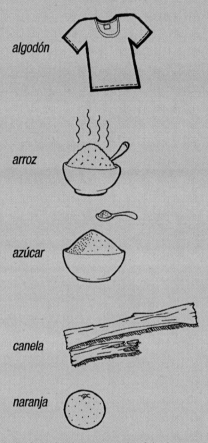

algodón

arroz

azúcar

canela

naranja

Year 5 pupils were each asked to bring in an example of the item and to find out something about how it is used, e.g. for making clothes, for flavouring food. Children then learnt how the item was cultivated and how it was processed for consumption. Although the task was mainly conducted in English, the impetus was awareness of cross-cultural etymologies in language and a sensitivity to the richness of cultural mingling. The Year 5 teacher who set up the project told us how surprised he had been that pupils had such little awareness of the Moslem empire compared to, for example, the Roman empire, and hoped that this project would go some way towards redressing the balance. In the same Year 5 classroom pupils had each designed an *azulejo* ceramic tile (though drawn on paper) and a lower part of a wall had been covered with their designed squares in the Moorish style still popular in Spain (*un zócalo*).

These projects exemplify Byram's *savoir être* because they broaden children's understanding of what 'Spanish' means in relation to their own British perspective, *savoir apprendre* because the children are set a research task to find out about given everyday objects as cultural artefacts, and *savoirs* because the children see how these items contribute to a collective, historical identity of Spanishness. The work on the Moors' influence in Spain not only encouraged a broader understanding of the Arabic Islamic heritage in Europe but also affirmed the vitality and richness of Islamic culture, a particularly worthwhile objective in today's climate of suspicion and intolerance towards followers of the Islamic faith. Many children feel alienated from narrow cultural epithets such as English, British, European and so we believe a key objective of intercultural education is to redefine these terms to include pupils rather than to describe given characteristics. In this respect, the relatively new subject area of Citizenship education links naturally to the cultural strand of primary MFL.

Citizenship and MFL

The 'non-statutory' framework for citizenship was introduced into English and Welsh primary schools in 2000 with provision becoming statutory in 2002 so that it is now fully integrated into the curriculum. We believe that MFL has a key role to play in broadening the scope of citizenship beyond the limits of national boundaries. Research led by Coffey (2005) into the perceptions of London school children to Europe and European citizenship revealed that many children from minority ethnic backgrounds equate European identity and languages with white, Christian populations that they may feel excluded from, often preferring instead to align themselves with their parents' place of origin, for example 'I'm Jamaican', 'I'm Somali'. Many school children questioned were unaware of the Moslem contribution to cultural life, not only historically but in modern-day France, Germany and Spain. The more pupils learn about the multicultural make-up of all modern European nation states, the greater their affinity for a shared European identity, not at the exclusion of other identities but, rather, as another strand to their integrated identity.

With a truly global language such as French, spoken over each continent as a mother tongue, it is relatively easy to present examples of different cultural and geographical contexts and many good course books now address this broader definition of a French speaker, by showing, for example, French-speaking Canadians enjoying winter sports in Québec, a Martiniquais child helping his father with the fishing catch, a Côte d'Ivoirien school room, a French Polynesian girl helping her mother cook the family meal and so forth. These images are interesting and help show the diverse contexts in which French is used but there is also a risk that they become internalised as romanticised snapshots of a different, exotic way of life unless there is some *inter*cultural preparatory and follow-up work. For example, as suggested above, an important initial phase for children confronting difference is that pupils are led to frame their own customs and way of living not as the indexical 'norm' but as one way of managing specific contextual circumstances. This 'frees up' the mind and allows greater objectivity when learning about how people in different social and geographic contexts manage the same universal challenges of eating, learning, making a living, maintaining relationships, finding spiritual fulfilment, having fun. Follow-up work might consist of comparing pupils' own lives with what they have learnt about other children's lives, but it is important that this is set up, as much as possible, as an unbiased analysis with the aim of providing a shared experience. As with all intercultural learning the ultimate goal is actual dialogue between pupils from different countries (more on this below), yet intercultural work can still be successfully managed within the class group, using images and information from the Internet and from other sources such as embassies and tourist offices. The following example illustrates how an object as mundane as a school bag can represent a cultural artefact for different uses in intercultural learning.

Year 2 children are the same age as school-starters in Germany, so it is a particularly appropriate time to look at the topic of 'schools'. The language learning in this topic revolves around revision of greetings and new classroom commands (*Schau her, hör zu, steh auf*, etc.), which appeals to their more 'bossy' natures! Towards the end of the topic, I bring in a real German *Schulranzen* and we compare this satchel to the kinds of bags British children bring in to school. The discussion and ideas from the children are often very rewarding. They notice how many reflectors it has on it and suggest they are to help keep the children safe in the dark. This leads into a discussion of lessons starting in Germany at 7.30 to 8am, often when it is still dark, and the fact that many more primary children walk unaccompanied to school in Germany compared with Britain. They comment on the large size of it and wonder whether that is so it can fit in a big packed lunch! This leads to a discussion of German children needing a *zweites Frühstück*, but finishing lessons in many schools in time to go home for a midday meal, which in turn leads to a discussion of the recent present of the *Schlüsselanhänger* sent to us from our partner school, and why children might be more likely than my Year 2s to wear a house key round their neck. We also look at the fact that the *Schulranzen* is designed to stand squarely next to the children's tables in class and, yes, that leads to yet another discussion, this time on how children in Germany are required to equip themselves with stationery, etc., and have it readily to hand in class. Using a video ('321 Los!'), we look at chapters on 'hellos' and 'goodbyes', which show scenes of children setting off to school with their *Schulranzen* and having them next to their tables in a classroom. I ask the children to look out for certain things when watching the video, e.g. 'Can you spot a Schulranzen? Where in the classroom do the children store their bags? How do their classroom tables and chairs compare to ours? Look out for the delicious cakes in the bakery!' We watch the video together, and then discuss what they had seen. The children are always full of questions. They are fascinated by the differences and reassured by the familiarities (the 'They look just like us!' feeling). Then we watch the video again to remind ourselves of what we have discussed.

Watching a video is second-best to the children actually experiencing Germany but miles better than me just talking to them about it. At the end of a very busy, chatty lesson, which usually has the children buzzing with questions, I leave the *Schulranzen* behind for the children to try on over the next few days, they love this!

The above clearly illustrates how many perspectives can be exploited from a single item. The use of the authentic material incited interest and the children's natural curiosity led to further discussions. Although English was used in these discussions (other than for the vocabulary for the main items being discussed) the cultural input provided a highly motivating frame for the planned language work related to school and classroom language use.

As well as learning about different ways of life in 'exotic' locations, it is important to represent the reality of cultural diversity in modern western societies. For example, learning about the colourful cultural landscapes of French-speaking societies across the continents should not exclude the enormous cultural range within any French metropolitan city. Pupils are often surprised by the cultural, ethnic and religious mix of neighbouring European countries which are often represented in advertising by quaint, old-fashioned stereotypes. Having a more realistic picture of France or Spain today will appeal to young learners, especially when their own reality of day-to-day life immersed in cultural difference is addressed.

EAL pupils and bilingualism: building on diversity

Many modern classrooms are characterised by rich and diverse cultural and linguistic heritage. Even in all-white, seemingly 'monocultural' areas, there are often interesting family histories of immigration or other geographic movements which can be uncovered two or three generations before. Until recently, children who spoke another language at home, especially if it were not one of the western European languages, were considered disadvantaged at school, their bilingualism often seen as a drawback rather than an asset. This 'deficit' perspective has changed radically in recent times and now children are encouraged to celebrate their linguistic and

[handwritten annotation: this goes w/ schools choosing their KS2 language based on the most common community FL, e.g. polish, to encourage communication]

cultural backgrounds. Indeed, this development is now enshrined in the Key Stage 2 Framework as a key learning objective:

IU3.1 Children should be taught to learn about the different languages spoken by children in the school.

(Key Stage 2 Framework 2005: 76)

Increased awareness of the varied needs of children with English as an Additional Language (EAL) has led to effective, differentiated support strategies in language coaching which take into account different starting points in terms of age and previous exposure to English but also with reference to first language experience. For example, some pupils may already be successfully reading and writing in their first language and whether or not this is a language using roman script will affect the transition to English. Many of the strategies employed in EAL tuition are transferable to the primary MFL teaching context where reference to existing knowledge of language is made explicit and built upon. Making links explicit in this way is a development reminiscent of Eric Hawkins' forward-thinking work in the 1980s on raising 'language awareness' across the curriculum (Hawkins 1984) and ties in today with the call to embed literacy across the curriculum (as stipulated in the Key Stage 2 Framework). Seen in this light, MFL is redefined as more than foreign language teaching and becomes part of the child's whole language awareness, whether a first language English speaker or an EAL pupil.

[handwritten annotation: EAL / MFL links]

In cases where pupils' first language corresponds to the MFL of choice, pupils can be a rich, natural resource in primary MFL teaching. Such pupils can provide authentic language models and can peer-coach other pupils. We believe that this not only provides linguistic benefits but can also be a cultural enrichment in the celebration of diversity. One cautionary word we might add here relates to the reluctance of some EAL pupils to use their mother tongue with peers as they may feel this makes them stand out as 'different' when they really wish to just assimilate. Such reticence may be linked to parental pressure to 'get on' and assimilate through English or may result from some confusion themselves in language use. After all, bilingual pupils are still young children and, especially if they have spent a long time in the UK, their productive skills in the mother tongue may well be underdeveloped even if their aural understanding is instinctive.

By way of an example, let us cite two Spanish-speaking identical twins that one of the authors (Coffey) met recently in Year 4 of a London primary school. The two brothers were asked, separately, to recount the story of Little Red Riding Hood using pictures only. The boys were addressed in Spanish but were not asked to respond in any particular language. One of the boys told the entire story in English with only one or two difficulties in vocabulary gaps which he tried to explain in English or asked 'what's that?', but his brother switched freely between languages several times throughout the story, calling the grandma *the abuela* and the wolf *the lobo*.

Whenever he was unsure of a word or expression he used Spanish. The different responses illustrate how motivation to use English versus the mother tongue varies even between children with almost identical environmental influences and how these translate to different communicative strategies. In a multilingual classroom there is space for a variety of strategies to be developed and these can be adapted freely by first language English speakers as they engage with MFL learning.

Celebrating diversity or language teaching?

In many schools, especially where there is a sizeable cohort of bilingual children, cultural diversity is celebrated throughout the school by respecting different religious feast days, greeting children in a different 'language of the week' or by talk-ing about different cultural traditions in assemblies, etc. We fully endorse these affirmative enterprises; they are both culturally enriching and encourage children to accept difference; however, such initiatives are not to be confused with MFL teach-ing and learning. For MFL to be effectively taught a clearly structured programme of study is required that sends consistent messages and is pedagogically sound. Culture has a vital part to play in the success of this language teaching, but again this needs to be structured and planned to fit a scheme of work. Anecdotal and ad hoc exposure to words and phrases of different languages may serve to bond the school community and engender tolerance but, alone, does not constitute effective MFL teaching.

Instead, what we are proposing is that planned language development is dove-tailed into intercultural work throughout the MFL schemes of work and that both strands are underpinned by whole-curriculum links.

Making friends across the world

The ultimate goal of intercultural language learning is to arrange actual or virtual exchanges between schools. The pathways opened up by new technologies have made such exchanges increasingly manageable (see Chapter 8 for a discussion of the different ways these can be arranged). The benefits of having a partner school in a target language country are enormous, because they represent a source of material and a window on the parallel lives of pupils of the same age. For staff, too, partner schools offer great opportunities for teacher exchange (both for language and cul-tural enrichment). Within the EU, funding is available for teachers to spend time in a school abroad or to attend language courses and there are also wider global exchanges facilitated through schemes such as the 'North-South' school links projects developed by Save the Children in conjunction with the Central Bureau (Poudyal 2001).

Where we have seen MFL most successfully embedded in the cultural life of the school it has been underpinned by some form of partnership abroad, not necessarily between pupils, maybe only between teachers, often led by the MFL coordinator or a visionary headteacher. Initial contacts can be provided by such agencies as the European Schools Net site, the British Council, foreign embassy cultural and educational departments, or by informal word-of-mouth networks, but the ongoing success of links is only sustained through effective personal relationships, clear joint planning and flexibility. Although this chapter has dealt primarily with developing cultural awareness in pupils' learning, it is essential that teachers also develop their own 'interculturality', and learning from visits to schools abroad, where culturally different ways of teaching and learning are experienced, provides enormous value in terms of professional and personal development.

Conclusion

Language learning and cultural awareness are inextricably linked and this has been recognised in the current Key Stage 2 Framework for Languages where intercultural learning constitutes a key objective. In this chapter we have considered how culture can be defined within a language learning context to meet the needs of children today, that is, to understand and to accept as natural and enriching the differences which surround them. The whole-curricular dimension of cultural learning is emphasised as is the importance of self-reflexivity if children are not simply to learn that foreigners do things differently but rather that differences are understood contextually as rooted in specific historical and geographic circumstances. In this light, cultural awareness becomes truly 'intercultural' as children have a broader understanding of their own emerging identities. Embracing cultural diversity is important both for schools where ethnic and cultural mix is evident and for those where the pupil cohort appears culturally homogeneous because all children need to develop flexible and adaptable ways of engaging with others in a world of fast change where increasingly globalised identities contend with locally-framed experiences. MFL has a vital role in the school in developing empathy, as one Year 6 girl in East Anglia told us about her MFL learning: 'it's fun, you get to feel like you're French or German when you speak the words'.

Issues for reflection

- Is the cultural diversity within your school/class already recognised and celebrated?
- Is there any linguistic diversity among pupils, e.g. EAL pupils, which can be exploited for MFL learning?
- How is the ethos of your school embedded in school traditions and practices? Is there scope for extending these to draw on a wider range of cultural and linguistic sources?

- To what extent are your pupils encouraged to think about the origins of the customs and routine habits which define their culture as British (or other)?

- How is MFL linked explicitly to Citizenship Education, e.g. in schemes of work?

- Are there further opportunities for including MFL in cross-curricular cultural learning, e.g. in art such as in the example for Spanish or RE such as in the example for Italian?

- Do you already have a partner school abroad or belong to a network? What practical limits may shape the type of partnership exchange? What would be the benefits to your particular context, for example, in terms of pupil engagement and CPD?

10

Transition from primary to secondary – continuity, cohesion and progression

WHILE IT IS important that children's trajectories of learning provide continuity from their primary schooling into the secondary phase in all subjects, it is vital to ensure that the initial interest in and enjoyment of primary MFL is maintained and that primary and secondary teachers work together to ensure that learning is sequential and coherent. Transition needs to be seen and understood in a wider context. The concept is based on liaison, defined as discussion and other links between primary and secondary schools, and transfer, understood as the actual move from one phase to the other. Liaison, transfer and an awareness of needs and expectations of all parties involved are the key elements of a structured dialogue on issues of the process of transition enabling stakeholders to develop a suggested framework. Transition then is the concept that embraces all the cross-phase deliberations and procedures. It comprises mini-transitions throughout the primary phase as well as the major point of transition from KS2 to KS3. Transition and its aspects are the focus of this chapter which itself is part of the ongoing dialogue.

Key issues

- Primary and secondary teachers of MFL need to conceptualise the foreign language learning pathway as a continuum of learning.

- MFL teachers in both phases benefit from a mutual awareness and understanding of teaching and learning approaches appropriate to the age level and from working in collaboration.

- Cross-phase liaison between teachers is essentially concerned with the continuous and continuing development of the whole child as well as, in primary MFL, language learning.

- Transfer documentation on children's primary MFL learning needs to be informative and useful to provide a basis for progression.

- Liaison provides an opportunity for teachers to show leadership on a cross-phase basis. The headteacher and Senior Leadership Team have a role to play in supporting primary–secondary liaison in their school organisational arrangements.

- Primary and secondary MFL teachers and other relevant parties need to put into place a regular and open dialogue to plan the progression of pupil learning and the enhancement of teacher subject knowledge.

Introduction: avoiding 'horrible things'

'At secondary school, the French teacher might say horrible things if we get on to harder things and we have no idea what they are talking about.'

(Year 6 ten-year-old boy at end of Summer term)

This genuinely felt fear of 'horrible things' anticipated by this pupil can be prevented when modern foreign languages teachers from both the primary and the secondary sectors communicate with each other. 'It's good to talk' according to telecommunication advertisements and the communication between teachers will open opportunities to provide a joined-up approach to primary and secondary MFL learning.

As a subject, primary MFL requires special attention given its relatively fragile place in the curriculum with entitlement status only at primary level (not to mention its vicarious position at secondary level KS4) and on account of its newness, at least until parity of subject is attained and until primary MFL is well embedded in the curriculum.

Furthermore, primary MFL is not just a question of learning 'a little French' but a part of the child's whole language development project and therefore liaison is essential.

There are actually many points of transition as the child moves through her or his school career (and indeed in life outside of school) – not just one solitary transition at the end of primary and beginning of secondary schooling for the young learner (although this is a very obvious and critical one) (see Figure 10.1).

We see primary MFL as a foundation stone for ongoing learning and an important step in preparing pupils for the progression from primary to secondary. Secondary schools can also benefit from a structured joined-up approach in that they have the opportunity to build on previous learning outcomes and ensure that appropriate challenges for pupils are set from the start.

When devising a framework for a successful transition, teachers need to consider the primary to secondary transfer within the context of a series of transitions that make up the child's school career. Awareness and inclusion of the needs of all

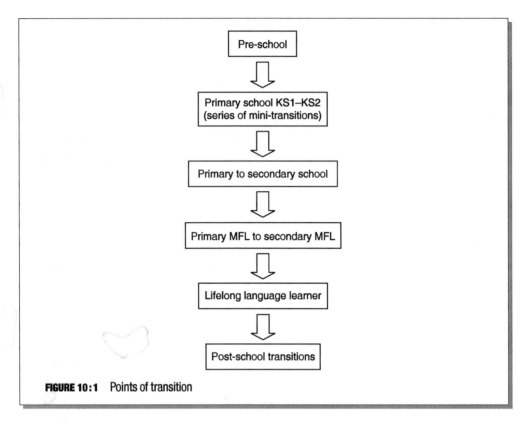

FIGURE 10:1 Points of transition

stakeholders in their communication and collaboration will lead to an effective dialogue which provides a basis for a smooth transmission from primary MFL to secondary school MFL for the main beneficiaries – the pupils.

Issues of transition, then, are more than communication and collaboration between teachers at the surface level – they are about the whole child and his/her long-term development at a deep level of consideration. This perspective will form a basis for planning a coherent if not always entirely seamless continuum of learning, for learning is never without its surprises, challenges and deviations. Learning, like a tree, grows up towards the light but develops interesting side branches and complex root systems as learners engage in different language learning experiences in different contexts. One very obvious example is that some pupils will take up a different language at secondary level to the one or those offered in the primary school.

A la recherche du 'tronc commun'

Transition has been the focus of research of Erika Werlen and colleagues at the University of Tübingen. They undertook some large-scale research in collaboration with several other institutions during the period 2001–2006 into primary English as a foreign language learning context and progress made in early foreign language learning. The pupils were aged from 6 to 9 and were learning English or French as a foreign language. Werlen's intention was to try to identify apparently significant factors promoting the progressive learning of a foreign language at primary level, leading to the identification of what she calls a 'tronc commun'. Some 470 primary schools in BadenWürttemberg were involved in this comprehensive exploration of teaching approaches and learning styles, infrastructures of school primary MFL provision and their impact on learning, issues of progression and transition to higher year groups. A great many classroom interventions were planned as part of this research, including older, more advanced learners coaching younger, less proficient learners.

Although this research has been devised for and is conducted in a different context, we consider it useful for the UK as it focuses on transitions and coherence throughout the child's school career. Werlen (2006) considers that the focus on learning needs to take a long-term view of the child's whole school life, a perspective of long-term learning that she plots onto a model comprising vertical and horizontal axes (see Figure 10.2) designed to mesh, flexibly, in order to promote cohesion on the *tronc commun* at various points:

The vertical cohesion axis is concerned with transitions of the traditional kind and easily identifiable ones such as moving from one year group to another (and ultimately from one school to another), but also transitions from systems and routines such as the inevitable shift from informal holistic assessment by the teacher of younger pupils to more formal assessment structures that impact on the learning

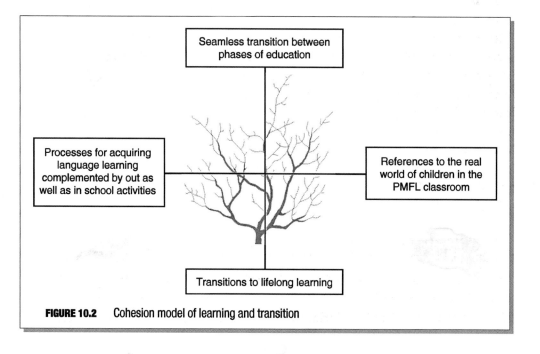

Seamless transition between phases of education

Processes for acquiring language learning complemented by out as well as in school activities

References to the real world of children in the PMFL classroom

Transitions to lifelong learning

FIGURE 10.2   Cohesion model of learning and transition

of the older ones. Such transitions are tangible, visible and manageable; they comprise the organisational stuff of school life and how primary MFL is managed across the whole school as discussed in Chapter 2 about primary MFL as a whole-school learning project; they are about systems, structures and procedures.

The horizontal axis focuses more on the children, their development and their needs. It lays emphasis on the classroom as one site of learning among myriad others outside of school and on how primary MFL teachers should, according to Werlen's assertions, create classroom language learning contexts that reflect the children's life experiences. This could be through the everyday life in school or by exploring the realms of the children's imagination with story-telling in the foreign language, for example. The curriculum, while rich in different topics, subjects and approaches, has cross-curricular dimensions and internal cohesion. The transitions on this axis are individualised, learning-centred and negotiable; they focus on children's needs and their growth.

As a primary school deputy headteacher with responsibility for early years commented, demonstrating an awareness of the horizontal axis:

> 'There are many mini-transition points starting with the transition from home to school. This transition is huge, especially if the child has not had the opportunity to attend nursery school. You can see this sometimes when a child has been accustomed to baby talk at home and then has to use more formal language at school. Within the KS1 stage, there is a major transition from the Foundation Stage that is play-based to the National Curriculum which is more formal, subject based, structured and includes literacy and numeracy although the current trend is back to more cross-curricular and more creativity. This provides a structure for KS2 which also provides new opportunities such as after school clubs, sports, networking with other schools, community activities, more work in the Arts and so on. Oddly enough, when I first started teaching, the third year was called the transition year between infants and junior classes but the immediate jump from KS1 to KS2 makes that transition more difficult now. The whole thing is like the change from nappies to trainer pants and then ordinary underwear thank goodness.'

It seems to us that much of the teacher transition discourse, where it takes place, focuses more on issues arising from the vertical axis, such as schemes of work, resourcing and assessment. There is scope for extending the transition discussion agenda to include issues deriving from considerations on the horizontal axis as well as exploring more comprehensively points of crossover. As Pagden writes (2001: 9):

> For a child to succeed there are some things that should stay the same throughout their time at school: most obviously, the combination of physical and social factors which ensures the child's right to feel safe and cared for. Other things should change progressively in order to support the child's growing competence and maturity: for example, the complexity of texts designed and/or chosen to foster the development of literacy skills.

Such issues would include pupil comfort level in primary MFL lessons and whole-school curriculum mapping and collaboration with colleagues. Indeed, we need to think about transition not just at the crucial KS2–KS3 stage, but as a series of mini-transitions that dot the primary school child's career on a continuous basis.

Hold the teddy, pass the teddy – mini-transitions in the primary MFL classroom

In a primary MFL context, children go through a number of mini-transitions, comprising a wide range of organisational to social transitions. Teachers teaching throughout the whole school are aware of these and integrate them into their teaching. One teacher of primary MFL throughout the whole school and thus responsible for learning transitions on the vertical axis, demonstrates sensitivity and awareness of these transitions and in doing so takes into account both the vertical and horizontal axis. The following examples range from transitions on an organisational, social and academic level.

Organisational skills

These skills refer to the children organising their day and materials.

- From carpet to sitting at a table

  'I teach Years 1 and 2 on the carpet, as it's much easier for them to easily stand up, but sitting at a table is easier for playing Question and Answer catch, as their coordination is better developed and less time is spent dropping the toy used for this activity, the Grüne Spinne!'

- From group work at tables to individual seat, and a tray for their material

  'At KS2 I can easily play two minutes of number Lotto, without preparing for it . . . they grab their rough books and a pencil from their trays under their table, and off we go! At KS1 I would need to be resourced fully in advance to do this as the children sit on the carpet with no equipment to hand. Having said this, I've done Lotto with Year 2, using a pre-prepared grid and handing out photocopies and pencils. Year 1 tends to be equipment like multilink or number bananas, which have to be given out by passing along the rows of children.'

- Coping with time and timetable: from having an afternoon playtime, to working right through from 1 to 3.15pm

  'Year 3 can get very tired in the afternoon, and also before lunch they get jaded. I swapped my Year 3 German slot with my Science slot to avoid MFL coming just before lunch when they were fading. It was Science 9 to 11.30 (with assembly and playtime breaks), German 11.30 to 12. Now German 9 to 9.30 and science 9.30 to 12. German lessons were much more sparky as a result, and science hasn't suffered.'

  'In PMFL in Year 1, evening was new English vocab for some children, so "Guten Abend" means nothing until they are clear on the idea of "evening". I put it down to the fact that at that age, once the afternoon is over, it's tea and bath and bed, with no real evening to speak of, i.e. straight from

"Guten Tag" to "Gute Nacht!" Older children need to be secure in reading a clock before introducing telling the time in German. I would usually expect a fair few Year 5 children to be wobbly on time-telling still.'

Social skills and growing up

- From responsible for self, to showing responsibility for others

  'These include forming relationships with other pupils, moving from classroom to whole-school assemblies, taking responsibility for other children. Our older children have opportunities to be responsible for younger or more vulnerable children, e.g. sitting among the little ones in assembly as good role models, or shadowing a vulnerable boy at playtime, or helping a wheelchair-bound child with her coat, etc. . . . some older children might sometimes sing a PMFL song when playing with the younger children at break.'

- From being relatively uninhibited at KS1 to the beginning of adolescence in Year 6

  'Silly songs can still work at Year 6, providing the atmosphere in the classroom allows this. Silly songs at Year 1 are a must! Some of my current Year 6 are becoming shyer at doing role-plays for the class. I know they are capable, but one or two are starting to be less willing to "perform", more "cool", so it is harder to assess what they can do.'

- Linked to the above, some children are becoming less comfortable with the opposite sex, e.g.

  'A lovely "touchy-feely drawing weather symbols on backs" lesson would go down a treat in Year 3, but in Year 6 some girls would not wish to be partnered with a boy, only a best friend for such an activity (bra-straps are awkward!).'

Learning skills

- From thinking of oneself to thinking in a group/class about tasks. The children move from being lone-players, to knowing the sort of behaviour required to play a group board game (MFL dice/snakes and ladders work best after Year 3)

  'At KS1 when the children are passing, e.g. a teddy to say "Guten Morgen" to, they are still learning to pass an object, to be fair, to take turns, not to snatch, etc., and are largely oblivious to the other children if they have hold of a particularly lovely teddy! My Year 2 topic on toys was most enjoyable, but passing them round sometimes took ages, as children gently rocked the dolly, or vroomed the toy car! By KS2, they pass things round quite quickly and efficiently. At Year 1 I once had a disastrous lesson with large 12-sided foam dice to help learn numbers. The children were so fascinated by the dice, and had to put so much concentration into rolling them, and were so hopeful that the dice would come to them next from across the circle, that any language learning was swamped by all these other things! I tend to keep equipment and activities really simple at KS1, whereas at older KS2, sometimes you have to pull out a few stops to "wow" them and grab their attention!'

- From doing the best for the teacher, to being more responsible for their own learning, their targets

'PMFL at KS1 is a lot about them looking forward to me coming, and enjoying making lots of lovely German sounds, and I almost always tell them how brilliant they are at some point. With Year 6 the other day, they knew their aim was to use good pronunciation for and confidence with numbers to 36, and they were responsible for asking me for help with the bits they needed to improve on. Praise plays a large part here too, but it's also important they know when it's not up to scratch, and what they have to do to get there.'

■ From individual to recognising 'the other'

'A child moves from being a person who thinks of number one, to maturing to include consideration for number two and number three. (MFL links with use of first, second and third person. With the little ones, emphasis is on "ich", moving to "du", eventually onto "er/sie/es". I haven't spotted much of a role for "wir" at primary level yet!)

■ Transitions also occur on the level of motor-skills when learning to write

'Using a pencil to being allowed to write in pen.'

■ From being a non-reader to a reader

'With obvious implications for reading and writing in MFL, some Year 3s will be non-readers still, or very poor readers, so the MFL KS2 framework encouraging copy-writing is a bit worrying.'

Thus, then, do Werlen's theoretical axes of cohesion translate to the practical transitions from home to school, nappies to trainer pants then pants, hugging the teddy to passing the teddy, pencils to pens, primary MFL for pure enjoyment to learning targets, unbridled exuberance to incipient 'uncool', cuddly toys to board games and so on. Add to this the potentially seismic transition from primary to secondary school and conversation between all parties involved becomes urgent to embrace the well-being and continuing and progressive learning needs of the children as well as to enhance subject dialogue between the language teachers concerned. The key purpose of such a dialogue is to continue to close the gap between the two phases as far as primary MFL is concerned and to build on the mechanisms for general primary–secondary transition procedures that have been developed over the years.

Mind the transition gap! The current situation

Any transition is, as can be seen from the examples provided in the previous section, a complex situation consisting of many aspects and different stages. Within the context of the transition from primary to secondary school, the concerns and needs of all need to be heard and attended to. Lorraine Flynn, as headteacher of a secondary language college, a strong promoter of primary MFL and its links with secondary school, refers to this need as 'opening dialogue, closing the gap' between teachers in the two phases, stressing that 'Effective dialogue, which takes in the generalists' skills and knowledge (for example, those of the literacy coordinator), is vital to developing successful models to ensure our primary children remain motivated as they move through the Key Stages' (Flynn 2005: 4).

The current situation, although improving, is still fraught with difficulties as the concerns that the stakeholders involved express show. There is a primary school teacher who regrets missed opportunities for visits from her school to a secondary school due to financial and geographical reasons:

'We have an open invitation to visit a secondary school but no visits yet due to distance, cost and time.'

And one of her colleagues is concerned about secondary MFL imposing their scheme of work on their colleagues in primary schools:

'They ask us to use a certain scheme of work to suit them.'

This one-directional dialogue can lead in some instances to secondary schools simply ignoring the foundation that has been laid in the subject area and teaching MFL as if the children were new to the subject; as one primary headteacher observes:

'In spite of the good work of some really enthusiastic colleagues in both primary and secondary schools, too many of the secondary schools just start at the beginning again and ignore what the children have done.'

This statement could however also be interpreted as attempts made by secondary MFL teachers to ensure that the children from different feeder schools start from the same level in the subject.

There clearly is a need for support for primary MFL from the leadership level in secondary schools, as an LA adviser points out:

'For me it is a question of leadership at secondary level. We need support for primary languages from the top and it isn't always forthcoming. There are issues to do with school organisation such as choice of language, groupings and the strategic overview of the place of MFL.'

Even more disconcerting than the criticism made by the members of the professional group are the fears and concerns expressed by parents whose children have learning difficulties. This parent of a Year 7 child anticipates an increase of difficulties for her son:

'My son struggled with French at primary school as he is dyslexic and is having a really hard time at secondary school.'

And children who, like this Year 6 child, found the subject hard at primary level, and fear a lack of support and extra help:

'If we are struggling at secondary school, it will be even harder and we won't be able to get extra help in groups like we do here.'

A coherent scheme of transition from primary MFL to secondary MFL is, as can be seen by these comments, much needed and far from transparent to those parties most concerned. Devising a model for an effective dialogue on the issues relating to the process of transition will have to start in our view with the ultimate beneficiaries – the pupils.

Scary and hard work to come

If given the opportunity, pupils can provide insightful views on the subject of their learning and express their own, sometimes strong, views about their experiences of MFL learning. Interestingly, there was a striking consensus of opinion that emerged from two Year 6 pupil focus groups in London that we organised at the end of a summer term and a third group one autumn term in a school in the South East. All the pupils thought that MFL would

- get harder;
- involve more writing;
- involve less speaking.

Asking the pupils in the focus group discussions to elaborate on what they meant by 'hard', they linked 'hardness' to 'scary' textbooks that they had seen, writing – 'like describing yourself, my brother had to do a whole page of writing' – fearing that they might not understand what the teacher would be saying when speaking the target language and, by extension, 'getting homework that we might not understand and we would get a detention'. Some pupils had heard through the peer or sibling grapevines that some of the work done at secondary school was the same as in primary school. All had indeed been warned about textbooks and those children who had seen the textbooks used by their friends or brothers and sisters thought they looked 'hard'.

Among the interviewees there was one boy who felt he was already 'rubbish at French' and was worried about how he would cope at secondary school whereas the majority of children thought that having learnt French/German/Italian, etc., might be useful. They saw the use in that, in their own words, 'we will know what to do'; 'we know some of the language so we will recognise it'; 'even if we do German, the French we have done will give us a clue about learning' and 'we will know what the teacher is talking about'. This is an important point coming from the pupils about their primary language experiences serving as a 'learning to learn a language' experience. In spite of all the talk about 'getting hard', the children exhibited determination and indomitable stoicism, and had good ideas effectively about improving transition and closing the gap.

Closing the gap: opening the dialogue and moving towards a framework

1. Foundations of dialogue – perspectives from the teaching staff

The dialogue to close the gap, while taking into consideration the very real concerns of those involved, has already begun among pupils, primary school teachers, secondary school teachers, parents, trainers, advisers and others with an interest and stake in the process.

In instances where heads and colleagues involved in the primary MFL adventure have planned primary MFL bridging activities and/or helpful transition arrangements, their enthusiasm and transition problem-busting skills are tangible. One head of MFL reported positive impressions gained on visits to primary schools and the extent to which this has had an impact on her planning:

> 'I went to visit one of our feeder primary schools and watched the AST PMFL teach and saw what they had covered over three years and realised we would need to change our scheme of work. We have since begun to amend our teaching approach with Year 7 to be more in line with what we saw at primary school. It was a revelation.'

Visits to feeder schools can be extremely profitable for secondary school teachers at an early stage of their career as this Newly Qualified Teacher (NQT) points out:

> 'I go to teach Year 6 at one of our main feeder primary schools once a week and I can honestly say it is the highlight of my week. I love it. I try to do similar things with my Year 7 and 8 classes.'

Lesson observations can be a very effective means and form an essential part of the dialogue on transitions – as one primary school teacher comments:

> 'The head of MFL from one of our secondary schools comes in fortnightly over the summer term and teaches Year 6. I find it interesting to watch her and the children can see that what they will do in Year 7 is not too different from what they are used to.'

It is beneficial when a school has a member of staff whose enthusiasm can start the dialogue on transition off, using networking skills, as the following example provided by a secondary headteacher shows:

> 'We have one teacher who is ideally placed to liaise on primary–secondary languages as she used to teach in a prep school and she is really keen to work closely with some of our feeder primary schools. In fact she has already made a start with the school just down the road as part of our school cluster arrangement.'

2. Towards a structured dialogue

So what are the key elements for a structured dialogue between primary and secondary teachers from which both sides benefit? Our discussions with teachers show the following issues:

- Secondary teachers knowing what primary MFL content the primary school covers and which skills have been developed and to what extent (we think it would be useful for primary teachers to be acquainted with at least KS3 schemes of work, in particular Year 7).

- A discussion about respective teaching approaches (to identify the areas of expertise of each and to find common bridging ground).

- A consideration of the best possible permutations of languages on offer.

- To agree a baseline coverage (to which primary colleagues would be oriented and on which secondary teachers can build and ensure progression rather than use guesswork).

- The sharing of materials (in order to familiarise themselves with the resource bank and perhaps share these with the pupils? (see section 4 below)).

- Problematic areas – and a search for solutions – and identifying what works well (how teachers can help each other and share good ideas).

- Agreement on primary MFL profiling data on pupils (to decide what transfer information would be useful and in what format and to identify learning and other needs of pupils – one way to avoid 'horrible things'!).

3. Foundations of the dialogue: the family support group

The impact of the transition from primary MFL to secondary MFL reaches beyond the school, and pupils seek and receive help from their parents and siblings as this Year 6 pupil states:

> 'I don't think it will get harder if we learn really hard at primary school and I have my brother and sister to help me when I am at secondary school. My dad got me a German dictionary.'

A parent describes her experience with the transition from primary MFL to MFL at secondary school:

> 'My daughter always enjoyed French when she was here [at primary school] – and my son does too – and she is really enjoying French in Year 7 at the high school. I know a bit of French and the teaching seems to be really inspirational.'

4. Pupils' perspectives on transition

In the focus group discussions, pupils were asked for their ideas about improving transition. Transition was explained to them as the move from primary to secondary school and what teachers might do to make it easier for them to continue to make progress and to know what they were doing. Among those ideas were:

- Looking at some of the textbooks that they would be using at secondary school but with their teacher at primary school would help deal with the 'scary' factor as they could see what would be expected of them.

- More regular French lessons, and French used by more members of staff across the school (see Chapter 2).

- More focus on writing and more opportunities to write as a way to prepare for secondary school. Even where the primary MFL teacher does not explicitly embrace this, we have seen children reading and writing in almost every school we have visited. Writing provides immense opportunities for extension and differentiation and the Key Stage 2 Framework is inclusive in this respect.

The children enjoyed doing small amounts of homework for French and project work and would like to do a bit more.

Some children expressed an interest in independent study and suggestions included researching cultural information and making tape recordings of speaking.

Above all, the children were anxious that teachers at secondary school find out what the pupils know and can, and conversely cannot, do. One child said it would be helpful if the teacher would ensure the pupils understood what they were saying especially if they were always speaking in French 'as sometimes they sound like they are talking to other adults'. One 11-year-old girl said: 'Teachers need to get into the child's mind and see our problems.'

The observations and views put forward by the stakeholders show, we find, a remarkable consistency concerning the issues surrounding the transition from primary to secondary modern foreign language teaching. These points need to be considered when devising a framework for transition.

A framework for transition

It would, taking the results of our findings and Werlen's research into consideration, indeed be very short-sighted to focus at the KS2–KS3 transition only. In the light of the multi-transitional language learning journey that the pupils have to undergo, we suggest that teachers take all four Key Stages into consideration. At the point of KS2–KS3 transition, it is vital that teachers plan transfer information that can guide and inform the next stage of learning provision. We have detected a certain vague-ness in some instances, as Cynthia Martin of the University of Reading put it in a personal correspondence: 'The information can sometimes be rather restricted to topic areas – 'greetings, ages, pets and colours, typical early Year 7 fare'. Scottish colleagues who complete a High School Transfer Card and include a section for French – or other language – for each pupil, have worked on integrating MFL in some detail into the subject pupil profiling, drawing on a data bank of useful statements. At the least, the transfer portfolio would include a report as for other subjects, class teacher's and/or observer's notes (e.g. Higher Level Teaching Assistant, visiting sec-ondary school colleague), a sample of work, European Language Portfolio, school MFL 'passport' or other purpose-designed instrument. Assessment is therefore a very important part of primary MFL provision within an assessment for learning framework and for the provision of useful data on pupil progress (see Chapter 7).

Teachers, in order to develop the transition framework, need to be in each other's classrooms from time to time and to work collaboratively and in imaginative ways. They can create a forum on transition in which their opinions will be heard and where they are respected as experts in their own field and feel involved in a constructive dialogue. Furthermore, it is incumbent on all teachers to take some responsibility for the continuing motivation and for the progression in learning throughout the child's entire MFL school career and her/his social progression in terms of self-confidence and self-efficacy. Joined-up thinking and collaborative action are important as never before as there are issues with the popularity of MFL at certain stages, and not just at secondary level, and also with the current alarming drop-out rates at 14+. While children may decide not to continue their foreign language studies, they will have been exposed to the skills required to learn an MFL and be able to build on this at a later stage of their lives.

A framework of transition builds the foundations of a constructive dialogue between all parties involved and will take the issues outlined above into consideration and work towards a possible resolution of these.

Conclusion

Given the frequency of certain concerns, the key issues for conversation between teachers can be summed up in the form of frequently asked questions (FAQs). The responses we provide are based on our discussion with teachers.

FAQ 1: Isn't it unfair that primary teachers have all the fun with oral methods and games and we (secondary teachers) have to do writing and grammar or we can't cover what we have to?

> Some secondary teachers and also some Year 7 pupils have commented on this but this can be avoided if primary and secondary teachers work together so that their teaching, especially in Years 6 and 7, demonstrates coherence and plans for progression across the phases. Fun in learning can still be part of the more intensive MFL diet at secondary level. That secondary teachers are sometimes aggrieved is understandable. It is they who have a major task in making changes to be able to respond to the needs of incoming children with their very varied primary MFL experiences.

FAQ 2: How are we at secondary school supposed to cope with children coming from over 30 feeder schools when some have done some French and some haven't? That's why we often start from scratch.

> You have to start somewhere so start with a small group of willing schools on very practical planning issues then spread this to others or at the very least disseminate

your planning and create e-mail and other networks. Most LAs have organised their schools in clusters, learning groups or other networks so mechanisms exist for conversations to take place as well as for peer observation. It is vital not to destroy children's sense of achievement or their enthusiasm by not acknowledging and validating what they have done.

FAQ 3: We really want to liaise with our colleagues but how do we find the time?

It is useful to construe time as a flexible resource. The introduction of primary MFL into primary schools needs some prioritising on the part of primary and secondary teachers in order to make it a success. Time can be found by creative timetabling and through leadership decisions that enable teachers to undertake the necessary visits and networking.

FAQ 4: (From pupils) Why do teachers when we go to secondary school start all over again when we did a lot of the topics at primary school? It's boring.

It is indeed frustrating and disappointing. However, the message is getting through and secondary teachers talk much more about what pupils have done at primary school in their language lessons and will be able to build on at secondary school. Many secondary school teachers are impressed with the work being done in the primary school which means that they can move ahead at a faster pace.

FAQ 5: So, who is supposed to be in charge of coordinating transition?

Leadership is of the essence (see Chapter 2) and the role of headteachers in their management and support of primary MFL is crucial. It requires shared leadership from primary MFL coordinators and secondary teachers with responsibility for liaison. Recent restructuring arrangements of posts of responsibility in English schools, adaptable in any school context, have seen a shift to whole-school and team leadership roles that provide an opportunity for enhanced internal and cross-phase dialogue on learning and teaching. Coordination requires the engagement of all those involved, both at school level and at LA level where advisers have a key role to play in ensuring a well informed and well resourced area framework.

FAQ 6: Specialist language colleges (SLCs) and designated Pathfinder LAs have been funded for transition but how can the rest of us who have not had funding manage?

We have been able to learn from the experiences of the SLCs and the Pathfinder LAs about transition but now *all* LAs are receiving funding for the purpose. There are many simple common sense solutions that do not have a huge cost element such as making contact with colleagues, making occasional visits to each other, swapping materials and looking at each other's schemes of work to see where adjustments can be made. Some schools jointly plan special thematic and cross-curricular MFL events as a bridging activity (we have heard, for example, of French Days and MFL Treasure Hunts), time and cost effective as well as memorable for all concerned.

Taking all the issues, opportunities and challenges the transition provides into consideration, it seems to us that the transfer from primary to secondary MFL needs to be seen within the context of whole-child development and whole-language policies, especially literacy. All the partners involved in this process want support from LAs, training institutions and others to enable them to close the transition gap. Therefore, a dialogue between all involved will focus on creating and sustaining progression, ensure a successful transfer and establish a workable framework. These elements will then form a platform on which a structure for continuous professional learning based on mutual trust and a willingness to learn from each other can be developed. This is also reflected in the following statement from the Key Stage 2 Framework:

> *Primary teachers should be encouraged to think about the skills they bring to language teaching . . . Little by little working in partnership with secondary colleagues and other providers, primary teachers can improve their own subject knowledge and in time build progression from simple routines to more sustained language learning.*

> **(Key Stage 2 Framework for Languages 2005: 69)**

Issues for reflection

- What creative solutions can be found to confront the logistical problems of time, funding and an apparently unmanageable number of primary schools needing support from secondary schools?

- To what extent are primary school children's fears of 'horrible things' and 'hardness' at secondary school real or unfounded?

- In what ways can issues arising from Werlen's horizontal axis be taken account of in primary MFL curriculum planning?

- What might constitute an ideal primary MFL transfer pack of information?

- Who should be taking a lead – and how – in ensuring appropriate, rigorous and coherent transition arrangements at all stages?

11

Training and professional development – establishing a community of learning and practice

PRIMARY MFL PRACTITIONERS have enjoyed great success in achieving their mission over recent years to make the subject a reality in the primary curriculum. The enthusiasm and deep-rooted belief in primary MFL as an entitlement for young learners have been vibrantly felt in the whole MFL community of practice. While secondary MFL has a strong and recognisable identity, the primary subject identity has been in transition as it has been framing its practice and defining appropriate well-grounded pedagogical principles and practices within the context of lively subject debate. Training and the continuous professional learning needs of teachers and others in the developing community of practice are the focus of this chapter. In our view, training is an essential tool to empower primary teachers, already expert in primary pedagogy, to undertake their role as confident and competent MFL teachers. This can be achieved by adopting a creative, eclectic approach when devising plans using teachers' prior knowledge and experience, and very importantly, their individual training needs as a starting point.

Key issues

- There is a need for a supply of well-qualified teachers to sustain effective primary MFL provision and to ensure enjoyment and confidence in teaching.
- The fundamental subject knowledge areas of language competence, cultural knowledge and pedagogical practice on a cross-phase basis are cornerstones of the professional learning agenda.

- Professional learning needs will be varied and need to be differentiated to build on existing expertise, prior experiences and knowledge, age and preferred learning style. These will include the needs of teaching assistants, governors, foreign language assistants and others engaged in the planning and delivery of primary MFL.

- Training forms an essential part of the development and enhancement of the subject community of practice.

- A wide variety of training opportunities are available to select from, ranging from provision from external providers to internal formats that include peer-coaching.

- There is considerable willingness to be trained and to develop MFL-specific skills.

- Co-ordination and support from those with leadership roles is crucial in creating a school culture that encourages a vibrant and empowering teacher learning community.

Introduction: a community of learning – and some unlearning?

A German landseer dog we know named Ossi undertook behaviour training and was duly, if rather incomprehensibly, awarded a certificate yet still behaves disgracefully in the house and equally appallingly when out for walks. His training was evidently inadequate and the core principles of appropriate dog behaviour have not been sustained nor internalised. Ossi has much unlearning still to do. In similar vein, one secondary colleague in discussion about the impact of primary MFL for him at Key Stage 3 commented: 'It [primary MFL] requires some unlearning of habits of a lifetime.'

There clearly is a need for a sustainable supply of confident, competent and adequately qualified teachers as the DfES 2004 research into primary MFL provision at KS2 showed. We would suggest that, alongside the continuing professional learning that will be required, in certain instances some unlearning may be necessary as MFL primary and secondary teachers work within a new paradigm of MFL teaching that requires some adjustment to their established constructs of or perspectives on teaching.

With a hint of concern that the current mission to establish primary MFL as an entitlement would be hindered by a dearth of such a supply of teachers, teacher training has been recognised nationally as a priority. Government has funded various kinds of training programmes (such as specialist Post-Graduate Certificate in Education routes) and other initiatives to this end, and there is also a wide range of training opportunities provided by private consultancies, national language organisations, LAs, embassies, EU projects and promotions and other international agencies (we should not forget that we are part of a larger international community). There is, even so, a danger that some money might be misspent if individual requirements are ignored. As one headteacher commented:

> *'The government has spent thousands of pounds (or maybe millions!) training primary teachers to deliver French. However, for those primary teachers who had no French to start with (I know a few) they still lack the confidence to teach French to their pupils and often leave it out of their weekly plans. When they do decide to do it, they are often teaching words incorrectly. While I thoroughly enjoy teaching French, I cannot provide a level of French that would have been given by an expert!'*

This chapter will not advertise, describe in detail or evaluate these initiatives but consider more broadly the professional learning needs of teachers and others associated with the primary MFL project which will support the development of a well-defined and well-grounded community of practice.

Such a community provides dynamic and flexible parameters for teacher learning, acknowledging the varied strengths, needs, experiences and motivations of the participants in this community. We loosely associate such learning with Lave and Wenger's seminal work (1991) on the concept of the 'community of practice', drawing on their notion of 'situated learning' through participation in professional activity in which participants have a shared understanding about what they are doing (see Chapter 6). Much effective primary MFL practice has grown in a bottom-up way from experimentation in classrooms and dissemination of such practice. Its learning-centredness, we consider, is at the core of our primary MFL learning community. Primary MFL practitioners, alongside secondary specialists or the increasingly common cross-phase practitioner, increasingly enjoy a shared and evolving discourse concerning subject knowledge and pedagogical expertise.

The learning-centred approach needs to be enhanced by a training framework that is available to beginners or those who desire or who would benefit from expert tuition or/and coaching. This would be achieved by, in Lave and Wenger's terms, a process called *legitimate peripheral participation*. In this process, newcomers to the community, i.e. inexperienced teachers, move from peripheral to full participation via a wide range of activities, resources, arenas of mature practice, other learners and ample opportunities for practice. Learning in this sense is experiential rather than abstract.

We find the 'community of practice' metaphor a useful and relevant learning perspective for primary MFL given its natural vibrant coaching context for language teachers. We would contend that not all teacher learning is socially situated and that cognitive styles of learning and individual reflection for example, also have their place. Teachers, as do their pupils, learn in their own individual ways. Furthermore, abstraction and generalisation have an important role to play in the theorisation of what makes effective primary MFL practice and ensure an adequate theoretical foundation for it. We suggest that training should comprise learning opportunities of the widest kind and that providers, be they external agencies, training institutions or in-house within schools, bear in mind that learning and training needs differ from individual to individual. We would assert that Lave and Wenger's perspective, in its emphasis on top-down induction, does not give due credit to two-way learning, with experienced teachers learning from and refreshing their knowledge from more inexperienced practitioners. This can be seen in the following comment made by a very experienced generalist and primary MFL teacher:

> 'I have considerable experience and have built up quite a stock of songs, materials, activities and the like over the years but I am still learning. I enjoy being in the classroom with our NQT who trained on a specialist primary MFL course and I pick up something from her every time I watch her. She switches from language to language and the children do too. I would never have thought to do that. But then I don't really know another language apart from French but I have picked up the songs from the Reception class children.'

In considering training needs, it is always useful to identify and audit the varied needs of individuals as a starting and monitoring point. This can be done in a simple way such as devising, for example, a questionnaire (as we did to illustrate this point) to capture teachers' individual needs and concerns regarding training and using them as a basis for a scheme of school-wide training.

Auditing primary MFL training needs

We asked the primary MFL coordinators of two primary schools, one in the north of England, one in the south, to audit the training needs of the staff. This included all teachers and TAs and any other helpers who might need to make a teaching and/or support contribution to the KS2 primary MFL entitlement. The coordinators used a questionnaire to elicit information about perceived foreign language capability and the capacity to contribute to the teaching of primary MFL.

The results gave a clear message that there is a great deal of goodwill on the part of these non-specialist teachers who teach or are about to teach some primary MFL. Most teachers evaluated themselves as having basic knowledge of a language, mainly French. Of 19 teachers who responded to the question, 12 had various levels of qualification in French, 5 had some knowledge of German and 2 had basic Spanish (see Figure 11.2). They indicated in their answers a surprisingly high level of confidence to be able to teach simple structures and notions such as numbers, colours

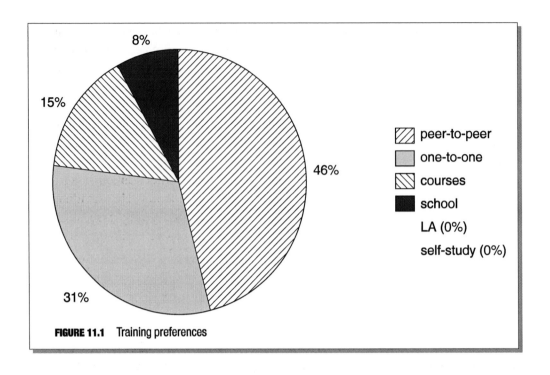

FIGURE 11.1 Training preferences

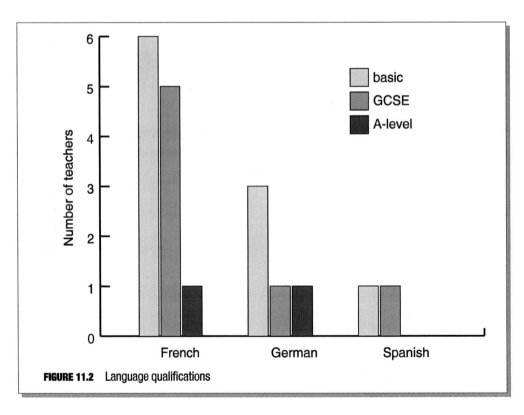

FIGURE 11.2 Language qualifications

and greetings, reflecting the strength of the primary generalist. Confidence is also an issue when it comes to looking at preferred training options since the majority would prefer peer-coaching and one-to-one, followed by courses (non-specified). Some teachers told us that they needed a coaching situation with which they would feel comfortable as opposed to language tuition where, in the words of one teacher 'I might be pounced on'. This is an interesting comment in the light of similar feelings expressed by some older adolescent pupils who also dislike being 'pounced on' in language lessons.

It can be seen from these illustrative audits that teachers are enthusiastic and keen to 'have a go' but at the same time are aware of and very clear about their individual training needs. Building on such findings, individualised training programmes can be devised to ensure that competent and effective – 'fit for purpose' – teaching takes place in the classroom so as to provide quality provision and pupil learning outcomes. The question then arises: what makes an effective primary MFL teacher so that training and continuous professional learning can be oriented towards a construct of effective practice?

The review of research conducted by Driscoll and one of the authors of this book, Jones (Driscoll and Jones *et al.* 2003), explored the characteristics of effective primary MFL practice. As indicators of effective practice, it identified the exploitation of the skills and knowledge of the primary generalist teachers who are active participants in the primary MFL community of practice. Such teachers are able to provide an enjoyable and, at the same time, challenging primary MFL learning environment and adopt an appropriate teaching approach that relates to the learning needs of pupils. The review also highlighted the importance of the skilful and selective use of resources, especially visuals that provide a powerful support for the young learner.

The research of Erika Werlen (2006) has also contributed to a definition of effective primary MFL teaching practices. Teachers, Werlen suggests, should be able to provide good language models themselves and make use of and build on the children's experiences as core 'content'. Using authentic materials, the teachers will help the children to see parallels with their mother tongue, and, according to Werlen, see mistakes, for example from carelessness, and errors based on a child's inter-language, as an opportunity for learning and, thus, make children feel secure in their learning. Good communication about learning that takes place with other teachers and parents would also indicate quality of practice.

Training needs, then, would seem to focus on certain key skills and knowledge areas:

- linguistic competence;
- the development of confidence to use the language;
- up-to-date cultural knowledge and intercultural understanding (see Chapter 9);
- aspects of methodology appropriate to the age range;

- an understanding of children's learning and language learning strategies (see Chapter 6);
- knowledge about foreign language learning;
- the critical reviewing of materials and an understanding of their role as a resource (see Chapter 3);
- communication skills.

HEI training programmes are comprehensive in their coverage. There is, however, a detectable preponderance of focus on a rather narrow range of teaching techniques of the 'fluffy bunny' kind in some short course provision. Although this is important, it needs to be developed in a broader pedagogical context. The course information we have investigated – and there are a great many offerings – indicate a wide variety of models for teachers, teaching assistants and other non-specialists to choose from. These range from a series of sessions to intensive weeks; day, weekend and twilight, and now include online interactive learning – all in all quite a range of 'courses for horses' or should it be 'horses for courses'? The concept of 'andragogy', i.e. adult learning, implies, as in Law and Glover's (2000: 249) words: 'an acceptance of the importance of more focused and individualised learning strategies, rather than simply treating everyone homogeneously, as a group with common needs and experiences'.

This does not mean an end to collective learning and shared reflection, which are very important, but that it is also important to recognise ages and stages in teachers' life and career cycles when considering professional learning needs and ways to meet those needs. This ties in rather well with the advent of the European Professional Development Portfolio that will provide a unified approach to recording a teacher's professional learning engagement which will be entirely a question for the teacher to negotiate, albeit coordinated by the relevant members of the school leadership team within the framework of a school's professional development programme.

Horses for courses and courses for horses

Higgins and Leat (2001) introduce this colourful metaphor to distinguish between a 'one size fits all' type of training (prevalent in the past and largely of the differentiated 'one shot' type of course) and longer-term differentiated courses or other training provision. The 'one shot' course is largely discredited now since research has shown they have very little impact on teacher learning. However, the occasional 'one shot' course, if well targeted and prepared (intensive days such as are provided by embassies for example) can serve as useful triggers for an engagement with a more continuous and sustained type of professional learning and provide an opportunity to network as well as to browse through available materials. Trawling through some of the many training opportunities available, there is no dearth of possibilities and it

FIGURE 11.3   Horses for courses and courses for horses

should be possible for all teachers to create their own training programme according to their needs and the practical aspects of their lives. We are recommending such an approach, eclectic and individualised, based on the auditing of a teacher's needs, which should of course mesh with the training needs of the school as a whole and its School Learning Plan and keying into as many formats as possible.

There are a great many types of training available in addition to the format of 'the course'. These formats include peer-coaching, the network concept and practitioner research which we suggest are particularly suitable for developing the primary MFL community of practice in that they continue to develop the bottom-up approach and encourage continuing teacher ownership on the basis of school need.

Peer-coaching

Peer-coaching, or classroom support, crucially recognises the expertise of one's colleagues and acknowledges the usefulness of exploiting the internal know-how in the school. Peer-coaching can always usefully feature as part of staff development activity and is particularly helpful where curriculum and teaching are the focus, as in the case of primary MFL. We have found in practice examples of successful peer-coaching which include the following.

- Some of the outreach work of ASTs, for example where secondary teachers team teach with primary colleagues to develop the capability of the latter or vice versa; we found primary ASTs in secondary classrooms rather less common. We would classify primary classroom 'takeovers' by secondary colleagues where the primary teacher is little involved as top-down and recommend a two-way transfer of learning so as to achieve maximum benefit.

- The efforts of primary coordinators, be they ASTs, specialists or not, to provide customised support for their peers in school on a needs/request basis, for example language pronunciation, introducing a particular song or game, questioning, ideas for embedding the target language into another subject.

- Peer support from school to school. Examples of this include 'picking the brains' of colleagues in another school on a particular issue, as in one case where a school has devised simple teacher-friendly schemes of work. The easy way would be to expect colleagues to hand over their precious work; the collaborative approach involves mutual school visits, lesson observation, and discussion about how the schemes of work are devised and used. The schemes of work can then be adapted by the visiting colleague. In another case, one school has successfully planned its primary MFL provision across the whole-school curriculum map, thereby solving the seemingly tricky issue of 'finding time in an overcrowded curriculum for primary MFL'. The enthusiastic coordinator is keen to share her experiences and support others to put in place a similar approach.

Primary MFL has, with its experimental approach to early language learning, used the opportunity to unlock the subject leadership of a great many talented teachers and peer-coaching is fundamentally about sharing, empowering and promoting subject leadership. It is a form of training that is so much richer when it can be shared for the benefit of the many rather than the few or hidden under a bushel in one classroom! Linguistic up-skilling is clearly a high priority as stated in the Key Stage 2 Framework:

> In developing a strategy for building capacity in language capability across the school, Head Teachers and senior managers might like to consider how to use the support available from secondary specialists and native speakers creatively and flexibly in order that both children and teaching staff make the best use of this undoubtedly valuable resource.
>
> **(Key Stage 2 Framework for Languages 2005: 21)**

Clusters and networks

In the spirit of cooperation, schools often network or cluster together, either informally or through the platform of an official school cluster arrangement, and make use of available expertise as in the following example:

'As a cluster group (six primaries and one secondary) we are given funding from our LA to have three professional development meetings per year. During these sessions, our secondary French colleague organises a vocabulary brush-up from different aspects of our PMFL programme. This gives primary teachers the opportunity to revise their own French and ensure they are pronouncing words correctly before teaching them to the children. During one session we also invite a French speaker from Edinburgh to come and work with us. This is a great ongoing development for us and keeps up the enthusiasm.

However, as we have now appointed a French-speaking teacher to work with pupils for one session a week in our primary school, we are very lucky to have expert advice on hand. I really think that using specialist teachers is a great asset to teaching primary children French.'

In another example, a school cluster has a more structured programme led by the LA adviser but the emphasis is always on sharing practice. The cluster has an intranet for teacher discussion and for the posting of materials for downloading and one teacher, who had interestingly made little use of it, due to time constraints, commented: 'At first I felt a real novice but gradually I have become confident enough to make my own suggestions to colleagues.'

Clustering and networking, however tightly or loosely, provide opportunity to share not just 'good practice' (however subjective the perception of 'good'), but the processes that lead to such practice. It shifts the learning mindset from what Huberman (1993) calls the 'lone wolf' style of working to a 'pack of wolves' collaborative effort that can synergise efforts and activities, perhaps integrated in research projects, thereby cutting out time-wasting and unnecessary 'wheel reinventions' – very important for busy primary school teachers.

Practitioner research

It is but a short step from the classroom investigations mentioned previously to something a little more structured that would merit the name of practitioner research. Our concept of practitioner research involves teachers, alongside other colleagues, researching their own practice in classroom contexts that are meaningful and urgent to them. Working with a definition of research as 'systematic self-critical enquiry', the primary MFL community of teacher learning has embraced research in this sense, no less than any other subject, and includes a nucleus of teacher research in various forms. These include:

- research centres focusing on early language learning and promoting small-scale research in schools or groups of schools;

- a large number of students attracted to aspects of primary MFL for MA and PhD theses, researching effective teaching and the eternal quest for the holy grail of language acquisition researching issues such as 'the younger the better'.

- LAs engaged in action research to develop materials and assessment schemes for example, and researching the impact of policies such as transition;

■ individual teacher research in teachers' own classrooms as they research their own practice from the 'inside-out', as Cochran-Smith and Lytle (1993) call it.

A recent example of individual teacher research we have come across includes an investigation into children's learning styles in the primary MFL classroom, conducted by a primary MFL teacher, that involved lesson observation, interviews with teachers and pupils and questionnaires to teachers, pupils and parents. These data sets enabled the teacher researcher to draw tentative conclusions about what was working well and to suggest areas for development. A staff meeting presentation and discussion led to an action plan (that included improved planning, more formative assessment practices and a focus on creative use of the target language). This was then included in the School Learning Plan as a whole-school learning objective for primary MFL.

Teachers, who may think research is something only academics engage in, are in fact, as Brighouse and Woods (1999: 42) write: 'natural researchers, in the sense that all teaching is based on inquiry and the response of the pupils provides ready evidence as to the effectiveness of various teaching and learning approaches'. Primary MFL teachers have already demonstrated an immense capacity as deeply reflective practitioners for research over the last 40 years as to what makes effective primary MFL practice. The 1960–70s Primary French experience, it could be said, was never a failure but a challenge to the community of practice to have another go at primary MFL.

Conclusion

There are training implications for both primary and secondary colleagues in helping them to become effective MFL teachers within the evolving context of cross-phase learning. Primary schools also need support to enable them to embed the new learning arrangements within and across the whole curriculum and extensive professional development to support this. Organisational and infrastructural arrangements are scarcely less for their secondary colleagues who will need, for example, to rewrite at least parts of their schemes of work and adapt assessment and teaching to ensure continuity and progression of MFL throughout the pupil's school career. Effective and continuous MFL provision will require teachers to adopt new 'ways of knowing' (e.g. about children's learning in age ranges other than those they teach), and, indeed, new habits (e.g. a reappraisal of how grammar is taught).These will, in turn, require professional development opportunities with specific attention, as emphasised in this chapter, to individual teachers' professional learning needs, as well as focused training for others in the community of practice, such as teaching assistants, foreign language assistants and governors, to enable them all to make a well-informed and appropriate contribution on their way to becoming effective primary MFL practitioners.

The role of leadership, as stated in Chapter 2, is vital, and where professional development is concerned there is need for careful coordination, budgeting and monitoring; as one primary teacher commented: 'The head needs to support us by being in lessons, providing/arranging appropriate training and being fully supportive of staff teaching MFL.' Where the subject is developed in a web of shared leadership with teachers fully involved, then the exciting primary MFL project – for it is an ongoing, open-ended learning project for pupils and teachers alike as lifelong learners – is increasingly sustainable and, as a whole-school project, an essential part of the modern primary school curriculum. This requires a warm collaborative school culture that promotes teacher as well as pupil learning with 'time for teachers to reflect and develop ideas and resources' (a further comment by the above teacher).

Primary MFL is not only rather special but has developed in a special way, building a substantial knowledge and skills base that needs to be taken into consideration by secondary schools as well. It is a chance not to be missed if continuity and progression are to be assured. And, as our final word, we wish to stress that primary school teachers who are already expert in pedagogy for the age group, ought not to feel anxious as they develop their foreign language subject knowledge to a stage where they feel competent and confident enough. Instead, we would encourage primary colleagues to enjoy learning a language 'together' with their pupils, albeit several steps ahead, in such a way that it is manageable and fun for them too.

Issues for reflection

- Why is it that even with a qualification, many potential primary MFL teachers lack confidence in their ability to teach primary MFL?

- Undertake a simple primary MFL training needs audit in a school, with the whole staff, a Key Stage or a group of teachers and compare your results with those in this chapter and with the results in the DfES (2004) survey into training needs.

- Devise a professional development programme that would take on board the identified training needs.

- How would you define the developing discourse of cross-phase subject knowledge? What do MFL teachers talk about and what are their concerns?

- How would you describe 'effective' primary MFL practice? What does it look like and is it possible to generalise?

- Identify and compare two training formats, one that was evidently successful and the other not so successful, and reflect upon the factors that made the successful one work.

References

Barthes, R. (1990) *Improving Schools from Within: Teachers: Parents and Principals Can Make a Difference*. San Francisco, CA: Jossey-Bass.

Barton, A. (2002a) 'Teaching modern foreign languages to single-sex classes', *Language Learning Journal*, 25, Summer, 8–14.

Barton, A. (2002b) 'The gender effect', in Swarbrick, A. (ed.) *Teaching Modern Foreign Languages in Secondary Schools*. London and New York: RoutledgeFalmer.

Baumann, A. S., Bloomfield, A. and Roughton, L. (2003) *Becoming a Secondary School Teacher*. London: Hodder and Stoughton.

Behrman, E. H. (2002) 'Community based literacy learning', *Reading: Literacy and Language*, 36(1), 26–32.

Black, P. J. and Wiliam, D. (1998) *Inside the Black Box*. London: King's College London.

Black, P., Harrison, C., Lee, C., Marshall, B. and Wiliam, D. (2003) *Assessment for Learning. Putting it into practice*. Buckingham: Open University Press.

Brighouse, T. and Woods, P. (1999) *How to Improve your School*. London: Methuen.

Browne, A. and Haylock, D. (2004) *Professional Issues for Primary Teachers*. London and Thousand Oaks, CA: Sage.

Burstall, C. *et al.* (1974) *Primary French in the Balance*. Windsor: NFER.

Busher, H. and Harris, A. (2000) *Subject Leadership and School Improvement*. London: Paul Chapman Publishing.

Byram, M. (1997) *Face to Face Learning 'Language-and-Culture' through Visits and Exchanges*. London: CILT.

Cheater, C. and Farren, A. (2001) *Young Pathfinder Series (9) The Literacy Link*. London: CILT.

Clarke, S. (2000a) *ICT in Modern Foreign Languages*. Cambridge: Pearson Publishing.

Clarke, S. (2000b) *Using the Internet: Modern Foreign Languages*. Cambridge: Pearson Publishing.

Cochran-Smith, M. and Lytle, S. (1993) *Inside Outside. Teacher Research and Knowledge*. New York: Teachers' College Press, Columbia University.

Coffey, S. (2005) 'A cross-cultural framework for Citizenship training within the MFL PGCE', *CILT LINKS*, Spring, 4–5.

Comenius, J. A. (1657) *The Great Didactic*, translated by Keatinge, M. W. New York: Russell and Russell (1967).

Council of Europe (2001) *Common European Framework of Reference for Languages: Learning, Teaching, Assessment*. Cambridge: Cambridge University Press.

Cox, M. J. and Abbott, C. (2004) *ICT and Attainment: A Review of the Research Literature*. Coventry and London: British Educational Communications and Technology Agency (BECTA) and DfES.

Cox, M. J. and Webb, M. E. (2004) *ICT and Pedagogy: A Review of the Research Literature*. Coventry and London: British Educational Communications and Technology Agency (BECTA) and DfES.

Creemers, B. P. M. (1994) *The Effective Classroom*. London: Cassell.

Cullingford, C. (1995) *The Effective Teacher*. London: Cassell.

Day, C. *et al.* (1998) *Developing Leadership in Primary Schools*. London: Paul Chapman Publishing.

De Bóo, M. (1992) *Bright Ideas for Early Learners*. Leamington Spa: Scholastic Publications.

Dean, J. (1992 [1983]) *Organising Learning in the Primary School Classroom*. London and New York: Routledge.

DfEE/QCA (1999) *Modern Foreign Languages: The National Curriculum for England*. London: QCA.

DfES (2003) *Fulfilling the Potential: Transforming Teaching and Learning through ICT in Schools*. London: DfES.

DfES (2004) *The Provision of Foreign Language Learning for Pupils at Key Stage 2. Research Report 572*. Research undertaken by Driscoll, P., Jones, J. and Macrory, G. London: DfES (Nottingham: DfES Publications).

Dobbs, J. (2001) *Using the Board in the Language Classroom*. Cambridge: Cambridge University Press.

Driscoll, P. and Frost, D. (eds) (1999) *The Teaching of Modern Foreign Languages in the Primary School*. London and New York: Routledge.

Driscoll, P. *et al.* (2004) *A systematic review of the characteristics of effective foreign language teaching to pupils between the ages of 7 and 11*. London: EPPI – Centre, Social Science Research Unit. Institute of Education, London.

Drummond, M. J. (1993) *Assessing Children's Learning* (1st edn). London: David Fulton Publishers.

Dugard, C. and Hewer, S. (2003) *New Pathfinder (3). Impact on Learning: What ICT Can Bring to MFL in KS3*. London: CILT.

Earley, P. and Weindling, D. (2004) *Understanding School Leadership*. London: Paul Chapman Publishing.

Edelenbos, P. and Johnstone, R. (eds) (1997) *Researching Languages at Primary School. Some European Perspectives*. Scottish CILT.

Flynn, L. (2005) 'Transition: Opening dialogue, closing the gap', *Modern Foreign Languages*, CILT's Bulletin for secondary language teachers, Issue 9, Autumn, 4–5.

Fullan, M. (1991) *The New Meaning of Educational Change*. London: Cassell.

Fullan, M. and Hargreaves, A. (1992) *What's Worth Fighting for in Your School?* Buckingham: Open University Press.

Gardner, H. (1983) *Frames of Mind: The Theory of Multiple Intelligences*. New York: Basic Books.

Grenfell, M. (2002) *Modern Languages Across the Curriculum*. London and New York: RoutedgeFalmer.

Grenfell, M. and Harris, V. (1999) *Modern Languages Strategies in Theory and Practice*. London: Routledge.

Grey, D. (2001) *The Internet in School*. London and New York: Continuum.

Harris, A. (2003) 'Teacher Leadership and School Improvement', in Harris, A. *et al. Effective Leadership for School Improvement*. London: RoutledgeFalmer.

Harris, V. (1997) *Teaching Learners How to Learn; Strategy Training in the ML Classroom*. London: CILT.

Hawkins, E. (1984) *Awareness of Language: An Introduction*. Cambridge: Cambridge University Press.

Hawkins, E. (2005) 'Out of this nettle, drop-out, we pluck this flower, opportunity: rethinking the school foreign language apprenticeship', *Language Learning Journal*, 32, 4–17.

Higgins S. and Leat D. (2001) in Soler, J. *et al. Teacher Development. Exploring Our Own Practice*. London: Paul Chapman Publishing.

Hobsbawm, E. and Ranger, T. (1983) *The Invention of Tradition*. Cambridge: Cambridge University Press.

Huberman, M. (1993) *Lives of Teachers*. London and New York: Teachers' College Press, Columbia University.

Hurrell, A. (1999) 'The four language skills', in Driscoll, P. and Frost, D. (eds) *The Teaching of Modern Foreign Languages in the Primary School*. London and New York: Routledge, pp. 67–87.

Johnstone, R. (1994) *Teaching Modern Languages in Primary School. Approaches and Implications*. The Scottish Council for Research in Education.

Jones, J. (2005) 'Foreign languages in the primary school in England: a new pupil learning continuum', *Francophonie*, 3, 3–7.

Keating, M.W. (trans.) (1967) *The Great Didactic* (J.A. Comenius). First published 1657. New York: Russell and Russell.

King, L. (National Director of Languages) (2005). Conference notes taken at 'Spanish: the Primary Challenge', 25 November, London.

Kohonen, V. (2004) 'How can the European Language Portfolio (ELP) Promote Transparency in FL Education', *Associação Portuguesa de Professores de Inglês* (Portuguese Association of English Teachers), Autumn.

Kramsch, C. (1993) *Context and Culture in Language Teaching*. Oxford: Oxford University Press.

Krashen, S. (1984) *Principles and Practice in Second Language Acquisition*. Oxford: Pergamon Press.

Krashen, S. and Terrell, T. (1983) *The Natural Approach: Language Acquisition in the Classroom*. Oxford: Pergamon Press.

Lave, J. and Wenger, E. (1991) *Situated Learning: Legitimate and Peripheral Participation*. Cambridge: Cambridge University Press.

Law, S. and Glover, D. (2000) *Educational Leadership and Learning. Practice, Policy and Research*. Buckingham: Open University Press.

Leask, M. and Pachler, N. (eds) (1999) *Learning to Teach Using ICT in the Secondary School*. London and New York: RoutledgeFalmer.

Lee, J. *et al.* (1998) *The Invisible Child: The responses and attitudes to the learning of Modern Languages shown by Year 9 pupils of average ability*. London: CILT.

Lee, W. R. (1971 [1965]) *Language-Teaching Games and Contests*. Oxford: Oxford University Press.

Lenneberg, E. (1967) *Biological Foundations of Language*. New York: Wiley and Sons.

Light, P. and Littleton, K. (1999) *Social Processes in Children's Learning*. Cambridge: Cambridge University Press.

Loveless, A. (1996 [1995]) *The Role of IT: Practical Issues for the Primary Teacher*. London and New York: Cassell.

Macaro, E. (2001) *Learning Strategies in Foreign and Second Language Classrooms*. London: Continuum.

MacBeath, J. (1998) *Effective School Leadership. Responding to Change*. London: Paul Chapman Publishing.

Martin, C. (2000) *Analysis of national and international research on the provision of modern foreign languages in schools*. London: QCA.

McLaughlin, B. (1985) *Second Language Acquisition in Childhood: volume 2. School-age Children.* Hilsdale, NJ: Lawrence Erlbaum.

Morgan, C. and Neil, P. (2001) *Teaching Modern Foreign Languages.* London: Kogan Page.

Nias, J. *et al.* (1989) *Staff Relations in the Primary School.* London: Cassell.

OFSTED (1999) *Inspection of Initial Teacher Training: Primary Follow-up Survey 1996–98.* London: OFSTED.

O'Malley, J. M. and Chamot, A. (1990) *Learning Strategies in Second Language Acquisition.* Cambridge: Cambridge University Press.

Oxford, R. (1990) *Language Learning Strategies. What Every Teacher Should Know.* Boston: Heinle and Heinle.

Pachler, N. and Field, K. (2002) *Learning to Teach Modern Foreign Languages in the Secondary School 2nd Edition.* London and New York: RoutledgeFalmer.

Pagden, A. (2001) 'Continuity and progression from 3 to 11', in Cockburn, A. (ed.) *Teaching Children 3 to 11.* London: Paul Chapman Publishing.

Poudyal, R. (2001) *Bridging the North–South Divide: Linkages and Learning between the South and the North.* London: Save the Children.

QCA *Schemes of Work*: MFL KS2. http://www.standards.dfes.gov.uk/schemes/primary_mfl/?view=get (accessed 14 September 2005)

Satchwell, P. and de Silva, J. (1995) *Young Pathfinder Series (1): Catching Them Young.* London: CILT.

Scrimshaw, P. (2004) *Enabling Teachers to Make Successful Use of ICT.* Coventry: British Educational Communications and Technology Agency (BECTA).

Senge, P. (1990) *The Fifth Discipline.* New York: Doubleday.

Sergiovanni, T. (2001) *Leadership: What's in it for schools?* London: RoutledgeFalmer.

Sharpe, K. (2001) *Modern Foreign Languages in the Primary School.* London: Kogan Page.

Sharpe, K. and Driscoll, P. (2000) 'At what age should foreign language learning begin?', in Field, K. (ed.) *Issues in Modern Foreign Languages.* London and New York: RoutledgeFalmer.

Shaw, S. and Hawes, T. (1998) *Effective Teaching and Learning in the Primary School.* Leicester: Optimal.

Singleton, D. (1989) *Language Acquisition and the Age Factor.* Clevedon: Multilingual Matters.

SOIED (2000) *Modern Languages 5–14: National Guidelines for Teachers and Managers.* Learning and Teaching Scotland.

Stoll, L. and Fink, D. (1996) *Changing Our Schools.* Buckingham: Open University Press.

Street, B. (1993) 'Culture is a verb: anthropological aspects of language and cultural processes', in Graddol, D. *et al.* (eds) *Language and Culture.* Clevedon: BAAL and Multilingual Matters, pp. 23–43.

Tierney, D. and Hope, M. (1998) *Young Pathfinder Series (7): Making The Link.* London: CILT.

Tomlinson, B. (ed.) (2003 [1998]) *Materials Development in Language Teaching.* Cambridge: Cambridge University Press.

Torrance, H. and Pryor, J. (1998) *Investigating Formative Assessment. Teaching, Learning and Assessment in the Classroom.* Buckingham: Open University Press.

Trethowan, D. (1991) *Managing with Appraisal.* London: Paul Chapman Publishing.

Vilke, M. (1988) 'Some psychological aspects of early second-language acquisition', *Journal of Multilingual and Multicultural Development*, 9, 1–2.

Watson, D. (1993) *Impact – An Evaluation of the Impact of the Information Technology on Children's Achievement in Primary and Secondary Schools.* London: Department for Education and King's College London.

Webb, M. E. and Cox, M. J. (2004) 'A review of pedagogy related to ICT', *Technology, Pedagogy and Education*, 13.

Webb, R. (ed.) (1996) *Cross-Curricular Primary Practice: Taking a Leadership Role*. London: Falmer.

Wegeriff, R. (1996) 'Collaborative learning and directive software', *Journal for Computer Assisted Learning*, 12, 22–32.

Wegeriff, R. and Scrimshaw, P. (eds) (1997) *Computers and Talk in the Primary Classroom*. Clevedon: Multilingual Matters.

Werlen, E. (2006) *Wissenschaftliche Begleitung der Pilotphase Fremdsprache in der Grundschule*. Project reports available on www.wibe-bw.de

White, I. (2005) 'The myth of Howard Gardner's Multilple Intelligences', *Ioelife*, 9(1), London Institute of Education.

Wood, D. (2004 [1988]) *How Children Think and Learn*. London: Blackwell.

Index

David Fulton Publishers

Geography 3-11
A Guide for Teachers
Hilary Cooper, Simon Asquith and Chris Rowley

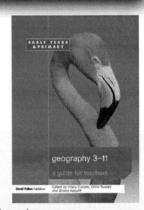

EARLY YEARS & PRIMARY

The advent of the *National Primary Strategy* has produced a welcome reminder to teachers of the importance of geography within the primary curriculum. This book aims to encourage this renewed awareness and to support teachers in teaching primary geography in different and exciting ways. It will show that children have an entitlement to learn about geography and this can be achieved in a lively, creative fashion uplifting for both teachers and children.

It covers:

· Planning for &assessing progression in learning
· Inclusion
· ICT and drama
· Indoors, outdoors and beyond

This book will help both trainee and experienced teachers to integrate geography as an essential part of the primary curriculum.

Contents: Introduction; Theory, practice and research: A rationale for primary geography and overview of recent developments; *PLANNING AND ASSESSMENT*; Are there different types of geographical enquiry?; How can we plan effectively to foster progression in geographical understanding? *CONCEPTS OF PLACE*; Sustainable education: What's that all about and what has geography fieldwork got to do with it? How can children connect to a distant place through drama? *INCLUSION AND THE GLOBAL DIMENSON*; How can we put inclusion into practice in geography? How can children develop an understanding of the global dimension? *VALUES, ENQUIRIES AND CROSS-CURRICULAR APPROACHES*: Is geography suitable for the Foundation Stage? How can geography make a significant contribution to a coherent and meaningful Key Stage 1 curriculum? How can geography have a significant place in a restructured Key Stage 2 curriculum? Reflections on teaching geography

Hilary Cooper, is Professor of History and Pedagogy at St. Martin's College.; **Simon Asquith**, is a lecturer in geography education at St. Martin's College.; **Chris Rowley**, is Senior Lecturer in Environmental and Geographical Education at St. Martin's College.

£17.00 • Paperback • 196 pages • 1-84312-421-1 • May 2006

How to order from David Fulton Publishers

Our books are available from your usual supplier, but if it is more convenient, you can order directly from us.

1.	**Tel:**	0870 787 1721
2.	**Fax:**	0870 787 1723
3.	**Post:**	David Fulton Publishers
		The Chiswick Centre
		414 Chiswick High Road
		London
		W4 5TF
4.	**Email:**	orders@fultonpublishers.co.uk
5.	**Web:**	www.fultonpublishers.co.uk

FREE P&P to schools LEAs and other organisations

£2.50 per order for private/personal orders

David Fulton Publishers

Science 5-11
A Guide for Teachers
Alan Howe, Dan Davies, Kendra McMahon, Lee Towler and Tonie Scott

PRIMARY

This uniquely organised book combines three vital strands of science teaching - an understanding of curriculum, subject knowledge and appropriate pedagogy. Within each chapter, the book provides a synthesis of ideas about teaching and learning that focuses on answering the question 'How should I best teach this area of science?' and addresses important themes such as:

- Progression
- Scientific enquiry
- Developing children's understanding
- Classroom management

Practical and innovative, this text will be invaluable to both trainee and qualified teachers needing to develop both their subject knowledge and their ability to teach primary science confidently and effectively. It provides a valuable starting point for anyone wishing to teach science in a creative and inspiring way.

Contents: Science, teaching and learning; Materials and their properties; Sound; Forces; Electricity; Light; The Earth and beyond; Humans and other animals; The green kingdom: plants; Living things in their environment; The end of the beginning.

Alan Howe is Senior Lecturer in Primary Science at Bath Spa University; **Dan Davies** is Professor of Science and Technology Education, Primary PGCE programme leader and Principle Lecturer at Bath Spa University; **Kendra McMahon** is Senior Lecturer in Primary Science at Bath Spa University; **Lee Towler** is Senior Lecturer in primary science at Bath Spa University; **Tonie Scott** is Deputy Head Teacher of Bishop Henderson Primary School, Somerset, and a visiting tutor for Bath Spa University.

£18 • Paperback • 244 pages • 1-84312-319-3 • 2005

How to order from David Fulton Publishers

Our books are available from your usual supplier, but if it is more convenient, you can order directly from us.

1.	**Tel:**	0870 787 1721
2.	**Fax:**	0870 787 1723
3.	**Post:**	David Fulton Publishers
		The Chiswick Centre
		414 Chiswick High Road
		London
		W4 5TF
4.	**Email:**	orders@fultonpublishers.co.uk
5.	**Web:**	www.fultonpublishers.co.uk

Free P&P to schools LEAs and other organisations

£2.50 per order for private/personal orders